The Lone Twin

Lone Twins forge the courage and the strengths
that enable them to make a unique contribution to life.

Joan Woodward
November 2009

THE LONE TWIN

Understanding Twin Bereavement and Loss

REVISED EDITION

Joan Woodward

FREE ASSOCIATION BOOKS

First published in 1998
Revised edition published 2010 by
Free Association Books Limited
One Angel Cottages, Milespit Hill, London NW7 1RD

ISBN   978-1-85343-200-2   pbk

A CIP catalogue record for this book is available from the British Library

Designed and produced for Free Association Books by
Chase Publishing Services Ltd, Sidmouth EX10 9JB
Printed and bound by CPI Group (UK) Ltd, Croydon, CR0 4YY

Contents

Acknowledgements

My thanks go first to Dave Whitnall and Alison Stewart for computer help in preparing the new edition. I am grateful to Jill Deeley for joining me in proofreading and supporting me through the last two years as we have worked towards this revised edition. My thanks also go to the publisher Trevor Brown for going ahead with this edition in spite of the recession. Above all I want to thank all the lone twins who have offered to contribute more stories. Some are new and some are updates, but they all help to increase our knowledge of the effects of twin loss on the surviving twin.

1
INTRODUCTION

I am delighted to have the opportunity that this Introduction gives me, to add more to this book after a gap of 20 years since the first meeting of 'The Lone Twin Network' and nearly ten years since the book was first published. In thinking about the most important issues to include, I looked back to my original 'Conclusions' to recall what it was that I hoped then that this book might do. I wanted it to be the start of bringing serious attention to the significance of twin loss and its effect on the surviving twin and their family. At the time, I felt this loss had been not only ignored, but positively denied by many professionals.

SIGNIFICANCE OF THE LOSS

All these years later, having met so many more lone twins, I am more than ever convinced that the *enormous significance of the loss is the most important issue*. It is a unique one which above all is highly individual in its nature, with many different factors determining the severity of its impact on the surviving twin as well as their family. As in other cases of loss of an important Attachment Figure, there are four main factors which largely determine the outcome. The first is *the situation prior to the loss* (for example, the family's attitude to the twins, which would include their expectation of the twins' arrival, the twins' closeness or distance and their general well being). The second is *the kind of personality or temperament of the survivor.* (Is he or she shy, nervous, lacking in confidence or emotionally strong and with a good sense of self?) The third is to do with the *actual circumstances of the death.* (Was it expected, was one twin ill for a long time, perhaps leaving the other feeling neglected, or was the death sudden and a great shock, or possibly very traumatic in nature, such as a suicide, or murder?) I am grateful to Paula Watts for sharing a very traumatic story, as these particular experiences need to be better understood. The fourth, is *what sort of other close Attachments are available to the surviving twin.* (Are these supportive and sensitive, or making the twin's loss feel worse?)

GREATER AWARENESS

There is no doubt a greater awareness now of the significance of twin loss than there was ten years ago. I think that this is largely due to a big increase in articles, radio and television programmes as well as the spread of the Network. Many web sites hold information as well. The well-known researcher Nancy Segal in the USA has, through her many books, added knowledge to our understanding of twin relationships as well as twin loss. She believes the loss to be highly significant and queries whether for some lone twins it is greater even than that of the loss of a spouse (Segal 2000). Others have written autobiographical material about their loss (Jones 1987; Farmer 1988).

In spite of this, there is still ignorance. At a recent book launch for the publication of a book about the loss of a twin through drug taking (Burton-Phillips 2007) someone in the field of education said to a few of us from the Network, that she did not see how a twin who lost their twin at birth could possibly be affected. She asked, 'How would the surviving twin know?' I asked her to imagine how *she* might feel if told during her childhood that she had been born a twin, but due to her 'taking all the food' during the pregnancy, her twin had not survived. I suggested that perhaps worse, she might have had her parents make it clear that they wished her twin had been the one to live. Less dramatically, she was asked how she might feel missing someone all her life who 'should have been there' to share it. This question was put by a lone twin who added that she had also had surviving twins born to the family to watch growing up as a pair, while she was without her twin sister. The educationist was honest and said she had never thought of those things before and then freely admitted our comments made her think again.

All sorts of research into twin loss continues quite rightly to be done, but there was one very recently that I feel obliged to comment on as the findings hit the popular press (Lummaa 2007). This study was based on a comparison between 377 sets of same-sex twins with 155 containing a male and female twin. It showed that these female twins were less likely to marry and have children and when they did, they had fewer of them. Because the findings also applied to those female twins who lost their twin brothers at or around birth, the researchers attributed the discrepancy to the effect the testosterone from their brothers had on the female twin while a foetus. This led to some suggestions that this made such female twins more masculine, and so unattractive to males, less likely to marry and so less likely to have children. I believe that this kind of interpretation of facts can be highly misleading. It was immediately queried by the Twins and Multiple Births Association, who have hundreds of twins as members.

I have now met many female twins who have lost their brothers. I believe that for some of them it has been hard to bring another 'man' into the pair, if their twin brother survived into adulthood, but this in my view could well be so, because of these females all living in a patriarchal society where males are valued in so many families far more than girls. I would expect this to be even more so in pre-industrial Finland where this study was set. For some female twins who lost their brother at or around birth, it could feel like a 'betrayal' of their dead brother to make a close relationship with another male. I have seen no evidence of 'maleness' in these female twins. I agree with the researchers that some of these female twins may indeed be 'disadvantaged', but I believe this to be determined far more by cultural and psychological factors than by hormonal ones. This kind of study makes me more than ever aware how careful researchers need to be as they formulate their conclusions.

DIFFERENCES DUE TO AGE AT LOSS

The second issue of importance that again needs confirming, is *how differently the loss is experienced according to the stage in life the loss occurred*. In some ways it would be far more exciting to be able to say all sorts of new issues have emerged over the years that were not apparent at the beginning. On the other hand, it is rather reassuring, that as more and more twins have come together and shared their stories in remarkably open and honest ways, that these confirm the earlier findings. I think all the twins who have attended any Network meetings would agree that an essential part of each meeting is for twins to get together with others whose loss was at the same stage in life. I also believe that most of the lone twins in the Network would acknowledge a deeply-held sense of a loss that they all have in common, regardless of when it happened. The members of the Network also have different issues that they want to discuss at these Meetings, which often cut across the age at which the loss occurred. That is why being able to choose which different group they would like to join where they can share talk about issues of importance to them, is also valuable.

Those in the 'loss at birth' group have nothing tangible to hold on to in the way of photographs etc. and have had their sense of loss all their lives. Those who 'lost their twin in childhood' have memories to recall, photographs and sometimes other things that belonged to their twin. These two groups have one very important fact in common and that is the parental influence on the response to the loss. The group whose 'loss occurred in adult life' have a deep sense of loss that is the most comprehensible to singletons. Many of these lone twins are able to understand the feelings of envy held by twins in the other two groups. They wish that they could have had at least some of their adult lives with their twin.

THE GROWTH OF THE NETWORK

Over the years since it was founded, the Network has grown steadily with many of its members actively contributing to this. At the moment the membership is around six hundred, with some members leaving and new ones joining. For a long time there has been some pressure put upon the Network to have a website, and very recently this has become a reality (www.lonetwinnetwork.org. uk). It is in its early stages and no doubt will change as time goes by. There is a hope that the Network will come to be better known, but that it will not become enormously enlarged as the current size provides manageable meetings. Many lone twins meet now as old friends after knowing each other over many years, as well as wanting to welcome new members. This could be much harder to do, if numbers greatly increased. The 'Twinless Twins' (a similar organisation in the USA) have had to organise their meetings over a period of days as they have grown bigger. They have incorporated family members as well, all of whose voices need to be heard.

I hope that lone twin networks will grow up in other countries, as the need for them gets more widely recognised. I was privileged to be invited to play a part with another lone twin to help start a Network in Scandinavia through the generosity of Abalone Glahn who has a twin web site. Because the UK Lone Twin Network is listed on many health websites as well as our own, it is easy to locate information.

I still believe the Network's future may eventually be served best by becoming a registered charity, but this can only come about when enough members want to make this happen and it may make too many demands on individual members. Currently enough members work hard to maintain the confidential list of members which is a unique and remarkable document as it holds a summary of each member's history of loss. Members of the Committee organise annual and regional meetings, manage a library, a directory of therapists who are knowledgeable in the field of twin loss, sell discreet badges and above all keep an up-to-date database as well as looking after the finances. I believe this to be a remarkable achievement by a group of people who have to cope with the inevitable emotional ups and downs that serious losses always leave in their wake.

When I let it be known to the Network that there was the opportunity for a revised edition of this book, there were some interesting responses with some 'new' stories as well as some 'up-dates' on previous ones, which provide an additional dimension to this edition. Some lone twins who did not wish to add further stories, asked me to stress the importance of the Network in enabling lone twins to be aware of others, which helps them stop feeling that they are the 'only ones in the world'. It may take some lone twins a long time after the original bereavement to pluck up the courage to attend a meeting. Gary Orange's story of his response to a meeting after many years as a member may encourage other lone twins to feel it is not so daunting as they may imagine.

One of the most controversial issues that a few lone twins have raised is a belief that they lost their twin early in their mother's pregnancy, even though there is no objective evidence to 'prove' it. This issue is one that holds such strong and divided views, that I have brought them together in a new section in this edition. I have tried to describe both up-to-date 'scientific' views on the subject and the views of others who disagree. There is also a new addition to the section on 'Therapy' from the member who is a therapist and has looked after the directory of therapists.

THE FUTURE

I can only end this Introduction by saying how glad I am that I had the opportunity to do the original study and to present it to an International Forum and that that enabled me to set up the Lone Twin Network and to put together the first edition of this book. I am very aware that there are fields that still await progressing. The most important to me is how to extend support in an appropriate way to young people under the age of eighteen who are too young to join the Network as it is established at the moment. There is also a need to bring together parents who have recently lost a twin at birth, with surviving twins who have reached adult life. On two occasions under the auspices of the Multiple Births Foundation at Hammersmith Hospital, such parents met up with adult lone twins who had lost their twin at birth. They were able most sensitively to offer understanding and some helpful suggestions to the parents at a time when their distress was very great.

Because sadly there will probably always be lone twins in the future, I can only hope that the Network continues to develop and that this book continues to be helpful to future lone twins, their parents, partners and friends.

2
THE BEREAVED TWIN STUDY

THE BEGINNING

'The trouble with you Joan, is you can't do anything by half.' This remark made to me when I was sixteen years old by an exasperated school friend brought me up with a jolt! At that time of my life feeling 'only a half' was a barely conscious perception, but looking back with hindsight, I can see how paradoxically my fierce struggle to disprove it by trying to be 'much more than a half', has never really left me. It was many years later that I was to hear other lone twins tell me how they had very painful feelings of being 'only a half' after their twin had died.

All through my life I have been aware of having many different feelings that did not seem to be shared by my singleton friends. It was this awareness that, quite late in life, made me question how far these feelings might be due to the death of my identical twin sister when we were three years old. Earlier, during two lengthy periods of psychoanalysis, neither of my Freudian analysts had considered her death as having any great significance in my life.

Within a few weeks of my sister's death, I suffered three particularly traumatic experiences in the streets around my home. At this point I went 'on strike'! My sister had disappeared in a taxi never to return and it seemed to me that 'life out there' was terrifying. I apparently announced that I was not going out of the house again. My mother, who was remarkably progressive for her day, took me off to see a well known child psychoanalyst. I remember my visits to her quite well. The apocryphal story goes that I reported how I wished that she would 'just let me play with her toys' (she had a wonderful doll's house) and 'stop asking me rude questions'! No doubt just as my subsequent Freudian analysts did, she too saw my fears in terms of my sexual fantasies. In spite of this, her interventions must have been helpful to me, for she strongly recommended that I start school immediately. This gradually broke my fear of going out and I can still remember my first day at school and everything I did in it very clearly. As with most people who have had a deeply traumatic experience early in life, many subsequent events have at times both forced the memory of the deep loss feelings to conscious awareness, as well as reinforcing my ability to face them.

The motivation to discover more about the effect on twins of the loss of their twin came from two further sources. The first was the recognition that I had never knowingly met another lone twin, so that all my knowledge was highly subjective. I knew that I would have to meet many others to come up with any valid findings. The second was that by the 1980s I had already completed and published three major research projects, so that I felt relatively competent to embark on a further one. This time I was determined to do it on my own, though I was appreciative of having The West Midlands Institute of Psychotherapy, of which I was a full member, willing to provide official auspices for the Study.

At that time, I was also seeking an alternative theoretical base for understanding not only about possible responses to the loss of a twin, but more about the whole grieving process. I was looking for a connection between the experience of deep loss and its effect on the formation of a 'sense of self' or identity. I was very interested in how this 'sense of self' develops and what factors tend to make it fail. I wanted a theoretical framework that would challenge the Freudian views that had dominated my training and which had proved to be so deficient in leading to any deep comprehension of both my own loss and the many varied losses experienced by the people I was working with.

John Bowlby's Attachment Theory, with which I had become familiar by the end of the 1970s, provides the fundamental concept of 'Attachment' as *'Instinctive Behaviour, built in to all of us as human beings, provides the protection and security we must have to survive. When this is unwillingly broken or threatened, it leads to virtually all the emotional disturbances that humans suffer from'* (Bowlby 1971). For me, only Bowlby's work, with further understandings from Alice Miller and Jean Baker Miller, has stood up to the rigorous examination of the many twins' responses to their loss and also provided invaluable pointers to helpful therapeutic interventions.

THE STUDY'S SAMPLE AND MAJOR FINDINGS

The Bereaved Twin Study began in the usual way, with punching keywords into a computer at Birmingham Medical School's library, to find out what work had already been published on the subject of twin loss. So much had already been published on the loss of spouse and loss of children, that I was expecting to find a number of papers on twin loss. I was very surprised to find at that stage that there was nothing, so the field was clear! I wanted to focus the study on how twins actually experienced their loss and to have each twin categorise the severity of the loss for themselves. I hoped to discover what they each felt were the worst aspects of their loss and if anything had helped to ameliorate it. I decided against postal questionnaires and to interview each twin personally in his or her own home whenever possible.

Lone twins were sought through notices in many local places and newspapers. It was not until a letter was published in a women's magazine with a vast circulation and getting a 'slot' on a TV programme that the sample reached the figure of 200. This could not provide a guaranteed typical sample of lone twins as all had volunteered, but it was likely, as a research statistician advised, to be a 'reasonable sample'. I visited 219 lone twins, men and women in England and Wales (Scotland was left out as too distant in terms of time and cost). The lone twins' ages ranged from 18 to 92 years. Some had lost their twin at or around the time of their birth, some in childhood and others in adult life. Ninety of them were identical (monozygots), 111 were fraternal (dizygots), 18 did not know their zygosity. The Study was presented to The International Congress of Twin Studies in Amsterdam in 1986. It was subsequently chosen for publication in the Journal of their Proceedings (Woodward, 1987). This gave the Study international status, but more importantly for me, it gave recognition to the unique loss of a twin.

The clearest finding of the Study was that the loss of a twin is a very profound one. Eighty-one per cent of the lone twins interviewed described their loss as having either a 'severe' or a 'marked' effect on their lives. The severest effect (with inevitable exceptions) tended to be experienced by those twins who lost a twin of the same sex, whether they were identical or not. The cause of death also affected the severity of the loss feelings. This was particularly so for those twins whose twin had died in a very traumatic way. Some had their twin commit suicide, two had their twin murdered.

The finding that created the most interest and surprise was that when the group that defined their loss as 'severe' was put with those whose loss had a 'marked' effect, there was a significant correlation with the loss having occurred *before the age of six months*. I believe that this is due to two factors. The first is that at this pre-verbal age the surviving twin cannot speak about the loss or grieve in a way that is properly acknowledged or shared. They have no knowledge themselves with which to understand such a loss and are engulfed with the feelings. Second, at this age the parental influence is at its height, so the surviving twin is not only coping with his or her own feelings, but also with his or her parents' response to the loss.

Eight themes emerged from the Study that were of particular interest. In order to understand these in the light of Attachment Theory, it is necessary for readers who may not know Bowlby's work, to introduce some of his basic thinking first. The themes will then be described. They reveal how important Bowlby's views are to understanding why so many twins have experienced the loss of their twin in such a variety of painful ways.

JOHN BOWLBY'S ATTACHMENT THEORY

Bowlby never actually studied or wrote about Attachment Theory in relation to twins, but he was very interested in and supportive of the Bereaved Twin Study, even though it took place near the end of his life.

Bowlby defines Attachment Theory as: 'A way of conceptualizing the propensity of human beings to make strong affectional bonds to particular others' (Bowlby 1979: 127). He came to this conclusion after years of observing the relationship between babies and children and their mothers. He chose to study the maternal bond because of its universality. It also meant that his findings are applicable across many different cultures. The importance of this 'propensity' in us all to make such bonds, is in Bowlby's view due to humans being determined by *instinctive behaviours,* just as all other animals are, in order to ensure their survival. It is the humans' need for protection that leads to the absolute necessity for them to be safely 'attached' to a 'caretaker'. Bowlby believes it is from this that a child develops a secure and valued 'sense of self', conscious of his or her own separate sense of identity, which, as he puts it, enables the child to 'explore'. He means by this that such a child grows up able to act with confidence and a proper awareness of both self and others and most importantly can in turn make bonds with others and become a capable 'Attachment figure' as a parent. Bowlby believed that an 'Attachment' with firstly a 'caretaker' (generally the mother, but it could be the father or other person) – created mutually, with deep pleasure experienced by both in the bonding – sets the pattern for the proper development and good mental health of the child as he or she grows into adulthood.

With twins, because of the existence of two babies, the Attachment process is different from the one that occurs for singletons. There seem to be three possible problematic variations. The first is when a strong Attachment exists between the twins, when they seem to form a self-contained unit. This can lead to an early form of language and communication between each other, which is not understood by anyone else. This can lead to mothers feeling 'shut out' and rejected, so that they tend to withdraw, leaving the very situation they dislike to develop even more strongly. Other siblings in this situation can also feel 'shut out' and are left feeling either resentful or they too withdraw. They may turn even more strongly to the parent, which tends to maintain the twins' isolation and separateness from the caretaking Attachment figure. A second variation comes when the mother or caretaker makes a strong Attachment to one of the twins and not the other. This leaves the other twin's access to the vital Attachment with his or her mother only available via the Attached twin. This tends to occur most often when mothers over-value a boy twin at the expense of the girl. When this does occur, the wanted son tends to develop in confidence and ability and the daughter tends to hold back and gets even less attention and valuing, making the situation even more extreme. The third variation comes when each parent is strongly Attached to a different twin. This can sow the seeds for a split in the family.

If those advising families with twins are aware of these possible Attachment variations, they can help parents of twins to recognise them and try to support such parents in ways that will enable both twins to get equal Attachment with their mother, or the caretaker figure. This will enable both twins to make proper Attachments with others as they develop. Bowlby believed that the greatest need for Attachment occurs up to the age of three years, but the need continues in varying degrees throughout life.

From Bowlby's recognition that proper Attachment lies at the heart of the development of a 'sense of self', comes an understanding of why it is harder for twins to gain this strong sense of their own separate identity. Ideally, this sense is reflected back to them through their mother's loving, caring and valuation of them. The difficulty for twins is not necessarily caused by the problematical variations already described, nor that twin babies are less valued than singletons. I believe it lies in the deep paradox that exists in every twin relationship. This is due to the fact that their 'sense of self' is built on the concept of being a 'pair'. They are defined as 'the twins', part of a twosome, yet this definition challenges a concept of a single identity. To have this means, in a sense, being without their twin, but this in turn requires a denial or loss of their sense of twinship. Bringing up twins requires a lot of open talking about this conflict, giving opportunities to arrange not only 'togetherness' which can provide happiness and security for them, but also opportunities to have Attachments on their own. This enables them as they grow, to know of a separate, competent 'sense of self' as well as deeply appreciating the existence of each other. This is easy to write about as a 'goal', but in practice is not so easy to carry out.

Failure of Attachment, that is, a lack of affectionate bonding between a baby or a child and its caretaker, or the *unwilling* loss of a primary Attachment (and this may include a twin through death), can lead, as Bowlby describes, to a state of 'Separation Anxiety'. In his view this almost inevitably results in expectations of similar losses to come. The 'loner' syndrome may develop when a person remains detached from others in order to protect him- or herself from the pain of possible future loss, through not risking making any other deep Attachments. This kind of behaviour is often seen in children whose primary Attachment figure has died, or left them, or even threatens to do so. Children whose parents for a variety of reasons are unable to provide appropriate Attachment, often leave their children seeking it for the rest of their lives in ways that are frequently debilitating, or worse, self-destructive.

Sometimes the loss of a twin in childhood can produce in the surviving twin some of the feelings more commonly created by parental abuse. This is because a young child trusts his or her parents, believing in their capacity to take care of him or her. When a twin dies, this ability to keep the child safe appears to fail. This can be experienced by the surviving twin as something the parent 'could' or 'should' have been able to prevent. This loss, experienced between the ages of about two and eight years can expose the fallibility of parents in a very sudden manner, often leaving a child feeling very frightened and insecure. I believe this is particularly so for a twin, though it may also apply to other siblings, because the surviving twin is so close to the child that has died in both age and proximity. All sorts of fears can arise in the survivor, leading to questions such as 'Could it happen to me?'. The concept of death due to disease is not easily understood by small children. They may instead fear the child died because he or she was 'bad' in some way. This again can set up fears about it happening to them if they are not 'good' and can lead to very placatory behaviour. As the function of Attachment is to make children feel safe, protected and able to thrive, a terrible paradox arises for all abused children, that the very people they turn to for their protection are those who abuse.

The Study showed that a few twins whose parents, for desperate financial reasons, were genuinely relieved that only one twin survived and went out of their way to make that twin feel especially wanted and valued, recorded no 'severe' response to their loss.

It is now possible to turn to the eight themes that emerged from the Bereaved Twin Study and to see how far they can be understood in the terms of Bowlby's Attachment Theory.

1. THE EFFECT OF PARENTAL ATTITUDE

There were two major ways in which parents *tended* to respond to the loss of a twin at or around the time of birth, or later in childhood. One was the very understandable response of being over-protective of the surviving twin. Many extreme examples of this were described to me, which, in Attachment terms, would suggest that the parents of these twins were themselves people who had suffered from some loss of Attachment experiences. This resulted in them being patterned strongly into the expectation of further loss to such an extent that their own fears took priority over the needs of the surviving twin. These fears then made it hard for such parents to increase the sense of security so badly needed by the survivor. In some cases the parents made demands on the twin that was left to meet the parents' needs in a variety of ways.

One man in his forties said he was 'so cosseted' by his mother after his twin brother's death that he could 'never leave her'. He never wanted to go to school and attended so irregularly that he never learned to read or write properly. Bowlby would describe this as an extreme example of an 'Anxious Attachment' giving rise to 'Separation Anxiety' and leading to this child having to 'parent his parent', with disastrous consequences for him. A woman whose twin died around the time of their birth said that she was not sent to school until she was seven years old. Later, she bitterly regretted not being allowed to work away from home because of her parents' anxiety about her. One woman in her sixties described how after the death of her twin sister, she was 'kept little – always ill', and sent to a private school where she said that she 'never caught up'. This sense of being the 'ill, weak one' was described more frequently by female lone twins than male ones. One woman described how she was 'not allowed a bike' and another was 'not allowed to go swimming'; yet another said her parents were so anxious about her that they would not allow her to go to the local library for fear of her 'picking up germs'. Some of these young women were kept at home not able to believe in their normal health and strength and they described deep feelings of loneliness as they grew up.

When the mother's grief for the dead twin was overwhelming, it sometimes led to the surviving twin feeling deeply devalued. As one twin put it, 'Lacking part of the self, I never felt right on my own.' One described her mother as so distressed by the loss of her twin daughter that she was incapable of taking the surviving daughter to school. This over-possessive protectiveness generally tended to leave the survivors immensely lacking in confidence, with some feeling that they were unable to fulfil their potential.

One or two described how they had challenged this parental response. One man said that when he decided to get married, his mother refused to come to the wedding. A young woman who dared to leave her very over-protective mother had both her parents refuse to speak to her.

The other contrasting response by parents, which appears to be the opposite of over-protectiveness, was to reject the surviving twin. I believe that both these responses come from the same source. It occurs when parents feel unable to tolerate their sense of helplessness in the face of severe loss. This is not a condemnation of these parents, but rather an attempt to try and understand their feelings in terms of their past experiences which left them very vulnerable.

There were so many sad stories of lone twins feeling deeply rejected, but these were much more evenly shared between the men and women than were the stories of over-protection. Many of the lone twins spoke of their parents making unfavourable comparisons between them and their twin who had died. They felt that they were the 'fat one' or the 'small one', picking up the implication that their parents wished that they had been the one to die. One man in his seventies said that he was the smaller, weaker twin. His mother had told him he 'should have been the one to die', meaning probably that she expected him to do so, rather than his brother. He took it to mean that she wished he had died and his twin had survived. Later he had a severe breakdown.

The worst response came from twins who felt in some way responsible for the death of their twin. One woman in her thirties was told, at the age of twelve, that she had been a twin. She was informed that her twin had died as a result of being kicked by her in utero. She felt deeply rejected by her mother and later attempted suicide. A young man of twenty-four was blamed by his father for his brother's death which occurred at birth. He said that his father 'beat him black and blue'. This man's father had also been a twin who lost his twin brother. This man was able to talk very openly about his feelings that he caught from his father's anger and distress about his own loss of a twin brother which he had never been able to express until the death of his twin son. One woman described how she was brought up believing herself to be 'a murderer in the eyes of her mother', as her twin never fully developed. A man in his forties was told that he 'took his brother's strength'. One of the most painful descriptions of rejection came from female twins who lost twin brothers and were left feeling hopeless because they could never be 'the long sought-after son'. These women all described themselves as having great difficulty in achieving a good 'sense of self'. A few twins described how their mother had had another child as a 'replacement' for the lost twin. This child then became the adored, wanted child and the surviving twin had deep feelings of being cast aside.

2. GUILT

Feelings of guilt were expressed in many different ways. They were spoken about by twins who lost their twin in adult life nearly as much as by those whose twins had died very early in life. Guilt feelings were inevitably strong in those twins already described, who felt responsible for their twin's death, or believed that their parents wished that the twin who had died had been the survivor. One of the ways that guilt feelings were expressed by many of the lone twins was in their attempt to 'live for two', to try and make up for their parents' loss as well as their own. One man in his seventies speaking of this said, 'I must keep going, I must never let the side down.' Sometimes guilt over being the survivor led men in particular to put themselves at risk on an endless path of dangerous sport. Some of the twins who lost their twin in adult life, spoke with huge regret at not having appreciated their twin enough when they were alive, or felt that they had not taken enough care of them. One woman, referring to her identical twin sister said, 'How can I have fun when she is dead?' Some of the most painful guilt feelings came from those twins whose twin had taken his or her own life. The grief and fear that they expressed thinly covered anger as well, which for some was too hard to acknowledge openly. For some twins, to speak of being the bigger, stronger, more capable twin was also an anguish, and experienced in some sense as a burden in that they had not been free to choose. One or two twins were actually able to express that there had been times when they had wished their twin 'out of the way' and then felt huge remorse when their twin had died.

3. NEGATIVE ASPECTS OF BEING A TWIN

The basis of these feelings was always the struggle for a separate 'sense of self' and a feeling of needing their own identity, made harder because of the existence of their twin. I believe that some sense of this struggle occurs in every twin couple. Those twins who lost their twin at birth or in very early childhood never had the opportunity to experience this ambivalence to any high degree, so that nearly all of these feelings were expressed by twins who lost their twin in adult life. There were two main variations on this theme. One came from twins who experienced themselves as the 'strong one' of the pair, and the other as a 'drag', often 'holding them back'. One twin spoke of how she had passed her eleven-plus exam. but was not allowed to take up her place in the grammar school because her sister failed it. The other variation came from twins who perceived themselves as the 'weaker one' of the pair, who felt that they had no chance to develop or to be fully themselves, because their twin was always the successful, admired, wanted one. As one twin put it, 'The sun shone out of his eyes, I was only the girl.' It seems highly likely that some of those twins who take their own lives have this feeling in an extreme form, believing in some way that they cannot find the space that they need within the twinship couple.

A few lone twins were able to express genuine feelings of relief following the death of a twin who had had a handicap or life-long illness.

4. CLOSENESS

This theme was spoken about a great deal by identical twins who lost their twin in adult life. It played an important part in their experience of their 'sense of self' found through the twinship. Some of the 'closeness' stories provided the most light-hearted moments in the Study's interviews. Twins who had looked so alike that they had been able to hoodwink their teachers and even their boyfriends or girlfriends, were able to laugh at such memories. One man delighted in sharing his memories of swapping places with his brother in a water polo match, without the referee being aware of what they had done! There were many stories of twins who 'knew how the other twin felt'. They would find that they had bought identical clothes when apart, or sent each other the same card on their birthday. They spoke of how they had been able to give each other a great deal of support at school or at work. The pleasure of being a twin came over very strongly. One elderly twin described how she and her sister had both wanted to go to Art School. They were forced to earn their living in very mundane jobs, but in the end both of them achieved high levels of skill and recognition in the art world, stimulating and supporting each other. This level of closeness and the reliability of offering each other equal Attachment, gave those twins a deep sense of self through their twinship. Some twins had lived together and never got married. A few had double weddings; one even honeymooned with her twin. Another described how she and her twin sister gave birth to boys on the same day and later both gave birth again to girls.

Some very interesting accounts came from those twins who were told in late childhood or early adult life that they had been born a twin. Without exception they said that they had known about it at some level of consciousness and, when told, felt 'everything fitted into place'. 'It made sense at once to my understanding of myself', was how one twin put it. How far this knowing is due to memories that begin in utero, or from many clues picked up from parents, including overheard conversations, is impossible at this stage of knowledge to ascertain. Just as these twins knew of the existence of their twin at birth, there were many descriptions from twins of knowing of their twin's death, before this was officially told to them. Some described having very strong premonitions of it; others described experiencing pain and fear at the time of their twin's death. These were so strong for some of them that they knew something 'dreadful' was happening to their twin. These experiences were not reported with hindsight but recorded by people who were present with them at the time. It left these twins awaiting a call with the news and knowing what it would be. We do not yet fully understand this level of closeness in twins, or how such knowledge is transmitted.

5. POLARISATION

Polarisation, like closeness, was an important factor for twins seeking a resolution to the twin paradox and finding their sense of identity separate from their twin, yet often retaining the twinship by complementing each other. As one man put it, 'my brother was brains and I was games'. It was from these twins that the perception of being a 'half' after the death of their twin was expressed most strongly. One man in his thirties said he saw his brother as 'good, gentle and clever' and himself as 'dim, noisy, but practical'. One or two men who had twin sisters saw themselves as the dominant one of the pair, who 'protected' their 'weak' sisters. Others said that their sisters were the lively, boisterous ones and they remained shy and quiet. Some of the twins spoke about how, after the death of their twin, they took over their characteristics, becoming more like the twin that had died. One twin whose brother died at the age of twelve became so like him that his family became convinced that he had his 'twin's spirit within him'. One elderly twin described herself as very quiet and her twin as the 'talkative one'. When her sister died in childhood, she became talkative to such an extent that she recalled her grandmother saying that she had 'swallowed the gramophone needle'. Her own memory was of her 'withdrawing'. It seems probable that the loss of a twin is generally such a devastating one, that the surviving twin takes on the characteristics of the dead twin in an endeavour to lessen the sense of loss. One of the most extreme expressions of this feeling came from a young woman who said that she wanted to take on her twin's name 'to stop being herself'.

6. THE WORST ASPECTS OF LOSS

This theme arose out of stories that were told to me of how the loss of a twin led to further losses. Sometimes these accumulated in a way that was utterly devastating for the survivor. One of the most extreme examples concerned a woman who lost her twin sister at a time when they were both married with children. After the death of her sister, she took over the care of her sister's children as well as her own. She said that she had no one with whom she could share her grief. She reached a point of utter exhaustion and distress which took the form of her suddenly being unable to speak. She was unfortunately 'sectioned' in a psychiatric hospital and while there, her husband joined up with another woman, divorced his wife and got custody of their children, so that she did not see them again for eight years. She came out of hospital with no husband, no children and no home. One middle-aged man described how his feelings of being an 'unwanted failure' following the death of his twin brother, led to a build-up of uncontainable rage and jealousy towards his sisters. This finally broke out when he attacked his wife. He was under a legal Order not to see her or his son and expressed a sense of utter desolation, at having 'lost everything'. Another man, whose identical twin brother lived in the same village, was left caring for his brother's children after his twin died and having to work very long hours to support them. There were two male twins, both of whose brothers took their own lives and the aftermath with their parents was severe. The father of one of them died soon afterwards as he 'never got over the shock'. The parents of the other were involved in a very serious road accident. This twin lost his memory for a while, was unable to sit any exams and said that he had 'lost his sense of belief in the value of anything'. He later went through a period of therapy and made a very good recovery.

The parents of some of the twins 'split up'; they themselves suffered from 'nervous breakdowns' and some felt very distressed and angry as their families seemed to so 'monopolise the mourning' that the surviving twins felt that their loss was denied. One lone twin whose twin died at birth, had another set of twins born to her family and grew up witnessing their closeness, making her continually aware of her own loss. The sense of endlessly seeking an Attachment that cannot be found, which for some lone twins goes on all their lives, seems extremely common. It appears to be particularly true for those twins who are rendered 'only children' by the loss of their twin.

7. THE EFFECT OF THE LOSS ON RELATING TO OTHERS

This was the theme that nearly every lone twin in the Study spoke about. The tremendous problem for so many lone twins in relating to others highlights the relevance of Bowlby's Attachment Theory in understanding the depth of this unique loss. When this Attachment is *unwillingly* broken it alters the surviving twins' sense of self to such a degree that it deeply affects the way they perceive themselves and so, inevitably, how they feel about relating to others. The most obvious feature of this loss, and one described so many times to me, was a deep, disturbing sense of loneliness. I believe that it is difficult for singletons fully to comprehend this, because they have never had this notion of twinship as providing half of the perception of themselves.

If a spouse dies, the sense of loss in the partner can be devastating, but the person does have a memory of themselves before they were married and some of them may marry again. If a child dies, this can be an agony for the parent that is beyond description, but some of them may at least be able to continue in their parenting role with other children, or even have another child. For twins, they have *never known what it was not to be a twin,* so that in some sense the twin loss is not comparable with other losses. I would never want to move into a competitive argument over degrees of pain from loss, and the Study highlighted how different these could be even among lone twins. What is of interest, I believe to most people, is how to understand why losses of Attachment figures distress us so much, and through that understanding, to discover good ways of providing support for each other, as well as changing attitudes in society, so that losses of all kinds, including twin bereavement, can be far more openly shared and spoken about.

One of the most common problems in relating is for those lone twins who subsequently marry and who have a sense of enormous dependence on their wives or husbands. This was described by a man in his thirties who had lost a brother at fourteen and who remained very fearful of his ability to cope if his wife should die or leave him. Other twins, who have had the kind of separation anxiety levels already described with very over-protective relations with their mothers, fail to make an equal adult relationship with their wives or can never face marriage at all. One twin, who had lost his twin in early infancy, found the death of his mother caused him overwhelming distress, from which he said he would never recover.

Another elderly twin so idealised his dead twin sister that he felt 'no woman could match her'. He said that to care deeply for another woman would feel like a 'betrayal' of his twin. He was in fact married, but admitted he did not feel close to his wife. This feeling of fearing closeness led to some twins in the Study saying how unwilling they felt about marrying or having children. Some who did, felt unable to sustain the relationship. One young man described how his inability to get close had led to the end of his marriage, leaving him with very mixed feelings. In contrast to this, there were some twins who looked to a marriage partner to replace, in some sense, their lost twin.

One young man described how his distress at the loss of his twin brother had been so severe that it 'drove his wife away'. This raises the issue which the spouses of some twins must recognise that there is 'another person' in the life of their partner who may be experienced as 'closer' than they are and who has known their partner all their lives. If a twin dies, the spouse of the survivor can feel devalued and less important than the spouse's dead twin.

One man in his late fifties, who had recently lost his twin brother, said openly that this loss was 'worse than if he had lost his wife'. There was evidence of some painful jealousy experienced by some spouses whom I met during the Study interviews, but one man admitted that he would have 'collapsed' at the loss of his twin brother if he had not had the understanding of his wife on whom he depended heavily.

Some twins find it very hard to be alone. As one lone twin in her sixties expressed it, 'I must have a very close relationship, it feels wrong always to be alone.' Some twins described to me how very hard they found it to mix with other people; that they feel themselves to be 'a lone twin', separate from others, 'like an observer'. A few twins had extreme anxiety about their own children, especially when they reached the age at which their parent's twin had died. This brought back painful memories of loss in a very sharp form.

All these different stories of pain and difficulties that arise from twin loss, confirm again Bowlby's belief that humans need strong Attachments throughout their lives. When these are broken unwillingly, the serious nature of the loss needs far greater recognition. To mourn this loss deeply does not imply an 'over-dependency', as it is so often perceived to be, with all the implied pejorative overtones.

8. AMELIORATING FACTORS

This final theme of the Study was one that I had hoped to find a great deal more about, but in fact there were very few positive descriptions of factors that helped the twins to overcome their sense of loss. Deep religious beliefs, seeking comfort through spiritualism and ESP experiences, convinced some twins that the 'spirit' of their twin remained with them and that they would be reunited eventually, which tended to soften their sense of loss. Many other twins with no such beliefs, described their struggles to get a new 'sense of self' through being the 'survivor' and finding strength through 'keeping going'. One or two mentioned an awareness of being the 'lucky one' to be alive and learning how to appreciate life more as a result.

A number of twins named children after their lost twin, which gave them a sense of playing a part in keeping their twin's memory alive. I fear that this could add a burden to those children, as they feel obliged to live up to someone else's ideal. The taking on of the characteristics of the lost twin already mentioned, was a way of easing some of the sense of loss for a few twins.

*   *   *

These themes confirmed two further beliefs that Bowlby held very strongly. The first concerns his conclusion that the loss of an important Attachment figure in adolescence can be as severe in its effect as losses experienced in childhood. He wrote very convincingly that from his observations, when the kinds of bonds that we make are either broken or threatened with breaking, deep patterns of feelings and behaviours arise that undermine our sense of self and can last a lifetime. Secondly, he believed that when adolescents have a loss of this kind, they tend to respond either by 'cutting off' from others, or to have an over-intensity of Attachment. Another of the most important of Bowlby's beliefs, which is highly relevant to the loss of a twin, is his conviction that *all emotional pain and fears that people feel, are due to actual experiences*. This is of such importance to lone twins because so often their experience of the loss is denied, or overshadowed by its effect on other members of the family. One of the disappointing discoveries of the Study was an apparent lack of therapists with either deep awareness, or real knowledge of the nature and significance of twin loss. Some lone twins have found very good and helpful therapists, many others have not. Some lone twins write of their experiences of therapy in a later section of the book.

Although all lone twins have one factor in common – living their life without their twin – the Study showed that there tended to be different responses according to the stage in life at which the twin died. For this reason, the next three chapters of the book have been divided into the experiences of loss at different times of life: the first at the time of birth; the second, childhood; and the third in adult life. Each chapter begins with a description of the themes that most commonly occur at each stage, which are then illustrated by highly individual and personal stories from twins who wanted to make their experiences more widely known in order to increase other people's understanding of twin loss. A few were involved in the Study, many were not. Each one was free to choose whether they signed their contribution or remained anonymous.

3
TWIN LOSS AT THE TIME OF BIRTH

INTRODUCTION

This chapter contains the most controversial view in the book. This is because many people including most psychiatrists and psychoanalysts doubt whether the memory of a twin's existence in the womb, or at birth, can contribute to the surviving twin's sense of loss. Attachment theorists believe that Attachment behaviour comes into being around six months of age. I believe this may well be the case for singletons, but serious research Attachment studies so far have not included twins or other multiples who are in a unique situation as they share the womb space with each other.

Since completing the Study and being in touch with so many lone twins, I am much more willing to believe that some form of Attachment occurs for twins both before birth and around the time of birth. The writings of Verney (1982), Itzin (1989) and Pionelli (1992), give credence to this concept. Pionelli in particular has observed the behaviour of twins before birth via scans. She noted how they related to each other and later found similar behaviour patterns occurring in them as babies. I was able to see some videos of her work and was astonished to watch how the twins in the womb related to each other so clearly; some positively and others quite negatively. It has to be seen to be believed!

I still maintain that it is the attitude of the parents of the surviving twin that has the most profound effect on their feelings concerning themselves. This seems particularly true when the truth about being a twin has been withheld and then when later they are told, they can feel devalued as a lone twin for whatever reason. Parents struggling to manage their own grief, perhaps unable to speak of it, or, as time goes by monopolising it within the family, tend to leave the surviving twin suffering a deep sense of isolation. On rare occasions this can lead a lone twin to be drawn seductively towards the twin who has died. This situation can leave such a twin with a very precarious sense of self that may take long-term help to change.

The stories that follow illustrate three themes. The first is the effect on twins of being told suddenly that they had been born a twin. The second is the great depth of some twins' sense of loss. These stories show how some of them have been affected all their lives and why it has led them to seek therapy. The third theme illustrates the strong urge in these twins to make a connection with their twin who has died. These stories describe the struggles of some lone twins to find facts about their twin; others tell of their efforts to discover where their twins were buried. Finding, and in some cases marking, or even just visiting the grave has enabled these twins to move towards a greater acceptance of their loss.

THEME 1
ON BEING SUDDENLY AND UNEXPECTEDLY TOLD THAT 'YOU WERE BORN A TWIN'

As the findings from the Study showed, some twins were told quite abruptly during their childhood that they had been born a twin. This information had never been openly spoken about before and tended to come out at a moment of crisis or tension in the family.

Most twins informed in this way felt shocked and deeply affected by it and yet, without exception, their overriding feeling was of being told some information that, in a sense, they 'already knew'.

It is difficult to separate out actual memory from the fact that many parents talk in front of children as if they were deaf or incapable of understanding. Small children do not always 'understand' in the adult sense, but they are often very highly attuned to the feelings and atmosphere in a family setting. It is possible that all such twins have at some time overheard references to their twin's existence, though this is likely to have created an even greater sense of confusion for them, if such important and sensitive information is then experienced as something that they are 'not to know'.

What seems of great importance to the surviving twins is that, having at last been told, they have a new opportunity to understand feelings about themselves, some of which were previously experienced as mysterious. They often want to ask questions and these too may be blocked. These twins are faced with a very deep sense of loss, but also a sense of feeling special and compelled to rethink their sense of self.

Story 1
A woman in her fifties who lost her brother at birth
I lost my twin brother at birth, fifty-one years ago. It's a long time ago, yet I live it every day of my life. I can remember the day my mother told me I was a twin.

I was eleven and we had just moved to a new house. We had made friends with a similar family of four children over the road. I was friendly with the younger son, Patrick. One afternoon he told me he was a twin, but his twin brother had died. When I told my mother she said 'Oh, you're a twin as well, he died at birth.' I asked to hear more, but didn't get very far. So I spent the rest of the afternoon sitting on my bed, thinking.

My twin was a boy – the long-awaited boy my parents had wanted who had, when I was eleven, just been born and was much celebrated. How must they feel about me? Surely they must have wanted the boy twin rather than me? I had elder twin sisters who always had each other, so I was in the middle, alone, yet for the first time getting an inkling of why I felt so alone. As far as my twin sisters were concerned I was very spoilt – 'wrapped up in cotton wool' one of them told me. Yet I felt little emotional support, somehow losing the thread of my relationship with my mother and retreating into my own world.

Once, when I was in my thirties, my mother and I talked about my birth and my brother's death, and there was tremendous grief and sorrow for us both. Expressing these emotions has helped me to acknowledge that in my birth there was also the death of my twin brother; and that I have nothing tangible with which to say 'This was my brother, Christopher.' So there is an emptiness and an incompleteness in my life. My fear of love and intimacy has affected any deep relationships I have. The consequence being I have never married or had my own children. This feels as if a part of me has never had the chance to blossom and bear fruit.

CYNTHIA WHELAN

Story 2
A woman in her thirties who lost her sister before birth
I only came to know recently that I was a twin. She died in the early stages of pregnancy. What amazes me is that that early experience left its thumb print on the whole of my life. When I look back on poems I have written, a lot of the imagery seems to have come from the subconscious memory of her. In living with what was, until now, a subconscious memory, I have struggled to find my own identity in re-experiencing the past, which I did through therapy. It is releasing the present and the future, as well as releasing me to be more fully me.

In the stillness of the blue before dawn
I cried out your name
with the desperation of a dying woman
The world heard my cry fall on
deaf ears
Spinning together thru the universe
The veil of the temple was rent in two

I journeyed onwards alone.
Now my soul pirouettes silently
Thru life, joined to your shadow.
And so this is goodbye
The moment I leave what has been for us
and move on into what is for me.
I go now into my world
To live and breathe and dance
To the rhythm of a music
I have written.
We move to the sound of different drums
and it is good that it is so.

CATE JACOBS

Story 3
A man in his fifties who lost a brother before birth

SOME THOUGHTS FROM A NOT TOO LONELY LONE TWIN

As one of a student gang doing A level re-sits with long summer afternoons to fill in Brighton, it wasn't long before we took to arcade life between opening hours – oh those innocent days of pinball machines! That was reality, nothing virtual about it. From there we quickly slid down the slippery slope and spent our time on the Palace Pier doing Candid Camera stunts: the fun we had getting two people, one at either side of the Pavilion, each holding one end of a length of string ...

One wet afternoon such sport was out and we spotted the bedraggled-looking tent of the fortune teller. I forget the good lady's name (and do not wish to enter into correspondence on the matter), but she, like us, was having a dullish afternoon of it, so we took turns to have half a crown's worth of her clairvoyancy.

I think the plan was that we should somehow set about ragging her, but as I entered the acrid enclosure the woman's studied tranquillity quickly hit the tomfoolery option on the head. She scrutinised me with the shrewd and neutral gaze of a housewife at a butcher's window. A silence spread between us – I felt like a pork chop that wasn't passing muster.

Her voice when she spoke had a gentle, almost weary tone that lent an inevitability to her words. She began with a few safe observations and I had no difficulty holding on to my cynicism, but then she got lucky on one or two details which I won't trouble you with here, and I began to take notice. I was quite unprepared though for her casual remark that was to illuminate so much for me.

'You're one of twins.' It was a statement of fact, not a speculation. I smiled and shook my head; perhaps I could get a refund. 'No, you are mistaken. I was born in June, under the Zodiac sign of The Twins. I am a Gemini.' That had always been my excuse for any feeling of duality. It was her turn to smile and shake her head. 'Are you? That wasn't what I meant.' She gave me some more of the pork chop scrutiny and went on, 'You like making people laugh, you like disguising yourself ... maybe you'll be an actor.' (With the A levels I was on the verge of failing, this was already my game plan.) I was keen to press her on this point, but my time was up.

The following weekend I mentioned the session to my Mum; we were agreeing that clairvoyants, especially on the end of piers on wet afternoons, are not likely to be that dependable. I said, 'I mean, she even thought I was a twin.' There was no pause before her reply, no theatrical awkwardness, only her usual candour. 'And so you should have been, my darling.'

These moments of dreams coming true, of doubts being confirmed, of fantasies come alive have a kind of slow-motion impact, don't they? As they settle into your memory bank their implications seem to ricochet through your whole personality. 'What?', I said. 'It's no big deal,' she answered, 'I had a miscarriage when I was five months pregnant with you. I was miserable of course, but the doctor came back a couple of days later and told me there was still a baby there – that I must have been carrying twins' ... Yes, it was a boy, I knew that.

Let me explain – things were different in those days. Mum had not deliberately withheld the information (that wasn't her at all). It was simply a gynaecological detail that would be of no physical or psychological interest to me or anyone else. In 1963 the world hadn't acquired its appetite for such pre-natal curiosity. What I am saying is, she wasn't to know how glad I was to hear the news.

Here's where it gets difficult. As I understand it, having a twin, or at any rate an alter ego, is quite a common fantasy of children, but in the action replay of my childhood, I know there was another me – a kinder, braver, cleverer me, a more lovable or more wicked me, a me I could follow or copy, a me who could take the other alternative and tell me about it later, another me to take the blame or credit. I am so glad that he wasn't just a fantasy, so glad I know about him. After all, we did have five quite crucial months together, albeit foetally.

It sounds fanciful I dare say, but at the extremes of life, the highs and lows that we all have, I sometimes find myself wondering if it's really me or him going through them? And whether it's him or whether it's me, the experience is somehow intensified – if it weren't we'd be letting each other down. He's not a ghost. So what is he? He's an alter ego, a secret pen pal, a second chance, a confidant, a mirror image ... someone who at the same time shares the load and doubles the responsibility.

Do I feel any sense of guilt that maybe I survived at his expense? ... Er no, not honestly, and I don't think he would either. Do I feel lonely, do I miss him? No, not really. Every now and then he tells me to buck up or take it easy, but mostly he minds his own business. I wish he'd been there during my childhood as something more than a fantasy, isn't that when twindom is at its most potent?

Aren't twins supposed to grow apart as they grow up? I probably wouldn't have liked his wife, and the likelihood is that nowadays we'd only be having lunch once a month to swap symptoms.

I think it's true to say that by the time I knew of my twin's existence we had already begun to go our separate ways, and if he doesn't like the way I've led his life – too bad.

SIMON WILLIAMS

THEME 2
ON EARLY LOSS PRODUCING PAINFUL LONG-TERM DISTRESS AFFECTING SOME LONE TWINS FOR LIFE

This theme of lasting sensations of loss in some twins whose twin died at birth has led to such queries as 'Would the twin have been so affected if they had not known about their twin?'; 'How can a loss so early in life make for such deep patterning, that some twins carry a sense of grieving into adulthood?' I believe that these stories provide evidence that some twins feel a deep sense of loss of an important Attachment figure when their twin dies at birth. These feelings seem to occur in twins whose sense of loss has become a large part of their sense of self. It has become a part of *who they are*, as well as *how they feel* about themselves. For some the sense of loss seems to increase as they get older.

Story 1
A man of fifty whose sister died at five days old

CAROL

There are no memories of you,
My sister, my twin,
No memories but remembrance
Of you, my twin,
Whose life was so short
that you had gone
Before anyone knew you.

There is no birth certificate
nor certificate of death
in the family deed box
Only a faded brown announcement
Of your quiet wartime funeral
When your barely-formed body

(Thrust into the world too soon)
Was laid to rest
In the Children's Corner
Of the daisy-strewn country churchyard,
A sad collection of tiny graves,
Unfulfilled potential
Unrealised expectations
Smashed hopes
And shattered joys.

There is no stone,
Just a grassy mound,
Anonymous
Unrecognised.

Our parents both dead
Our younger sister estranged
I alone know who lies there,
My twin,
Carol Eileen.
Fifty years on
Still I yearn for you
There is a void,
A longing,
A realisation,
That all my life
I have been searching
For you, my twin, my soulmate,
The unremembered one
The unrecorded one
the rarely mentioned one
But the unforgotten one.

Are you no more
Than a few minute fragile bones
In a country churchyard,
Mourned by no one but me
Or are you in another dimension
Progressed now into maturity!
Have you greeted our parents
Who were also denied you!
Have you shared, unseen,

The painful years of our lives?
Are you with me now
As I struggle with my anguish
And aloneness!
Have you shared my sorrow
And my joy!
Would that I
Could have shared with you,
My sister, my twin,
Carol Eileen.

© MARK REES

Story 2
A woman of fifty whose brother died at birth

I've been a twin all my life, even though my brother died within a few hours of his birth. Being a twin has been part of my consciousness and its importance to me has always been great.

I don't know when I was told I had a twin brother, it seems I've always known and when I was a child it seemed very important to me that others should be aware of this fact. I still have a deep and intuitive feeling – a conviction – that it matters. It makes me different, and that difference deserves recognition. He has been my life-long companion. His presence in my life has not been intrusive and only rarely do I imagine his life as it might have been.

Through the Lone Twin Network I have met lone twins who have been denied the knowledge that I have taken for granted and I'm grateful that my parents, especially my father, told me. My mother died when I was eleven years old and therefore I've never had an opportunity to talk to her about my twin. I come from a Northern working-class family where feelings were not discussed and I was born in an era when talking about dead babies was seen as positively damaging. As a mother of an adult daughter I can only guess at the pain and grief my mother endured. I can imagine that much of her grief had to be denied by feeling 'thankful' that one survived. My own passage in the early months was a stormy one, so there were long months of anxiety in that also.

It may be that some of that anxiety had its repercussions for me. My physical health as a small child was not good and by the time I was five I had developed mastoiditis, then a potentially dangerous condition. Whatever its origins, there was in my early years – and is still now – a part of me that tended to dwell morbidly on sadness. At a pre-school age I used to sit in our little kiddy's chair and in my sister's Toby Twirl Annual turn unfailingly to an illustration of a little dog with its foot caught in a trap and I would weep uncontrollably. Eventually I was forbidden to read that book. Anxiety about death has stayed with me all my life. I had neither the means nor the opportunity to express my feelings and even now, only lone twins who lost their twin in babyhood really know how I feel. Singletons cannot understand how losing someone only a few hours old can possibly affect one at all. I don't have any answers, but I do know it matters, and now that I have the LTN [Lone Twin Network] to support me, I don't need to deny that feeling any more, nor do I feel any need to justify it.

LIZ LLOYD

Story 3
A woman of seventy whose sister died at five weeks

'BUT THEN FACE TO FACE'

I had always known I was a twin, that we were born on a cold November night in 1924; my sister Edna had been born twenty minutes before me. Over the years, through childhood to teens, from teens to adulthood there had been that constant feeling of loss and incompleteness, which I couldn't share with anyone, which didn't make sense, so I pushed it aside, though now it was falling into place. I grew up knowing that my mother had a difficult home confinement, that she had no idea whatsoever that more than one baby was due until after my sister was born: it was a big shock to both my parents to be told there was another baby making its way into the world.

My father's 'Oh no, we don't want two – one's quite enough!' was ringing in my ears as I arrived – possibly it was the natural reaction, but now I'm beginning to realise that this rejection of my father's carried on into the future from that first day: there was never any bonding with him for me throughout his lifetime. Edna had the bonding and for him should have lived. I was the weaker of the two, and both of us weighed under four pounds at birth. So many times through life I've thought, 'If only Edna had lived.'

There had been little, if any, ante- or post-natal care for my mother; no scans, no tests and some incompetent midwife told her she could feed us both, even though her diet was mainly bread and milk – hardly nourishment for a mother and one baby, never mind two! My twin just slipped away at five weeks old. I remained small and thin and, as one aunt never failed to tell me, 'looked like a skinned rabbit' in my pram.

My mother was afraid to let the wind blow on me, but there must have been some north-country toughness somewhere in me because I am now in my seventy-third year and am still going strong. There were panic stations when at a year old I had suspected meningitis and I used to be quite proud of my lumbar puncture mark. I had my tonsils out at five and was plagued with asthma from an early age.

During my school years I always felt left out when there were twins in the school. There were several twins in the High School and one pair in my class – how I missed my twin and wished she was with me. If on an odd occasion I'd say,

'I'm a twin', the question would then be, 'Where's your twin then?' I'd say,'Oh, she died at five weeks old'; I'd get a queer look and a 'Well, you're not a twin then, there's only you!'

I have two daughters and a son – how I wished I'd have twins with each pregnancy, but it wasn't to be. While the children were growing up I still looked with a special yen at sets of twins around the village.

As the years go by I miss my twin more than ever and I know that however many bonus years I have left, in the not too-far-distant future my twin and I will meet again, that we'll catch up on those years we've missed, that the separation will be over and as The Good Book says, 'For now we see through a glass darkly – But then face to face'.

RUTH WEAVER

Story 4
A woman of forty who lost a stillborn brother

I was born in 1952, with a stillborn male twin, who, much later on, I decided to call Richard. It has helped me to give him a name, and talk to him as a person, but it took a long time to reach the right time to do so. I have no idea why he died, but I grew up with a sense of guilt: I felt that it must have been something I did … did I strangle him with the umbilical cord? It is much more likely that it was something to do with me, the girl twin, using up all the nutrients at the expense of the boy twin. I believe this is quite common, but I will never know if this was so in our case.

My parents tell me that I slept a lot as a baby, and had to be coaxed into eating – as an adult I have suffered from clinical depression several times and now wonder if these were the first signs of depression, as I was left in a frightening new world without the brother I had grown beside for eight months.

When I was four and a half my sister was born. I was absolutely sure she was going to be a boy – when she wasn't, I remember feeling that I would continue to have to be both him and me. Trying to be both of us felt a heavy load to have to pull into the future.

Being both of us for me, I think, had a positive side-effect – I feel I have grown up without much conditioning because I was taking in both male and female conditioning and rejecting a lot of it. I think that helped me to make the choice later on to study physics to degree level and to work in laboratories, although it could be argued that I was attracted to science because my male conditioning was stronger than the female. However, whatever the reason, I did enjoy scientific laboratory work, and also team sports, playing women's cricket to county standard. In childhood I remember long summer holidays riding my bicycle and climbing trees with my friends, typical tomboy activities. I also took on the male need for a stiff upper lip, and even now, after therapy, I find it very difficult to shed a tear in front of other people.

I remember suffering early anxiety when leaving my first school, aged seven: this took the form of feeling unwell for the last few mornings I had at the school. I believe this was the first time I showed any separation anxiety (fear of being separated from something or someone close to me).

This came up for me again when my grandmother died when I was nine. She was my last and favourite grandparent. She died one night very suddenly and I had no warning that this was about to happen. My parents were rather matter of fact about it and I wasn't invited to the funeral. I don't remember crying, just being very shocked, and soon afterwards I began to have dizzy spells at school, getting sent home during the day. I can now relate this to separation anxiety – and I believe my grandmother's dying stirred up very early panic at being separated from Richard. I believe there was a very close bond between us in the womb for eight months and that when he died (before we were born), and subsequently never appeared after I was born, the panic, loss and anxiety were overwhelming. Sometimes I get in touch with a sense of extreme loneliness. I have no way of telling whether singletons or twins ever feel so lonely, but I tend to think not.

LIZ DAWSON

Story 5
A woman in her early thirties who lost a stillborn brother

Mark is my twin brother. He died when we were born. He was actually dead by the time I was delivered. It may seem an odd thing to say, but he is my best friend. I have many friends who are dear to me, but I love none of them as much as I do Mark. He is my mentor, my confidant, my guardian angel, my counsellor, my friend, my guide. I feel all these things about him, yet I have never met him in this life; he has never spoken to me audibly, and we have never exchanged an earthly interaction.

I miss him more than words can say. Every time I reach a crisis point, a new experience, a memorable occasion, he is there with me in spirit. But I want him to be there with me in body. I would love to share our birthday together, to be able to remember Christmases with him, to experience beautiful places and happy events jointly. If only I had just one picture of him, or perhaps a tape recording of his voice. If only to know him in body, to have known what it was to share with him, to experience with him, to love and to laugh with him.

The place in which I feel closest to him is at his grave. I am able to chat about my hopes and fears, my failings and frustrations, the good times and bad. It grieves me greatly that he is laid to rest in a public grave; I would like him to have a headstone. I want those who pass his graveside to understand and to acknowledge his presence in the general scheme of things.

I would not want not to be a twin. I am special and privileged to be one; I am proud to be Mark's twin sister. Whatever else has been taken from us, no one can take that fact away. We will always be twins; we will always have been born together, have lived in our mother's womb for nine precious months together. I will always have the knowledge of his existence, and of his place in my life.

Recently I have tried to join him. I believe that he is in Heaven, with God, and I felt the need to just let go of this life and be with him forever. But I wonder now whether this is what he would want. Perhaps I should be living his life for him, be his window on the world; perhaps I should experience joys and sorrows for his sake, so that maybe he will know through me the thrills and pains and pleasures of human existence. My belief is that he is waiting for me; we will be together one day, and we will be overjoyed to see one another. But maybe the time is not right just yet. Maybe I have a lot more living to do on his behalf. The answer is unclear as yet

ELIZABETH DALLAWAY

Story 6
A woman in her fifties who lost her identical brother at nine months
I discovered about the Lone Twin network and the Lone Twin book in an article in Saga magazine just before I turned fifty. Reading the book helped me make sense of the first fifty years of my life. I found bits of me on every page.

I had grown up knowing I'd had a twin brother, Jonathan, also believing that I was responsible for his death. I'd felt a need to justify my existence with miserable consequences, I was often lonely and struggled with relationships whether with family or friends. I recall being so very envious of other twins. There were twins at both my primary and secondary schools; how I longed to tell them that I was a twin too, but never could. I have an enduring image of myself as living outside of everything, more spectator than participant, if that makes sense. My birth circumstances, though not secret, were never discussed; I knew nothing about how or why Jonathan had died or where he was buried. We were born at home, my mother often blamed the midwife for not getting her into hospital, and a local girl had been employed to help with the twins so she became surrogate mother for a number of years. Sadly she died young leaving four small children, so I never got to talk to her either.

I had two disastrous relationships and had been severely depressed off and on for many years. I'd lost all self esteem and confidence and was pretty reclusive when I attended the LTN conference in London March 2006 (quite an effort for me, I'm not sure to this day how I got myself there but it was obviously meant to be). Travelling all the way from Devon I arranged to stay overnight with a friend of 20 years and discovered she too was a surviving twin. I also found a wonderful counsellor at Palace Gate Christian Counselling in Exeter who helped me come to terms with a huge number of difficulties, many of which were rooted in my birth/family circumstances.

My father, who had never mentioned Jonathan to me in fifty years, read a letter I'd written to Saga thanking them for introducing me to the LTN. Then, after finding and reading the article that my letter referred to, he wrote to me confessing that he had never given a moment's thought to the possibility that I might be affected by my birth circumstances and dialogue began. I now know how and when Jonathan died, where he is buried and have his birth and death certificates.

Eighteen months on and I am no longer ill, have two new jobs, have left an abusive partner and bought a little home of my own, I've rebuilt damaged relationships with my three children and elder stepson, become a grandma and made new friends. I joined a writing group and have had a short story published. I have grieved and finally put my troubled past to rest and am much more comfortable with myself, I have also found a deeper faith which has helped enormously.

Sad to say that I haven't been able to mention any of this to my mother (she and my father divorced when I was in my twenties), and doubt that will ever happen, but at least my father and I have an understanding which has done us both good.

Jonathan and I were born on 30th June 1955. I was first born and Jonathan lived for half an hour dying of respiratory failure. He is buried in the churchyard of the village church where I was christened and married, 100 yards from our family home.

JO TURNER

THEME 3
ON SEARCHING FOR THE LOST TWIN AND STRIVING TO MAKE CONNECTIONS

For some lone twins whose loss occurred early in their lives there seems to be an endless searching for the missing person. This may or may not be something of which they are consciously aware. It certainly affects the way some of them relate to other people. It can leave for some a sense of living in an incomplete jigsaw. It confirms Bowlby's view of the need for Attachments being life-long. It has led some twins to go to great lengths to discover the graves of their twin and to carry out meaningful rituals of various kinds both to mark the spot and to give recognition to their twin through naming, having a plaque made, or a container placed in the cemetery.

I believe that these activities are of utmost importance for twins who have no mementoes of their twin, no photographs, nor any way of sharing talk about their twin in the family.

Story 1
A woman in her forties who lost an identical sister at birth

My identical twin sister died one hour after her birth and I've since been an only child. I was for many years a very timid, lonely, only child. In my infancy I preferred to be alone or with adults, rather than with other children, who always appeared to be extrovert, bold, daring, happy in their particular tribes. I always felt apart from them, isolated, different, and of course I didn't know why. Unfortunately, not only did I feel different, I also felt very inferior – my friends were always better; better people, better scholars, and certainly better sports people. My timidity became even more apparent in the school gym and on the sports field, or in any place where physical strength had to be displayed. I was reduced to a trembling mass of fear when faced with any danger. I desperately wanted a best friend, another little girl who could be the other half of me, the special piece of jigsaw that would slot perfectly into mine. My 'friends' at that time, however, were sturdy, self-confident little girls who didn't have the same fears as I. They enjoyed peril and, as a result, I became the butt of their teasing, and often their cruelty. My mother, to whom I've never been close, despaired of me. I preferred sitting alone in my room with a pen in my hand when I should have been outside joining in my friends' games.

When I was eleven and attended secondary school, I met Susan to whom I immediately attached myself and we were the best of friends many, many years; through school, college and later in adult life. As happens with most people, of course, our closeness became less intense with the passage of time and I was devastated. I couldn't accept that Susan could be anything other than my little piece of jigsaw.

In spite of my love of English, when I took my mock O levels I had a dose of flu and as a result, failed my English exam. Against my better judgement, I was persuaded to enrol at a business college. I passed my GCE O levels with flying colours.

There followed twenty years of absolute hell. I hated office work with all my heart and was no good at it. I left unsuitable jobs and drifted aimlessly into other unsuitable, low-paying work – shop assistant, barmaid, night club waitress etc. – and I was sacked several times from secretarial positions. My already low self-esteem took another nose dive every time an irate boss told me I was no good and sent me packing.

For a period of four years I was married to a man whose main pleasure in life was making me miserable. His nickname for me was 'silly cow'. However, because he went out alone every evening to the pub, I began writing stories in earnest and was published in certain magazines and also wrote for BBC radio. These successes in my life did not elevate me in my ex-husband's eyes. I divorced him in 1980 and met a man whom I formed a strong attachment with – thinking yet again that I'd finally met my other half. The elusive piece of jigsaw. An ugly brute, but warm, strong, affectionate and funny; and, most important of all, he made me feel wanted. He made me feel good about myself – he told me I was an 'interesting woman '; he made me feel proud of my body, my physical appearance.

I travelled overland to Africa with him, in an old, converted ambulance. We had many adventures together; hilarious, wonderful, extremely dangerous adventures. We were going to reach Zimbabwe, get married and raise a family. Yes, at last, I'd met my other half. Except our ambulance broke down in the deserts of Sudan and Tony sent me back to England, wanting to continue the hazardous journey without a female encumbrance. He intended sending for me when he had settled. I flew home from Khartoum, heartbroken, and spent the next four months waiting for his very infrequent letters – and the most important, final letter containing a plane ticket. His final letter, however, contained a few lines telling me he'd met another woman. I hadn't met my other half, after all.

That year, 1981, I met Pam, an Indian girl with whom I had an instant rapport. I felt very close to her, she was a warm and wonderful human being. She thought the same about me and we spent hours in each other's company, talking about everything under the sun. We decided to share a house together and I was very happy. Pam then got another job in another town and met new, more exciting people than I, and we spent less and less time together: it was becoming obvious that I was beginning to bore her. I was sacked from my 'perfect' job for incompetence. That was about the fifth time. Pam and I eventually left our house – after seven short months – and she went to London. I've never seen her since.

In 1983 I started writing my first novel. The publishing company where I'd worked was going to publish it. Then I returned from holiday and was told they couldn't publish it. I didn't feel worthwhile any more.

The following year I got a job as a secretary to a top architect in Leeds and was sacked after two months. For the seventh time. That was when I decided to do what I'd wanted to do twenty years before, teach English. I took a Teaching English as a Foreign Language course in Bradford and I've never looked back. I'm now teaching at an international language school in Paris, loving every minute {almost!} and writing. I've just finished my third novel. None of my novels has yet been published, but I'll never give up trying. I've recently written a lot of texts for my school, some of which will be used world-wide. My professional life, at long last, is successful and I thoroughly enjoy what I do.

I've never found that piece of jigsaw that would fit so perfectly into mine. I've got female friends here in France – although that's taken a long time. But the friends I've got are already partnered; they have boyfriends, husbands, families, lives of their own. I'm still only half a person; I'm still searching for the other half of me.

The key word throughout a twin's life, I think, is 'share' and lone twins are not excepted from this rule. I've always felt the need to share my experiences with a special person, the good, the bad and the banal. Because the original and real special person in my life isn't there, I've always had to have a friend with whom I can partake of the day-to-day events of my life. It's not possible for me to keep things to myself – as soon as I have wonderful or devastating news I must immediately pick up the telephone and share it. If the response on the other end of the line is less than enthusiastic, I feel hurt, let down.

Another strong feeling that's clung to me throughout my life is the fear of losing something. Whenever I begin a new relationship with either a male or a female I always think it's not going to last, I'm going to lose it, it's going to be taken away from me. It's the same with possessions homes, jobs, pets, etc. I live in deep fear of losing and never regaining these people and things in life that are precious; that I value and love.

A palmist told me I was looking for my soul mate, somebody who was like me. I still haven't given up hope.

SHEILA HEYWOOD

Story 2
A woman in her thirties who lost an 'interlocked' twin brother at birth
The discovery that I had been born a twin was made on a summer's day in 1973. What I could not possibly have known at that time was that it would take me a further twenty-one years to gather together the information that would shed some light on this discovery.

I found a letter which contained a never-to-be-forgotten line: 'Never mind about the other little one, you have a beautiful baby daughter ...' At first I thought this referred to a sibling but the date on the letter linked it to my birth. Reading this sentence was a turning point and a source of relief. Everything fell into place and made perfect sense. What I read felt familiar and was a relief rather than a shock or surprise, although it most definitely was just that. Instead there was a recognition that yes, this is true: of course I am a twin, along with an awareness that it confirmed what, subconsciously, I already knew. I am also quite convinced that had I not uncovered this letter and asked some questions, then the information would have remained a well-kept family secret.

As a child I can remember a constant feeling of something being lost or missing, though what this something might be, I could not explain. I recall a sensation of waiting – but for what (or whom?), I did not know. I needed to ask questions and make sense of my discovery. Such a topic is a sensitive one and to raise it can re-open wounds which have never healed. At the time I did not fully understand this so I was curious to find out all I possibly could.

At thirty-four weeks into what was my mother's first pregnancy an X-ray was taken. This established that my parents were expecting twins: although twins had occurred in the wider family, there had been no reason to suspect a twin pregnancy and no diagnosis to this effect had been made. Six days later, following an emergency delivery in the local hospital, I was born; my twin did not survive. The consultant later said that my twin and I were interlocked, and that in all his years he had only ever read about this obstetric complication, let alone been present at such a delivery.

As a twelve-year-old, all of this didn't mean a great deal. I knew that I felt myself to be something of a rarity, even a little bit special for being a twin and for having survived. Somehow I knew enough not to talk about this subject and although I put it away at the back of my mind, I never forgot about it. It arose, several years later, during both of my pregnancies.

In order to arrange my ante-natal care, my GP asked the usual questions pertaining to my medical history, including one relating to the incidence of twins in the family. Her eyes lit up when I mentioned that I was born a twin. It became clear that I could not provide very much information relating either to my own birth or to the circumstances of my twin's death.

When my first child was born I experienced for myself the strength and depth of that bond which forms between a mother and her baby. Only then could I appreciate for myself the enormity of the grief that follows the death of a baby, and the understandable hesitation of the parents in talking about this tragic event. During each pregnancy (and afterwards), I often considered what it meant to be half a twin. Questions formed in my mind in regard to my own birth and to the ante-natal care my mother received. Being the mother of two small children left me precious little time for reflection and so, once again, the subject was relegated to a mental back-burner.

I continued to speculate about my twin. I cannot recall when, or even if, I was told my twin's gender. I picked up a clue that my twin must have been male, though he was never referred to by name. I sensed that my twin was, indeed, male, a much-missed brother, and I considered it unfair of me only to refer to him as 'my twin'. As the one who survived, it gradually became very important that I should name my twin and in doing so I would both acknowledge and confirm his existence. Had he survived I had a strong feeling that my brother would have been called Patrick (in which case I would not have been Patricia), and so I quietly named my brother PATRICK TOMAS.

The thoughts and questions which I had carefully filed away reached a crescendo in June 1989. I had a strong feeling that my brother's death was somehow my fault. As I was never given the reassurance that this was not so, I lived with the consequence: namely, guilt. Was there a suspicion that my mother was carrying twins? Had any symptoms been overlooked which might have given an earlier indication of a possible multiple pregnancy? Could a much earlier X-ray have alerted the doctors to the situation? From the evidence available on the X-ray, and from the emergency which developed, why was a Caesarean section not done? I wondered whether a Caesarean section might have ensured a safer delivery and maybe my brother might have survived too. I wanted to know how it was possible that one baby could survive birth while the other did not.

I desperately needed to know every detail relating to our delivery and to the death of my brother. My search for these answers caused an ache in my heart. Not knowing meant I could not grieve as I needed to for my brother. My feelings, thoughts and especially my tears were put on hold.

I contacted the Registrar of Births and Deaths in the district in which I was born, in the hope that there would be a certificate relating to my brother, but there was neither a birth nor a death certificate. When asked about stillbirth records, I was told that I had left it too late to enquire, as after a given time these are destroyed. To be told over the telephone by a complete stranger that I could safely assume that my twin had been stillborn, and that I would have to learn to live with this was a most strange and numbing experience.

In July 1989, when it appeared that I could go no further and that my search for information had come to an end, I read in the *Independent* newspaper an article about lone twins. It was a timely discovery and a welcome relief to learn that I was not the only one whose twin had died, and that others shared and understood this experience. I immediately applied to become a member of the then Lone Twin Register (later to become the Lone Twin Network). When I met them, I could not have anticipated the openness with which other members told their story: this was a revelation to me. For so many years I had lived with my story which had had to remain a secret and could not be talked about. I envied birth loss members who grew up aware of (and were encouraged to speak of) their twin. My heart ached when I listened to them relate how their twin's memory was kept alive as an integral part of their family story. Having no information, I was even jealous of those who had always known of their twin's grave or who had discovered it for themselves.

The Network provided the support and the impetus for me to resume my search for information. Inspired by a fellow member's success, I too obtained a copy of my twin's stillbirth certificate. This confirmed the gender (male) and the causes of death: asphyxia, breech and interlocking of twins. It was wonderful to receive this official document which offered an acknowledgement of my brother's existence and a reference to the fact that we are twins. I wanted to know more and so I read midwifery textbooks and obstetric medical papers and learnt that interlocking of twins is a rare obstetric complication occurring in approximately 1 in 90,000 deliveries, or 1 in 1,000 twin births (Adams and Fetterhoff 1971). I needed to understand the problems which can occur during labour and the delivery of interlocked twins, and I found a relevant paper (Nissen 1958). The combined evidence of the medical paper and the stillbirth certificate point to the fact that in such a delivery, the first (vertex) twin normally survives, whereas the second (breech) baby rarely does so. This was an unexpected revelation. For years I had let myself believe that my brother had been born first, and now this was turned on its head. From being the little sister looking for her big brother, I learnt that most likely I was delivered first and so I am really Big Sister. It's funny to think that for as long as I can remember all I ever wanted was a big brother; recently I 'adopted' two close friends to be surrogate big brothers.

Armed with all this new information, and with the assistance of the hospital chaplaincy department and the cemetery superintendent, I located where my brother was buried. It is ironic that for many years my family and I lived not ten minutes' walk from the cemetery without ever being aware of the grave. There was no memorial to mark the grave and so I put in place a simple marble plaque bearing an inscription.

In finding and marking my brother's resting place, I have now come to the end of the physical part of my search. After all the doing, the time had come to stand back, reflect on what had been discovered and allow myself to respond to it. I promised myself that once all the letters were written and calls made, then there would be nothing to obstruct the emotional aspect of the search.

The mystery which had surrounded my brother's death is now gone. There is relief in knowing what caused his death. For years I had hardly dared to hope that I would locate his grave. With so many gaps in what I knew about my twin, I almost gave up hope of ever finding out what I was looking for, and this was painful as well as frustrating. To be a twin felt very negative. The loneliness which comes from being a birth loss twin is something which has never gone away, and although it is now less painful, at times I wondered if I would ever fully get used to it.

At one point I might have chosen the word 'incomplete' to sum up my experience of being a lone twin. I felt like a jigsaw puzzle which had one piece missing and this piece held the key to the whole picture. Feeling more positive, I am now able to focus on the nearly completed puzzle and not merely see that part which is missing.

I accept that I cannot change the fact that my family of origin is unable to speak of my brother and that his death remains a taboo subject. They can neither recognise, acknowledge, respect nor encourage my need to speak out. I feel that this silence serves to deny his existence: as we developed together for thirty-five precious weeks, I wonder about the significance of this. In the context of my home, church and friends I have found the freedom to break the silence.

That my brother was stillborn remains unchanged and, much as I might wish to, I cannot alter history. I am still learning to live with the reality of my brother's death. I am immensely proud to be a twin. I was born a twin and will remain a twin all my life: nothing will change this. The time spent together in the womb forged the bond which my brother and I continue to share. Though he died, it would be impossible for me ever to forget him. However much it may be ignored or denied, this bond cannot ever be altered or broken. I was thrilled to find this expressed so well in a wonderful line of poetry: 'We who have been are one another for ever' (Raine 1988).

The sadness of former years has been turned around and replaced by an inner calm. I feel so much more positive: I believe this to be part of the process of letting go of the negative (centred on bereavement, death and loneliness) and moving on. In releasing my brother, giving him back to God and allowing him to be at peace, I have found peace.

There are times when I am reminded of how much I miss my brother, for example on my/our birthday. I know two lone twins who celebrate their birthday on this same day, and a positive feature of what could otherwise be a difficult day is our common celebration and the support we receive from each other.

As a committed Christian, I accept the Gospel accounts of the resurrection, hold on to Jesus' promise about the gift of eternal life. If for a moment I thought that death is merely THE END, I would truly despair. I believe passionately that love continues beyond death and that life does not end when the body dies. There is a verse in scripture which reads: 'We want you to be quite certain about those who have died, to make sure that you do not grieve about them, like the other people who have no hope' (Jerusalem Bible 1974).

I have hope. The conviction I hold that one day I will be reunited with my brother means I have something to which I look forward. I celebrate what was and rejoice in what will be. There is no reason to lose heart; for the moment I have to trust and be patient.

© PATRICIA CURTIS

Story 3
A woman in her forties who lost her brother at birth

My twin, David, died a few days after birth. As a child, I remember being very lonely and desperately wishing that he'd lived. Although I knew he was the first to be born, and died as a result of a complicated delivery, very little else was said, and I went along with the family pattern of not talking about him. It was almost as if he had never existed. Why did I have so many questions, so much pain inside, when everyone else seemed to be OK? I would, as a child, and later as an adult, have loved an opportunity to talk about him – to be able to say how sad I was that he wasn't alive, and hear what others felt. A few years ago, I heard Dr Elizabeth Bryan describe feelings that a lone twin might experience and I was so relieved to hear that I was, in fact, normal. This gave me the confidence to trace David's grave, and put an end to my restless searching. I haven't found him, only his grave, but I now have a focus, and no longer find myself in mental anguish, travelling in circles of unanswered questions. I've been able to let go of him. My mother has been with me to the grave, an experience which she found very moving, but sadly my father felt it may unearth too much pain.

Had my parents been allowed to grieve for David, rather than be told that at least they had me, then maybe we as a family would have been able to talk about him, verbalise our questions and sadness, and thus work through our inner pain.

© SUE MARCH

Story 4
A woman in her fifties who lost her sister at one day old

Ever since I can remember I have asked questions about my twin sister who, I understood, had died when we were two days old. I wanted to know, why had she died! Were we identical! Where was she buried! All sorts of questions would go through my head. I have very dear parents. (Sadly my Dad died when I was in my twenties and I miss him a lot. My Mum is very special, she suffers with multiple sclerosis and lives in a home and we see her often.)

My parents never wanted to talk in any depth about my sister. I did have a very happy childhood and they said they were lucky to have me but they didn't understand that I desperately wanted to know more. I have no other brothers or sisters but I was lucky to have many friends. I always wanted and needed company and it was always important to me to have a close friend. I remember that I very often felt very lonely. This could be because I was an only child or because I was a lone twin: I will never really know. Some of the problems I had, especially during my growing years, I am sure were due to the fact I was a lone twin. I have always been searching.

When I was eighteen I met David. We were married when I was twenty-one years old and we have been married for thirty-two years. I have always said to him that he is my dear husband, my sister and my best friend. I am much happier when he is near me. Several of my friends would say it is because I am a twin. Maybe so, maybe not, but I know I am extremely fortunate to have him. We have a very close relationship and a very strong love and bond.

Over the years I have asked my Mum where my sister is buried and she said she was put in a coffin with someone else but she didn't know where she was. I had written to the hospital where we were born but to no avail. I felt that if I could find where my sister was I would feel more content and I could identify with her. I really did not know what to do.

My husband and I had a very difficult period in our lives: my Dad died and at the same time I discovered that my Mum was suffering with multiple sclerosis. We then moved to a bungalow so that we could look after my Mum, which we did for two and a half years until it became too difficult. During that difficult time we had given up hope of having children and had made enquiries about adoption. Then we discovered we were expecting Joanne and, sixteen months later, we had our twin daughters, Claire and Amanda! After six years of waiting we had a bumper bundle and we were absolutely overwhelmed with our daughters and felt very privileged. I often talk with Amanda and Claire about being twins and the bond they feel for each other. I am fortunate that all our daughters are very close and I am really happy about that. Also, they totally seem to know how I feel and are very understanding and supportive.

A close friend of mine came with me to St Catherine's House to see if we could trace my sister's birth and death certificates. Our surname was Grimes and I was expecting to find my sister, Mary Grimes. To my surprise our names were entered in the register as my sister 'Kathleen' and me 'Kathleen Mary'. I was so anxious to see the death certificate to discover why and when Kathleen died. The Registrar came and showed me the book and I could see my Dad's writing and she said that it was most unusual that he had registered us both giving us the same name. She died when she was one day old because she was so premature. Kathleen was 3 lb and I was 3¼ lb. I had a constant lump in my throat that day. What a day for me – many thanks to my friend Jay.

I got in touch with the Council and asked if they could give me any advice as to where she might be buried. As a result of this I was in touch with Mr Rice at the cemetery, who told me that Kathleen was in her own coffin, which made me feel so happy, but she was in a common grave. He said he would put a little marker on the spot where she lay. The following weekend David and I visited the cemetery where she is and there was a little white flag to let us know where Kathleen was. We were both overcome to find her after all this time. So we had a small marble stone made with her name on and the amazing thing is that now I feel that we are together and I can go and talk to her and take her some flowers from time to time. My daughters have visited Kathleen's special place too. The very sad thing is that when we discovered where Kathleen is we also found a family grave for my Mum's mother and my Mum's brother, who died when he was nineteen years old. My Mum knew they were there but would never tell me that Kathleen was nearby. I questioned her about this but she just said she didn't know. I must not upset my Mum now – it will not change anything – I am just so pleased that my sister and I now have a bond.

I have told my Mum about all this and have tried to help her understand how important it has been for me. We said we would take her to the cemetery, but she said 'no'. I have talked to her and said that I also understand how difficult it must have been for her. She didn't see Kathleen at all and didn't see me for a while and my Mum was in hospital for several weeks after our birth. When she took me home she had to wash me in olive oil and couldn't take me out for six months. I am a very fortunate person. But I sincerely wish that my parents had been able to talk to me more about my sister – what happened in December 1942, if we were identical and how they felt, as their feelings have to be considered. I think the greatest difficulty is that it must have been extremely hard for my parents to understand what an effect losing my sister, even though we were babies, had on me.

MARY HEIGHWAY

Story 5

A woman in her fifties who lost a brother at birth

At forty-one my mother hadn't known that she was expecting twins, though my future godmother had seen 'two little bluebirds in the fire'. The doctor thought she was gaining too much weight and put her on a diet.

After a difficult pregnancy I was born seven months prematurely, weighing 5 lb, and placed in an incubator. Then someone noticed another baby in the womb! My twin brother, weighing 4½ lb, survived a difficult breech birth whilst my mother was left in a state of total exhaustion.

Later, when the nurse came to show mother her 'lovely twins', she knew that something was very wrong with one of them. She remembers that one baby had a rosy pink face but the other was pale, its face reminiscent of her dying mother. Later that day my brother died. My mother felt that she should never have seen him. I was left alone in the incubator waiting to begin life as a 'singleton', a lone twin in disguise.

No one ever mentioned what had happened to my twin's body. I supposed it had gone down the hospital sluice. But later in life my mother did give me a death certificate bearing his name, 'Quentin Edward' and at strangely sad moments on birthdays I would quietly remember, I had been a twin once.

I think my mother feared that I would be distressed by my twin's death and, consequently, I was never allowed to cry, though I could rage freely at my much older brother and sister. Neither was I exposed to family funerals or to any situations of grief.

I attended my first local Lone Twin meeting in Purley in November 1990. I was very apprehensive about going since I assumed it was really meant for recently bereaved twins. But the welcome was so warm and with my 'Twin Lost At Birth' badge I somehow felt that I had found a new family.

Gradually stories of loss began to unfold. It was so strange to look around the room and sense amidst the men and women there twenty-six amputated existences, twenty-six people sharing the hidden pain of losing the closest relationship which can exist, that of being a twin. Very slowly, my own twin identity, which had always felt rather like a childhood fairytale, seemed to be creeping out of the shadows into the real world.

Now in the Lone Twin group people wept freely. I heard people speak of the grief process of the surviving twin. I didn't know if this had any application to me, but I did feel an unexpected quiver of unhappiness inside when I saw others sharing their twin photo albums over lunch.

We who had lost our twins near birth had no photos, no possessions, no gravestones on which to focus our grief. We had nothing like this to show our twin identity, nothing apart from our feelings which, I began to realise, I shared with a group of apparent strangers. We all shared the same loss of identity – we were no longer twins.

But some people who, like me, had lost their twins near birth, had tracked down their twins' graves! They told me something I had never known, that if a baby is full born there is always a proper funeral at the hospital. A knot inside me felt as though it was about to burst open. I suddenly realised I could now try to track down Quentin's grave.

The reality of that unique day exploded on my return home. I was overwhelmed by waves of tears and harrowing sobs. I found myself stumbling to find pastels and two large pieces of card on which to pour out my feelings. Both started with the same sweeps of purple and white, then one became progressively wilder with coils of green, deep purple sobs, tiny purple tears, deep green waves of emotion rolling out slowly calmed by the palest pink. Calmer now I let the other unravel, soft green soothing shading, two purple and white eyes, a beak and feathery fronds. A bird, with a calm, direct gaze emerged. Exhausted, I sat back and wondered.

Life is odd at times. About two years ago I joined an art group. I'd wanted to paint for years but had a block. However, this was a group which painted from the unconscious, i.e., you let your intuition choose the type of paper, paint, pastel, etc. and then you switched off your thinking process and let your hand draw something out of your feelings. Oddly enough, in the studio from time to time I used to create double images. I had no idea what they were about until, fortuitously, one emerged on my birthday, at which point they finally made sense. I told the group leader about my twin's death and he implied that these twin images were very important for me.

Well, these last two images certainly kept me grounded through what was, I suppose, the first explosion of grief for my twin's death.

A few days later I managed to pull myself together and wrote to our place of birth at St David's Hospital, Cardiff. I asked them to check their records to see whether my dead brother had been buried by the hospital, and if so, where. The reply brought both negative and positive news. The hospital records had been destroyed in a flood, but the local crematorium did have records covering the same period. I wrote an explanatory letter and sent it with a search fee to the crematorium.

Five days later came a reply, a yellow receipt for my cheque plus the documents I had never believed could exist, two papers which marked Quentin's final presence in the world. They indicated his name, Quentin Edward Lumley, his parentage, the family home which he had never entered, plus details of his grave, the section in the cemetery and his number in it. The transaction, for fifteen shillings, had been paid for by a W. Hans. I disintegrated into tears.

And then came a long pause, a psychological dilemma. How could I return to Wales to look for the grave without going to see my now ancient, widowed mother? Following the first Lone Twin meeting I had excitedly told her the events of the day and was both horrified and so disappointed to hear her words, 'I think you're silly, daft bothering about something like that which is over and done with for forty-five years. Concern yourself with things in the present.' I couldn't tell her what I'd done.

Four months later I attended another Lone Twin meeting. Two lone twins who, like me, had lost their twins near birth, told our group how they had succeeded in tracking down their twins' graves. They provided the spark that I needed. I telephoned the cemetery in Cardiff. A woman with a lovely voice answered. She must have heard my voice shaking as I told my story. She explained that the grave, since it was a communal one holding five babies, would not be marked, but she would arrange for a numbered label to be placed on it. She would also send me a map of the cemetery, a very large one, indicating the grave's position. As I replaced the phone deep crying rushed up from inside me with strange inner panting and gasping for breath. I wondered whether that was what being born felt like.

At the weekend I bought a day-return ticket to Cardiff. At the station my old school friend Jennifer was waiting to drive me to Cathays Cemetery, our conversation calming the rising anxiety I felt inside. The cemetery lay behind a very long, high, stone wall. The gateman pointed our way down a wide tree-lined avenue passing quiet areas of flower-speckled grass to Section EO. EO, the size of four tennis courts, EO, where numbers did not appear on many gravestones and where they did they stood in no logical sequence. I had reached my goal but it was like a haystack, how was I to find the needle? My heart sank. But I knew that somewhere close by, my twin's body was quietly resting. Jennifer and I split up and began our haphazard search for grave 1533. When desperation was beginning to set in, I spied an open patch of grass bearing a speck of white. Like a homing pigeon I stumbled over gravestones towards it, a cross marking the resting place of Quentin my tiny twin brother, parted more than forty years ago. I now stood by his grave. For weeks, in anticipation of this moment, I had expected to be overwhelmed by a storm of powerful emotions. What I hadn't expected was a sense of deep inner calm which now crept over me, an immense sense of being a twin, no longer a singleton but a lone twin. I arranged a bunch of daffodils on Quentin's grave whilst Jennifer took a photograph marking a moment in time. A moment which, quietly, was to change the course of my life. Now I'd be able to proclaim my twin identity with a new assurance, knowing that I could share this, one of the most moving experiences in my life, with others who would laugh and cry with me, bringing the sadness of immense loss into the warmth and care of those who had survived it.

© PENNY LUMLEY

Story 6
A woman in her fifties who lost an identical sister at birth

I was described as a 'mardy' baby, which means I was rather miserable. With hindsight I would guess that I was grieving for my twin sister Jacqueline, who was strangled by the cord during her birth.

I cannot remember a time when I didn't know that I was a twin. But in my family this was quite a talking point as my mother gave birth to a second set of twins two years after we were born. I had a brother and sister who both survived. I think that always knowing I am a twin made it easier to accept than if I had been told about this later in life.

The most difficult times in my childhood were when the three of us argued, two girls against one boy – then my sister would suddenly change sides and it would be The Twins against me. It always took me by surprise and if I went to my parents to have a moan and to say that I wished I had my twin to turn to, their reply, which was supposed to comfort me, was that if my twin had survived they probably wouldn't have had the second set! It never really helped me, but obviously comforted them.

I never really asked much about what happened to my twin, but understood that she, as a stillborn baby, had been buried with a woman at Lodge Hill Cemetery in Birmingham. When I was coming up to my fiftieth birthday I rang Birmingham Cemeteries and was sent a map of the cemetery marked with the position of my twin's grave.

My own children asked for more details than I ever did and my parents were always very open with them as they had been with me.

On my birthday I went with my father, sister and husband to look for the grave. It was a bit rainy but this seemed appropriate, and after a little searching we found the grave with a peg marker which the staff had put there to help me. I left a chrysanthemum, my birth month's flower, and a sprig of rosemary (for remembrance) on the grave. I took a photo, which is quite a comfort. It is the only direct link to my twin.

I don't think you ever get over the loss of a twin, even if you lost him or her at birth. There is always a feeling that you are searching for someone close enough to replace them, but of course you never can, and it is always a disappointment when you face the fact that you can't.

JILL DEELEY

Story 7
A woman in her thirties who lost an identical sister at birth

I cannot remember a time when I did not know I was an identical twin. My family have always talked about it, in what seemed to me a detached way. By that, I mean that it has always been discussed as an interesting fact, but not as something which could have affected me very much, although my parents thought that my continual crying as a baby might be to do with me missing my twin. I myself did not connect my feelings and experiences to losing my sister before birth until I was in my late twenties.

My mother did not know that she had been expecting twins until after we were born and neither did the hospital staff. The first hint that it was not a straight-forward labour was when my mother was told that there was a 'soft head', but the hospital staff would not explain what that meant. After twenty-two hours, they removed my stillborn sister. I was then delivered with forceps as I was becoming exhausted. I weighed 4 lb 11 oz and my sister weighed 4 lb 10 oz. I was in the premature baby unit for three weeks. My parents were concerned about my health and my mother was very unwell after the birth. For these reasons, my parents decided that they would not see my sister and asked the hospital to arrange a burial.

From the start, there appear to have been hints that the loss of my twin sister had affected me. I was a very unhappy baby, always crying and screaming. Often I would not be comforted or quietened by anything my parents did. As a toddler I couldn't be left alone without becoming distressed. I am sure that this was a symptom of my bereavement. From what I have been told, I seem to have been particularly unable to cope with being left alone, or in a place where I couldn't see anyone else. I think I had an in-built fear of being abandoned again, as I had been in the womb. The consistent crying and colic I experienced as a baby are certainly recognised signs of trauma in utero.

I seemed to settle temporarily when my brother was born. I was just under three years old. Maybe it was to do with having a replacement for my sister. However, I have never had a close relationship with my brother.

The other 'complication' with regard to my sister, was my grandmother's belief in and practice of spiritualism. Although she never claimed to have contacted my sister at spiritualist meetings, she would often make a passing comment when we went to visit her that she had 'seen' my sister about the house. I remember her talking about my sister in this way as long ago as when I was three or four years old. I don't think I was ever upset by it. In fact, I remember asking about what she looked like and being quite interested in what my grandmother had seen. However, I think that it could have been confusing for me. I do remember worrying about her reports of spiritualist meetings because I couldn't bring myself to believe that these things had actually happened and yet I couldn't believe my grandmother would lie to me either.

In a lot of ways I wish my gran was still alive so that I could talk to her about it now. She died when I was thirteen. When I first started feeling that my sister was very important, I felt that my gran could have done me a lot of harm, talking about seeing my sister as a ghost. However, there is a part of me now that is so grateful that she saw her as a real person and that she treasured her 'encounters' with her. I don't believe in spiritualism myself, but I'm sure that it was a great comfort to my grandmother, whether she actually saw her or only believed she did, and I don't begrudge her that. It seems strange, though, that it still took me so many years to become conscious of how much losing my sister has affected me.

The effects have been deep and intense, at the very core of my soul.

Perhaps the main result is that I have always felt very isolated and alone. I have had friends throughout my life, many of them close, but I've always felt an intense loneliness which nothing quenches. Although some of it is almost certainly due to other events in my childhood, I have always had a deep sense that it is much more than that. I have never understood why other people are happy with what seem to me to be superficial relationships. I've always felt that people never talk to each other at a level which really matters and that people are never 'themselves', which to me makes relationships pointless. I want relationships with other people which are empathic or even telepathic. I find it very difficult when someone doesn't instinctively know what I am feeling. This results in some considerable frustration at times, but now that I know it is because I am wishing that I had a replacement for my sister, I can handle it much better, although it doesn't prevent me from wishing it was so. I have found that other people become anxious when their feelings begin to merge with another person's. That type of closeness often seems unbearably intrusive to people who were born as singletons, but to me it is how relationships should be, I suppose because that is how my relationship with my twin sister was. Some lines of T. S. Eliot's play, *The Cocktail Party* sum it up for me:

> It isn't that I want to be alone, but that everyone is alone, or so it seems to me. They make noises and they think they are talking to each other, they make faces and they think they understand each other, and I'm sure they don't. (Eliot 1982: 131)

As a child and even an adult, before I began to suspect the effect of my sister's death on me I had feelings and images which I now believe were subconscious expressions of my feelings of loss. As a teenager, I would frequently draw a pale, thin girl with her arms outstretched as if reaching for something which wasn't there. I also had an incredibly powerful dream when I was about six or seven which is still very vivid. I dreamt that I was dead and I felt terrified. I was going to various adults, trying to get them to believe that I was dead and how frightened I was, but no one would listen to me. They all patted me on the head and told me to go away. Although part of the message seems to be the lack of understanding I felt, I think it must also say something about my dead twin.

More recently, when I was a day patient in hospital, I drew what is the most powerful image to me now, although incredibly, I didn't know why I was drawing it at the time. The picture is of a girl banging her fist against the mirror in frustration because there is no reflection of herself in it. This to me can be nothing other than an image reflecting my loss. There should have been a reflection – my identical twin sister – and she isn't there. The rediscovery of this drawing left me feeling shaken up and even now it makes me feel quite strange when I look at it.

My time as a day patient was part of a long treatment for depression and anxiety from which I have suffered on and off since I was a child.

Because I wasn't finding the treatment I was given for depression at all helpful in the early stages, I began reading a great deal about psychology and, in particular, pre-birth experiences in the hope of finding some 'answers' for myself. Alice Miller's books have provided me with a lot of answers about my feelings – I think she is wonderful. It was her recommendation of the book *Making Sense of Suffering* by Konrad Stettbacher (1990) that led me to read his views on the effect of a person's birth on their emotional well-being. I was scathingly sceptical at first and did not believe that those sorts of feelings and memories could survive into adulthood, but as I continued to read, feelings about my sister began to come to the surface. I found myself thinking, 'If the births he is describing are classed as traumatic, what was mine?' I shared the womb with my identical twin sister (there can be no closer relationship). I was then lying next to her dead body for several days without being able to understand why she had stopped responding to me. She then 'disappeared' (she was removed with forceps) and I was dragged into the world the same way and isolated in a special baby unit. Surely all of this was a deeply traumatic experience, especially since a baby has no means of comprehending what is happening except to have a severe sense of loss and fear, of bewilderment and of feeling suddenly very alone. A baby can not verbalise its feelings and experiences, so those feelings can be elusive even when the adult has learnt the vocabulary to interpret them verbally. I have certainly found that this has compounded the problem of coming to terms with being a lone twin, because the feelings it produces are so difficult to express.

Once I had begun to consider the effects of being a lone twin, I began to have very intense feelings of bereavement and despair, but I was afraid to trust my feelings. I still couldn't quite believe that my birth experiences could be affecting me now. However, I was determined to find out more about it so that I could discover whether it really is possible to have feelings of grief years after an event and whether it might possibly be contributing to my depression.

I contacted TAMBA (Twins and Multiple Births Association). I knew that this organisation is primarily for parents of multiple birth children. However, they did put me on to the bereavement group, who help parents who have lost one or both twins at birth or in childhood. They in turn were able to give me a few articles to read and put me in touch with the Lone Twin Network.

I joined the Network in December 1992. It has been helpful to read some of the articles they have been able to send me. I have also been to two of their March meetings in London. Both meetings were extremely helpful, even though

I did not find either meeting easy. I always find going to strange places and meeting new people very difficult anyway, and the meetings are always very emotional events.

Talking to other lone twins was far more than just 'interesting'. It brought all sorts of feelings even more to the surface. It had really got too much by the afternoon, but everybody knows what the feelings are like and everybody supports each other.

I have already mentioned the effect on my perception of relationships and my feelings of being intensely alone. This seems to be quite common among the lone twins I have met. There is certainly a general feeling of loss which even having friends and relationships does not completely address. However, it became obvious to me that I felt this more intensely than the rest of the group I was with. Someone asked me if I thought that being an identical twin had made a difference. All the other people in my group were non-identical twins. Of course, I had to answer that I didn't know. But, although I know some of my feelings may also be linked to other factors in my life, as I believe is true of most people, I have come away from the meetings with the impression that being an identical twin does seem to have increased my feelings of isolation. In a way, I suppose, it is logical. I teach quite a number of identical and non-identical twins and I do sense quite a marked difference in their relationships with each other. Identical twins have a particularly intense form of communication. It's almost verging on telepathy at times. For example, I teach one pair of identical twins who would often argue because they each accused the other of copying their work, which was extremely similar, both in ideas and in the way they expressed them. But I knew that they had been sitting at opposite ends of the room for the whole lesson and it took a while for them to realise and accept that they had not knowingly copied each other. I know this is a very common experience for identical twins and this makes me believe that in the womb, too, there could be a particular closeness. That is not to say, of course, that non-identical twins can't be very close. I am also aware that not all twins, identical or non-identical, get on – I have seen this in other twins I have taught.

Connected with the feeling of isolation, there seemed to be a very common experience in lone twins of an inability to cope with loss, be it bereavement or simply the ending of a friendship, for whatever reason. This has always been a severe difficulty for me. I cannot cope with loss and change and I have never done so, even something as minor as a friend moving away. The only way that I can deal with it is to suppress the overwhelming feelings and then, of course, they fester for months afterwards and longer. It was once pointed out to me that I always seem to be abandoned and this is how it feels sometimes. I am sure these feelings are all the more intense because they echo my original abandonment prenatally when my sister died.

However, paradoxically, I also feel that I abandoned my sister. This is an incredibly strong feeling at times and it makes me want to be able to hold her, protect her and comfort her. Although I know that a baby is in reality quite powerless over events, I feel as if, being the only one who knew her, I should have stayed with her, and that means that I desperately didn't want to be born. I think that I became very still and withdrawn in the womb after her death, as if trying to 'join' her, although I obviously wouldn't have understood that she was no longer responding to me because she was dead.

Difficulties in coping with loss and separation were too common at the Lone Twin meeting to be coincidence. I'm sure some people who are not lone twins also have difficulties with separation and loss, perhaps deriving from other factors in their personal history, but I'm convinced that the extent of the desperation which lone twins seem to feel regarding loss and the number of people at the meeting who expressed such intense feelings cannot be coincidence.

One person at the first meeting I attended, gave an account of how she always pushed herself relentlessly to give and give to others as if justifying her existence in some way. I certainly do find myself doing this and several others said they also identified with this feeling. As she pointed out, it's as if, subconsciously, we have to justify being alive because our twin did not survive and the only way of doing this is to endlessly give to others. I know that the reason I went into the teaching profession is because of the opportunities it gives for me to help the teenagers I teach. Of course, this is not a black and white situation. There is a right and proper part of me that genuinely wants to help the children I teach. But in the times when I have considered changing my profession, what has prevented me is that I see it as the only part of my life where I am making some attempt to 'atone' (I can think of no other word) for my existence, and most of the time, that still doesn't seem to be enough.

There seems to be a common feeling in lone twins that they are living for two, which in some ways must also be connected with the guilt of surviving, although it has a positive effect on some lone twins and gives them extra strength. Yet another aspect of lone twins which I noticed, was the large proportion of lone twins at the meetings who are in overtly caring professions such as nurses, teachers with a special interest in pastoral work and therapists. It also seemed unlikely to me that there would normally be so large a percentage of people in a group who had either had or were in the throes of therapy for one reason or another. Not all lone twins end up in therapy, of course, and other factors play a part in leading people to therapy too.

Most of all, though, the similarity between lone twins I have met appears to be the depth of feeling and empathy for others which we as lone twins seem blessed (or cursed) with. There is quite a bit of disagreement about when babies begin to have a sense of me/not me, which is central to the development of their personalities, but I wonder whether twins develop this earlier than singletons, as they have another person (a 'not me' experience) to relate to from the start. If so, then I wonder if this can account in part for this highly developed empathy. This is a characteristic which I sensed incredibly strongly at the meeting. If there had been any doubt in my mind about there being such a thing as 'lone twinness', it was certainly dissipated by seeing this empathy in so many lone twins.

But it does also seem that the degree to which lone twins are adversely affected by their bereavement can be partly governed by the way it has been handled as they were growing up. Those whose parents have openly acknowledged and grieved for their dead baby, as well as loving the surviving one, seem to cope better with the loss and be less affected by it in adulthood. Some families have perfectly good reasons for not wishing to dwell on their dead baby, but instead concentrate on the living one and I am not criticising them for this. My parents did not dream that it would have such a lasting effect on me. As far as I know, there was nothing known about lone twins at the time I was born and no one could have been expected to know that it would affect me in the way it did. Although things have improved in more recent years, there are still far too many people who know nothing about the subject. Nevertheless, a lack of acceptance of a dead twin while the survivor grows up, does seem to compound the difficulties for those twins both in childhood and adulthood.

I have met a few lone twins who say that they haven't been affected by the loss of their sibling in any way and these people often seem to have families who have been very up-front about the death. Having said that, it makes me smile a little that they have all, without exception, gone on in the course of the conversation to talk about several aspects of their lives in which they have experienced feelings that are, in fact, very common in lone twins!

Since joining the Lone Twin Network, I have had the opportunity to read some studies of pre-natal experience in general, from which it is possible to gain more insight into how lone twins feel when they lose a brother or sister in the womb. It was such a relief to read the proof that memory of pre-natal and post-natal experiences can remain and be recalled well into adult life. The books reassured me that the original event did affect me as I grew up and that the more overt feelings that have now been reawakened in me with vehemence are real and have a concrete and accessible origin. I even have a strong sense that we lay close together, with her back curled against my stomach. When I get flashes of this image, it feels so real. I can 'feel' her skin and the warmth of her body and everything is quiet and so peaceful. It's very hard to describe the feeling adequately in words, but it is extremely vivid and moving. I often had the physical feeling that I had something missing the length of my body long before I had these memories and I have always felt very vulnerable there. I have modelled the two of us together as I feel we were in the womb in an attempt to capture the 'memory' in a more concrete way.

For a long time after I had joined the Network, I felt overwhelmed by the feelings that I was experiencing. I cannot describe them as anything other than severe grief, which I should have worked through a very long time ago. I have largely come to terms with losing her now, but I still think about her a great deal and the feelings of grief can be re-triggered. It feels so strange to be having these feelings so long after the event, but I now know why I feel them. I am a twin and nothing will take that away from me, but that also means that I can never be completely free of the effects of losing my sister.

Apart from meeting and talking with other lone twins, I have also been able to come to terms with my loss through actively seeking to create concrete symbols and memorials to her. It helped me a huge amount to draw a picture of us together as babies and to give her a name. I obviously am unable to have a photograph of her, so this was the next best thing. I knew that some people found comfort in finding or creating a grave for their lost twin. At first I couldn't begin to cope with the idea of doing this myself. However, gradually I began to feel that I wanted to know where she was. I looked forward to possibly having a headstone put on the spot and taking a photograph of it. I had seen photos like this taken by two other lone twins at the March meeting. I wrote to the hospital where we were born and eventually the bereavement officer replied to me with the name of the cemetery where the hospital had buried her. I contacted the cemetery, hoping that they would be able to show me exactly where she was, but to my dismay, they wrote back to say that they could only show me a large grass area where the hospital buried babies and that they had no more detailed records. At first I couldn't accept this and all my plans of visiting her spot seemed completely meaningless. But eventually I decided to go and another lone twin friend said she would meet me there, which I was incredibly grateful for as I don't think I could have coped with it alone.

It felt very strange to be there and I couldn't stop crying although I didn't really know what I was crying about and I felt very detached from it all. Funnily enough, I felt fine on my way home, but it all came out at four in the morning, when I woke up in a panic attack. My friend picked up a fir cone from the area where Sarah is buried and picked me some lavender and since then it has helped to have those things because they came from the place where she is.

A few weeks later I decided to buy one of the necklaces which come in two halves and to bury one half in the cemetery as near to where she is buried as I could. I would wear the other half so that I would always have a connection with her. I got permission to plant a small tree so that I could put the necklace underneath it. I did this a fortnight later and I also put a plaque there, which reads 'In Loving Memory of Sarah Lucy Goode, stillborn 4/12/63, Twin Sister of Bryony'. I felt that I needed to name her and let the world know that my little sister is buried there. I had been wearing both halves of the necklace since I had bought it and splitting up the two halves was a very emotional moment. I wear my part of the necklace all the time now and find it very comforting to look at and hold. It gives me a real sense of connection with Sarah and makes me feel complete somehow. The wording on the necklace, which is commonly used by friends who are to be apart for a while, seems incredibly appropriate for my situation. It reads, 'The Lord watch between me and thee while we are absent, one from another.' I carry a photograph of the tree and cemetery around with me and that also helps.

I told my parents that I had done all this. I wasn't sure how they would react, since they had chosen at the time of the original event not to commemorate her and I know they did this thinking they were doing the best thing. But they were pleased I had planted the tree and put up the plaque and, even though they don't want to visit the cemetery at the moment, they now have copies of the photographs that I took there.

Despite having taken all these steps to reclaim my sister, and there is no doubt that it has helped, I wanted her stillbirth certificate. In a way it seemed like the only official evidence that she existed, particularly since I have no photographs or possessions that belonged to her. I had not realised, however, that stillbirth certificates are different from death certificates. They are kept in Southport and, unlike death certificates for children who have lived even a few minutes, they will not issue stillbirth certificates to anyone other than the parents. They argue that, in the case of a stillbirth, the parents are the only ones to have been directly involved with the baby and that it was not anyone else's business. I was devastated. It felt like everyone was conspiring to keep every little part of her away from me. However, with perseverance and several letters later, the authorities were persuaded that in the case of a lone twin, who had shared a womb for several months with their brother or sister, the surviving twin had a right to have access to their twin's stillbirth certificate. I was the first lone twin to obtain this certificate and several others have since been permitted to have them also. It has made me feel that her existence has been truly acknowledged.

Although Sarah will always be a very large part of my life, and the effects of losing her will mean that I will always feel that a part of me is missing, I feel much more at peace now and able to accept her death. My necklace will remain my most treasured possession.

BRYONY GOODE

Story 8
A woman in her fifties who lost her identical sister at eight days
Whilst walking along a long sandy beach in Spain during the summer of 2006, apart from enjoying the peace and quiet except for the soothing sound of the waves breaking on the sand, I came across lots of shells washed up on the beach. The shells were all different shapes, colours and sizes – each one beautiful in its own right.

I then came across a small shell, glistening in the damp sand, which almost looked as if it had Tiger's Eye markings. On closer examination the two halves of the shell were still 'together'. It looked like a beautiful butterfly, nestling in the sand. As I picked the shell up and looked at it more closely, it struck me that it was like a 'complete' set of twins and the rest of the single shells on the beach were like the remaining lone twins.

It then struck me that whatever we are, every day of our lives, there are always 'things' that will make us think of our missing twin, not that any of us ever needs reminding of our missing 'other half'.

Several years ago, whilst on holiday in Jersey, I experienced a similar feeling when I bought a gold bangle. The bangle comprised of two 'flat' strands, intertwined. Although I liked the style immediately, it was only the following morning that I realised that for me it symbolised two lives intertwined. Although my twin, Sandra, died at 8 days old, we had been closely 'intertwined' during our time together in the womb.

As I thought about this aspect further, I felt that being circular, the bangle represented the circle of life and the fact that although our lives are so closely connected, we only shared a very short time together in life, and it is only at the end of my life that Sandra and I will be reunited, completing the circle that once again will be 'complete'.

> In loving memory of Sandra Mary Langridge
> Mum, Dad and I miss you every day.
>
> JOAN BRINE

Story 9
A woman in her sixties whose twin brother was stillborn

For countless years, I have wondered just what life would have been like had my twin brother survived. My thoughts have wandered from the positive to, sometimes, the negative. Would we have got on – shared the same sense of humour, enjoying meeting people. Or would we have argued, to the point that neither could relent. These things are but small comparisons, a 'drop in the ocean' – compared to the underlying sense of loss and a part of me that remains forever somehow missing – an absence never to be fulfilled, in respect of a loving relationship, good and maybe not so good, between brother and sister. My heartfelt thoughts remain in place for there is no other way and this I must accept. Yet again, for countless years I have wondered where might be the grave of my brother. In this, my search goes through twisty roads leading to a cul-de-sac.

My birth came on 15 September 1940 in south-east London with my brother, stillborn, five hours later. Of the two of us he was the heavier but 'went too long'. Having survived, I was brought up as an only child. Historically, the period had become known as the Battle of Britain. German bombing had been relentless for days and nights and the hospital had received a direct hit. During these unending raids newborn babies were 'shunted' down to the cellars. In later years my mother described the memory as being, 'like Hell on Earth!' – refusing to go into greater detail, or speak on the subject any further. With only just surviving herself, her only additional comment was that, 'you lived each day as though it was your last'. Respecting her wishes, especially the impact of trauma, all the same has left me feeling 'in limbo' as to what might have happened to my brother.

My first 'bend in the road' appeared through my mother being only able to remember a little of the trauma. The second 'bend' arose as a result of a (student) friend wishing to use me as a guinea pig for her heraldic studies. Tracking down the registration of my birth – the registrar telephoned to tell me that they had no evidence of my brother being stillborn! He said 'you know what this means don't you?' (That is: my brother was alive!). Immediately, my imagination went into overdrive … wondering just what he would be like, or if he had a different name? I was both scared and excited! The Registrar passed my details on to the then, St Catherine's House in London. Eventually they telephoned to ask that I came to see them and brought a relative (my husband John). Once again, my imagination went into overdrive. …! On arrival we were ushered into a room aside from the main office – where I was told most sensitively that they had found my brother's Stillbirth Certificate deep in their vaults. Thanking them, I left and was faced with shock – namely the grief that surfaced took me by storm. Even now, some years later, the memory of that moment and slipping away of hope (with the possibility that he might still be alive) remains … and with it a certain 'lump in the throat'.

The third 'bend in the road' emerged when I began to search out where my brother might have been laid to rest. In trying to make contact with the hospital I came up against a no-go. The hospital had been turned into private apartments. Knowing where I might be able to track down the hospital records for 1940 presented yet further 'bends in the twisty road' and included 'the cul-de-sac' effect. Another 'bend in the road' emerges in wondering if my brother was buried in a nearby local cemetery. Where could I begin my search, especially since my brother had not been named? Consequently, I am unable to tell if my brother had a proper burial. And herein lies a further twist to my personal story.

Around twenty years ago I went on a week's course at an Anglican/Inter-denominational retreat centre at Crowhurst. During my stay, I talked with the house-minister Reverend Ray Jones about my brother and most of all my feeling a sense of limbo because of not knowing what might have happened to him, where was his resting place. In the Library at Crowhurst I came across a book concerning baptism for stillborns. Again, the subject was raised with Ray, following which a baptismal service was held in the chapel for my brother.

The experience was memorably profound and moving. I was asked to have two witnesses who after the service were in tears. I was numb, stunned by the impact of this unique moment in time. With just the three of us and Ray in the room, as he commenced the ceremony – the weather was dark and brooding, the wind howling through the eaves and shutters, the branches of a tree lashed against one of the windows, the rain pelted down hard. I was truly 'lost in time' and unable to remember the words, exactly, that Ray – so beautifully – presented. But at the end of the short ceremony an immense peace pervaded the room gone was the howling wind the pounding rain, the darkness. Instead the clouds parted, the sun came out and a beam of light slid through the windows on to the altar and a blackbird alighted on the branches that had earlier been thrashing against the window pane. His sweet song told me that 'all was well and would be well'. Emotions ran high – yet above all, I felt my brother saying 'Thank You'.

Finally, I have reached the proverbial 'cul-de-sac' with just one last 'brief encounter'. A few years ago I went on a Painting Course. During that residential week one of the participants was a retired Hospital Chaplain. One evening talking to him about his work, he mentioned the name of the hospital where I was born and where he was resident, especially during 1939 to 1964. He went on to speak about the Battle of Britain and how it was his 'job to go down to the cellars and bless all the babies'. Quietly I listened and quietly I did not interrupt and at the end I said 'I think you and I might have met before – only I would have been just this long (measuring the distance of some twelve to fifteen inches between my hands). 'I was one of your babies that you blessed' I concluded. His amazed response was 'Well I never!' Unable to remember further details of that period, he suggested I spoke to his friend who had become the Lady Almoner. Excitedly, I waited for her visit – but it never came.

And so having reached my personal cul-de-sac, it is time to close this account in memory and reverence, with love, to my dear brother, yet forever close.

AILEEN WRIGHT

4
TWIN LOSS IN CHILDHOOD

INTRODUCTION

The thirteen stories in this chapter illustrate five themes. They show how in many ways loss in childhood produces similar responses to loss experienced at birth. This group of twins shows equally strongly, how their parents' attitudes also affected the twins' responses. When the twin's need to express his or her feelings are blocked, or his or her feelings are devalued, the sense of isolation in the twin can be severe. Attachment theorists would describe this situation as likely to make great difficulties for the surviving twin to have a good or strong sense of self. Sometimes when this process of grieving is denied to the surviving twin, these children attempt to make very close compensatory attachments to pets.

Unlike the twins whose loss had been at birth, these twins all have some memory of their twin and many have photographs or objects which provide a greater sense of connection with their twin. The special situation of abandonment experienced by the twin when the other twin is seriously ill and has all the attention focused on them leading up to their death, is vividly described. There is also a description of one twin's reaction to over-protection.

THEME 1
ON THE GRIEVING PROCESS BEING BLOCKED

Story 1
A woman of forty who lost her brother at six years

Looking back, I realise that I have lived two lives – which has a certain irony since I am now only living half a life ...

In September 1957, my mother gave birth to twins – a boy and a girl. It was a perfectly normal birth and we were happy, healthy babies. People remember little things from their very early childhood, things that happened to them as toddlers, but I remember only two things from my first life. My twin and I were always chatting together after 'lights out' at night and this annoyed my dad no end. But I remember that suddenly it was only me who got smacked and my twin hardly even got told off. And the other memory, oh so vivid, was of driving home from school in the car. Mum was driving, my twin was beside her and Nan and I were sitting in the back. Nan started quizzing my mum about the lump on his neck. (Why do I remember it as yellow?) And that's all. All that I have left of my first life, which finished so suddenly and cruelly in June 1964 when my twin and I were just six years and nine months old; when all the lights went out …

My second life started the same day but now everything was different. Where there had been brightness there was an all-pervading dark. Where there had been two of us, now I was alone. And where there had been few or no memories, now I remembered EVERYTHING.

Apparently my twin had Hodgkin's Disease (hence the lump in his neck) and, later, leukaemia. He died in hospital but I still don't know which one and how long he was in there. I think it was all quite sudden at the end. My parents' friends used to pick me and my older brother up from school while my twin was in hospital, as I was not allowed to visit him. On that awful day in June, my parents arrived to collect us from their friends much earlier than usual. The radio was playing – I remember the tune – and we were just finishing tea. When the car drew up my parents' friends went ashen faced and hugged each other. I really didn't understand because no one had told me how sick my twin was. Mum and Dad came in and hugged their friends. I was bundled into the car and I suddenly realised that my twin had died, had gone from my life for ever. On the way home I remember – oh so clearly – how everyone sat in the car and I cried and sobbed and wailed, pushing myself into the far corner of the car, so alone. My mother turned on me and shouted that I must stop crying, must never cry again and that I would and must forget my twin. The overpowering darkness engulfed me and wiped out my first life forever.

During the following week my mother wrote to friends and relations and sent me with this dreadful burden to the post box, telling me not to speak to anyone on the way. My twin's best friend, John, and his mum, seeing me pass, came out to ask how my twin was. I wasn't allowed to speak but they knew and John ran inside.

About a week after my twin's death, my aunt and uncle were getting married. My twin and I were supposed to be page boy and bridesmaid. But my twin had died so another little boy had been found at short notice to replace him and my twin's clothes were adjusted to fit him. I had to be bridesmaid – it was all arranged and no one was to be let down. I tried to get out of it, I pleaded and begged and even rubbed chewing gum in my hair, but all to no avail. The gum was cut out of my hair and I was prepared for the big day. That boy and I walked down the aisle together behind the bride. I refused to hold his hand – he wasn't my twin. And at that very same time, on that very same day, while I stood dressed in an orange satin dress at a WEDDING, my twin's funeral took place … I've never seen photographs of the wedding or myself as a bridesmaid. Maybe someone realised, all too late, what they had done to me.

And so my second life carried on. Mum locking herself in her bedroom to cry every afternoon, with me forbidden to enter. I ran away from school every day, crying and screaming – I didn't want to go to school without my twin. I think it was a relief to everyone when I finally went to grammar school in a nearby town. It was a new start.

Growing up is hard when you are only half. I sought suffocating friendships in an endeavour to make myself whole again – but only served to drive my friends away. Friendships only caused me pain and disappointment but still I struggled on, looking for the impossible. How can you find anything so precious in the dark? I did, however, find solace in my dog. We were inseparable and she never let me down or disappointed me. My love never suffocated her and I could cry into her soft receptive ears without any fear of retribution. Then, in my teens, my parents bought me a pony and with my dog and pony I was finally able to escape the agony of human companionship.

My marriage lasted seven years but I had got it wrong again. My husband was a brother, not a lover. Why on earth did I keep thinking that I could replace my twin? It was at this stage of my life, when I finally reached an all-time low, that the fighter in me began to take over. Deep down I knew that I needed to start facing my loss if I was to have any chance of survival. I confronted my mother, I needed to know about my twin. How did he die? What did he look like just before he died? What was the date of his death and where were his ashes? My mother, sitting pale and drawn, gave up what she had claimed as her own for so many years. Not everything, but enough for me for now. The next day my older brother rang and told me never to put my mother through that again, never to talk to her again about MY TWIN! Too late, big brother, too late.

With my new-found knowledge I could, at last, visit the crematorium on the anniversary of my twin's (our) death. On this day the Book of Remembrance is opened to show my twin's name and the simple, impossible, statement, 'died age six and a half years'.

As a postscript, I should like to add that my parents and I are really quite close now. It's just that the subject of my twin is taboo. Things were different then from the way they are now. My parents were swallowed up by their own grief and no one came forward to offer them advice and support. Even though I ran away from school every day in tears, no one in the education system seemed to recognise the desperation driving that lost little girl. I love my parents but I miss my twin dreadfully and I hope, most fervently, that things really have changed for the better – that nowadays there would be much more support.

ANONYMOUS

Story 2

A woman in her fifties who lost a brother aged five years

We are all children of our time – I was born in 1942, in the middle of the Second World War. I imagine that I should say 'I' when I was born a twin. Perhaps this is because I don't know which of us was born first. Perhaps it's because he died aged five years on 8 August, 1947, so for virtually all my life I've been without him. And yet I haven't really. Once a twin, always a twin.

Until I was interviewed by Joan Woodward, I had not knowingly met another lone twin. It seems extraordinary now, but my family never spoke about his life and he faded into the background of my life. We were very poor, my parents semi-literate, and I was the strong, clever child. I remember reading *Peter Pan* before I started school and yet it was a home without books, paper, pencils. I sit now in my own home surrounded by an abundance of these. My brother and I started school together in Battersea (it's still there – I went to the centenary a few years ago and remembered crying in assembly, when we sang 'Morning Has Broken'). Did the teachers know why, I wonder? Later, I was bullied by some boys. Would my brother have defended me? Who knows. He was physically the weaker twin. We both had scarlet fever. He had ear problems. My sisters (seven and ten years older) say he was a nuisance to take out – wimpy – I was the goody-goody. But he was the only son. My father was in the army in France when we were born. He must have been in Germany, too. I still have a watch given to him for cigarettes. It hung on a nail in the kitchen. I dropped it once and was sent to bed without tea. My oldest sister worked in a sweet factory and brought me some coconut icing. Both sisters married in their teens. By the time I won a scholarship to grammar school, I was the only child at home.

I have no recollection of my brother's illness. I only know what I have been told. Other people's memories. Sister Jean: 'We went to the seaside for the day. He ran into the water and a wave came over his head. He was really quiet in the coach coming back. We said we should take him there more often.' Sylvia: 'He kept falling asleep during the days. Mum took him to the doctor who didn't think there was anything wrong.' Then he started having fits. He was taken to Tite Street Hospital in London and then transferred to Atkinson Morley Hospital in Wimbledon. No visits. No telephone at home. No time to say goodbye. I think my grandmother looked after me during the funeral – 'He's gone to heaven.' Later the word meningitis was used.

In 1997 I went to Atkinson Morley for the first time to interview a patient. I am a social worker. How peaceful it was: not at all what I had expected. I thought about asking whether their records went back to 1947, but I didn't. I didn't actually know the date in August though I do now. In January I walked into St Catherine's House, opened the register, filled in a form and the death certificate came in the post. 'Tubercular meningitis'. TB. Scourge of the 1940s. Aunty Connie always coughing. 'She kissed him on the lips', says my other aunt.

Too late to ask my parents what they thought. Is that why I pay such attention to details? Who knows.

Update
Since writing my story for the first edition, I have now had the opportunity to meet with a large number of lone twins, many of whom have become friends. I could not have envisaged this when I joined the Lone Twin Network in 1989. Neither could I have predicted that I would learn so much about the impact of twin loss fifty years after losing my brother.

I honestly think that, had I not been able to share my experience with others through Network meetings and correspondence, I might never have understood my emotional responses, particularly to convey the significance of my twin loss to those close to me. Even now, friends I have known for years are startled to learn that I had a twin. I find it easier to talk to them about it and they feel that they know me better.

It has been rewarding to contribute to the Lone Twin Network. Initially, by helping to organise the London meetings and then by creating a 'Library' of articles and recorded interviews with lone twins which I can share with members. Not everyone can attend meetings, so reading about the experience of others can be very helpful.

Another unexpected reward is that I had the opportunity to create a Remembrance Book. I offered to do this because I was studying calligraphy and thought that I would be able to carefully write out names and inscriptions as requested by lone twins. As the book evolved, I was asked to add quotations or poems which had a significant meaning or association with the lost twin. In doing this, I realised that I had never commemorated the loss of my own twin. I then began to feel that, in creating the Remembrance Book, I was actually creating a tangible memorial to my brother. Remembrance, which had once been so painful, was now a source of comfort as his name was joined by others. When it became full with entries, I found Christina Rossetti's poem, 'Remember Me When I Am Gone Away', and felt a sense of completion as I wrote it out for the frontispiece. Had I not linked with the Network, I think it is highly unlikely that I would have created a memorial in this way …

> Remember me when I am gone away,
> Gone far away into the silent land;
> When you can no more hold me by the hand,
> Nor I half turn to go yet turning stay.
> Remember me when no more day by day
> You tell me of our future that you planned.
> Only remember me; you understand
> It will be late to counsel then or pray.

Yet if you should forget me now for a while
And afterwards remember, do not grieve:
For if the darkness and corruption leave
A vestige of the thoughts that once I had,
Better by far you should forget and smile
Than that you should remember and be sad.

IRENE COPPOCK

Story 3
A woman in her thirties who lost her brother at two and a half years

I have always felt I had a foot in both camps, life and death. Death has been a friend, personified by my twin whom I've felt attached to through the mere fact of twinhood. I have often felt that growing up from childhood with death as an integral part of my consciousness gave me a strange stability and a useful perspective from which to evaluate the ups and downs of life. It also made me into one of life's completers and preparers!

My twin brother, Graham, drowned when we were two and a half. A few months later my parents adopted a baby boy, Richard, who was three years younger than me. I grew up feeling very close to him. We were told that I'd had a twin who'd died and that Richard was special because he was adopted. I also had two older sisters. I knew a little about my twin, and there were photos in the family album which hinted at his character and ways. That I'd been a twin was a fact that I took out and polished from time to time with curiosity and satisfaction at being that bit more interesting deep down. Like most sensitive children I sometimes felt lonely and that life wasn't fair. When I felt insecure, ashamed or hurt I sometimes felt that everything would have been all right if only Graham was still alive. At the same time I always felt a strong warmth, protectiveness and loyalty towards Richard, and I think he may have kept alive in me some aspects of twinness.

During my teens I had a lot of problems. Engulfing anxieties over schoolwork, long lonely depressive times, the huge black hole of claustrophobia for a year or so when I had to spend time alone with anyone but my mother or my brother. A suicide attempt and a personality that could alternately put itself through hoops to succeed and crumble with inadequacy and nerves. My parents had separated and divorced and life was more complicated emotionally and practically. And whether my difficulties were caused more by all the changes or whether I had them ahead all along by virtue of losing my twin I'll never know. But during those bleak years when intimacy caused me such anxiety and when I felt like a Walking Problem, I thought very often about this unknown twin whom I had shared my beginnings with – the person most like me in the world – and ached to be close to him.

From twenty to thirty I became much more animated and outgoing and better able to enjoy life. After I finished studying I started working and found I could talk to anyone about more or less anything. More useful in a way than all the exams I'd passed! I had as many friends as I wanted and had relationships with a number of supportive men, free now from any emotional claustrophobia. One of these relationships was a spell with someone who had an identical twin. I was in my mid twenties and doing far too much as usual and gradually, with all the pressures, my health broke down. Getting to know a 'real' twin I felt the curiosity that had always been at bay about my own twinhood forcing itself up like a volcano and taking control. Imagining (not necessarily realistically) the pain of each of my family when Graham died preoccupied me for months. I think much of my own separation pain after losing Graham was still buried under depression and anxiety. But I had one moment of success at bringing my need out into the open when during this time I told my father that I'd been thinking a lot about Graham. He responded by telling me about the day 'Ga' died, how he was given the news and had to come home from work and collect Ga's small dead body from a neighbour's house and then break it to my sisters. I had always felt awkward when there had been a passing reference to 'the twins', too awkward and sometimes too choked to say anything. But this was part of Graham's life being shared, both sad and absolutely fascinating. And most wonderful of all, though difficult at the time, my father cried a little and I knew that he still felt very sad about losing Graham. And most of all that he loved him.

I have been able to explore with other lone twins how losing a twin had affected my life. I realised both the advantages and disadvantages of my parents' attitudes. The general absence of highly emotional references to Graham or my own conscious memories of him had given me the freedom to develop, unworried by public displays of regret and without the restricting mould of a twin. However, without much encouragement to talk about my feelings, including about being a twin, I grew up feeling confused in many ways and often insecure and self-doubting.

I also went to a meeting of other lone twins with parents who had recently lost a twin and wanted to know what to do and what not to do vis-à-vis the remaining twin. I was amazed at how they knew to keep some clothes and toys of the dead twin to pass on to the remaining one. They had put photos up and recorded various details and anecdotes about the dead child to pass on to the remaining twin and other children in the future. Yet they were aware of the need not to let the home become a memorial to the dead child.

My breakdown and my experience of these 'enlightened' recently bereaved parents made me very angry and probably moved me out of my numbness. I felt indignant that I'd missed out on my rightful memories of my brother and myself – no entertaining anecdotes about our babyhood. The family fragmentation after my parents' divorce had put another veil over the past. It has taken over ten years to draw out more of Graham's story and I have regularly felt an anger so deep and a desperation so intense it's hard to describe. Sometimes I have seen it as a conspiracy of silence.

But the picture is changing as with time and practice my family have weathered the questions I ask from time to time about Graham and I am able to weather the waiting and trust that the process will continue. The most helpful change is losing my self-consciousness about asking, and feeling more resilient about trying to concentrate the minds of family members from time to time on this far-away time. There is beginning to be some laughter and happiness in the memories. I feel less sorry for Graham, whom nobody wanted to remember. And I mind less, inwardly, if people don't understand why I need them to try and remember him so I can get to know him. If they cry or I do, I accept it as a natural part of the process. I feel there is potential for real intimacy with members of my family if we can continue to learn to listen to and accept each other's feelings and talk about the past more easily. Also that there would be great benefits to our relationships if we could talk about death, especially as my mother and father and their respective partners get older.

I am in a relationship with a man whose wife died of cancer before we met. I feel very lucky to be with a man who values spending time to communicate and talk about feelings and is teaching me by example about intimacy and open-endedness. It means I can explore my own feelings around loss with someone who has his own call on the past and his own way of honouring it.

Last year I started writing to Graham, as a stranger and intimate, one and the same. I also started painting during times when he's foremost in my mind. I even wrote a couple of poems to him in a very sweet, sad state of mind. The rhythm of the poems was quite distinct and seemed to be performed in my mind. It feels important to have started a creative process like this which can come and go according to my need and can continue independently of anyone else's consent or understanding.

Last year around his anniversary I looked at the photos of Graham with my father and then with my sister. My mother managed to add to the occasions when we have discussed Graham, a busy written account of the most intense and harrowing years of her life, which included mothering four children, among them twins. My father tapped a store of happiness in his memories which I think he found precious and I found memorable. He suggested we carry on the remembering process. This openness and willingness to continue is more precious to me than any other aspect of the process. I have initiated with him a memorial of music whereby we dedicate a piece of music to Graham from time to time. There is not any rationale behind the choice of music, it simply feels appropriate in some way, and I hope will become a collection which we associate privately with Graham whom we loved and lost.

I am beginning to derive a secure sense of what Graham was like as a child. He was experienced by some as a 'disruptive' child, but I can't feel any negativity for him, only a real twinkle and fondness for the picture I have of him so far, and fascination and relief that other people's memories can build him into a real child for me. I think in time he will feel like part of my experience, rebuilt by others who choose to participate. Bit by bit the fact of twinhood and the name and the photos and now people's individual memories are taking shape as a real child, though long dead, whom I am beginning to feel I know and who is there in my memory for when I want to remember him.

Update

Writing again from the broader perspective of now, I remember as a child always being curious about the invisible. My mother had told me that my twin Graham was in heaven, and I was drawn to the Church, which seemed to be the only place which acknowledged the invisible or talked about death – and life beyond – albeit in a rather stylised way. The other place where you could find death talked about a lot was anything to do with the Holocaust, and for many years through adolescence and adulthood I was equally horrified and fascinated by it and read countless autobiographies of people who survived Auschwitz and other concentration camps. I think it was a way of vicariously exploring my own grief as well as finding out how people in infinitely more challenging situations survived.

I can see how lucky I was to have had a good education which gave me the means to express my feelings and gradually find my voice. I did a great deal of active emotional work (variously with lone twins, therapists, priests on occasion and always between whiles on my own) over many years from my late teens to mid-adulthood. I am very grateful to my parents for bringing us up to be adventurous and independent. In me I think this took the form of going on a long journey inwards, intuiting that it was what I had to do to improve my health all round, and having the strength to face up to the depths and learn the value of my feelings and crying my tears.

A lone twin I know lost her sister at the same age as I lost my brother and has had a fair amount of therapy. But the grieving work seems largely untouched. She feels the twin issue is at the root of her many problems but feels too scared to go into it. She was also two decades older than me when she found out about the Lone Twin Network.

I'm aware too though that in my case the inward work was not the whole story. What stopped me searching for Graham was going, several years apart, to two psychic healers at the College of Psychic Studies. When I 'found' him and 'heard' him through them I experienced an infinitely subtle but seismic inner shift with respect to him. I didn't feel sorry for him any more or try to find ways of rehabilitating his memory.

Over the last few years I've become close to my mother and enjoy an emotional intimacy and balance with her that never seemed possible before. She sometimes voices deep regret and guilt over the past. But we can at last communicate closely and enjoyably on an emotional level. My father had a major stroke and died suddenly three years ago. In spite of my hopes, it wasn't possible to explore emotions much with him over the years, though I'm glad to have tried. Sadly, it often felt like a rather tortuous relationship while he was alive. Partings with him at stations over the years I remember being particularly tense and difficult at times, not surprisingly perhaps I now realise. I feel greatly for my parents that they had to carry this burden of grief and guilt for so many years, largely in silence and without support. My sisters and brother have started talking to my mother to some extent about the past from their point of view and now it can happen occasionally that one of them mentions Graham in conversation.

For myself, I feel that the emotional and spiritual work I seem to have spent so much of my live doing had brought me relatively good stability. Life is certainly a lot easier these days. I seem to have left depression well behind, though I do worry, including about time.

Strangely perhaps I don't think about Graham very often, and it's rarely emotionally loaded when I do. I do feel, though, that being a lone twin has shaped my life deeply, and probably helped me towards my new path in life as a medical herbalist.

I see myself essentially as an explorer and I'm still exploring the invisible. I feel very different from most of my family, for whom the material world is all there is. Many extraordinary, beautiful and comforting things have happened to me from the invisible, both in churches and outside of them. So I know beyond any doubt that the invisible world is real and that one way and another I have all the evidence I need to know I'm being accompanied on my journey.

JUDITH LOCKE

Story 4
A man in his thirties who lost his brother at fourteen years

NICKY. NICHOLAS. NICK.

I spent fourteen years and nine months sharing my life with Nicky. And then on August bank holiday 1979 in Ireland a group of people decided to attack and kill my family. They thought it would improve things somehow. That group of people was the IRA. They planted a bomb on our small fishing boat, and set it off by remote control. Nicky died instantly. My grandfather, grandmother and Paul, our young Irish friend who was spending his school holidays looking after our boat, also died. By some miracle my mother, father and I survived, thanks to the holidaymakers who pulled us into their little boats, thanks to the brilliant Irish doctors and nurses, and their skills in the operating theatres.

We were lucky. We had all our limbs, no brain damage and a large close family and wonderful friends. And after a time the scars were few. The visible ones, that is.

Talking was the greatest cure, and I was good at that. I wasn't good at crying though. I did cry, of course, sometimes alone and sometimes with my family. But we were all so completely crushed by the bomb, we needed not just to survive, but to signal to others that we were surviving. And when we were all so devastated, it was hard to say, 'I'm hurting, I need more time, more energy, more support, more listening.' The one thing I wanted most was to give support and strength to my beloved family at the worst time in our lives – and the first way I felt I could do that was to show them that I was all right, I was coping, not to worry about me. I knew that they were very worried I might not be able to carry on as a lone twin, so I automatically felt I should give them the 'all-clear' signal as soon as I was out of hospital.

I fooled them, but worse I fooled myself. My emotional and mental scars were terrible, and they took years to come out because I clamped down on them and kept them from view. The years rolled by and eventually I admitted to myself that all wasn't right. Hearing in my head the sound of the bomb day after day was not normal or healthy, so I went to a counsellor and started doing what I should have done fifteen years earlier – setting aside the time and the energy to talk and think and admit to myself and others what was going on inside me. The only problem was that I was now thirty, and those scars were so deep and toughened that re-working the splinters slowly and painfully out of the old wounds was much harder than if I'd done it before.

What I needed then, when I was fourteen, was for someone to keep me talking and thinking about what was going on in my head and my heart. I remember my parents from time to time suggesting I visit a child psychologist, and I pooh-poohed the idea: 'I was fine', or at least I wanted to be, for them.

I met other lone twins, but one day I met David, with whom I got on so well that we became and remain each other's closest friend. We talk and understand each other, and we understand each other without always having to talk. We soon discovered that the loss of our twins was only going to be a small part of what we shared, but it was an acorn from which grew an oak. We were both younger than our twins, we were both identical, we were both so close to our twins that imagining life without them had been impossible. But after they were killed (his in a medical accident) we not only survived, we grew and flourished. We suffered enormous pain, but we gained enormous strength and capacity for life.

And now I'm ready for a new stage in my life – I've learnt enough and grown strong enough to grasp life once again and all that it offers with the excitement and energy that Nick and I did as children – and to look forward to a wife and children of my own one day, maybe even twins.

© TIMOTHY KNATCHBULL

Story 5
A woman in her seventies who lost her sister at three years
Having lost my mother in November 1926 when I was only two, it was doubly hard losing my twin sister the following November.

My aunt has told me what an outgoing and attractive child my twin Joan was – definitely the stronger of the two of us. Unfortunately, apart from photographs I have no recollection of her. I have always felt incomplete, as if a part of me was missing. I have missed her guidance and companionship. How different my life would have been had I not lost the two people most close to me. Maybe we'll meet in the next world. I hope so!

BARBARA BAYLEY

Story 6
A woman in her fifties who lost an identical sister at six years
Two baby girls were born in an upstairs bedroom, undetected, the first had the cord around her neck and was saved by the nurse staying next door. The second was thought by the mother to be the afterbirth. That baby was me. We were rushed to hospital to be incubated.

Now, more than fifty years later I look back to the early childhood memories I had tried to push aside because they were painful.

We had both returned from that hospital and were very close to one another, we were dressed identically and everyone called us 'the twinnies'. We were a double, we played games that only we understood and giggled at things that others did not understand. We were bought the same toys to play with.

Starting school was a milestone. We were in the same class but seated at separate tables. I was devastated. I can still recall the feeling of wanting to be with her. The teacher could not tell us apart so she pinned a 'hanky' on one of our school cardigans, I don't know which one because we would go into the cloakrooms and swap it – share it. We were the twins, two into one, we came as a double. We were so used to people not knowing which one was which that we answered to both names anyway!

I remember the day she became ill as if it were yesterday. I didn't want to go to school without her but wasn't given the choice. I went by myself for a few days and the teacher always asked 'How is your twin?' Then one day as I returned home from school I saw an ambulance on the roadside outside the gate. I ran, I saw my twin on my mother's lap in the front seat, cradled in a blanket. I ran but it went and I couldn't catch it. 'Wait for me!' My grandmother was there and read me endless Rupert stories as I cuddled on her lap. Even now my stomach churns with the memory when I see Rupert books.

I was told that my twin had gone to hospital 'to be made better' but one night I awoke to the sound of crying and as I descended the stairs I knew instinctively that my beloved twin sister was dead. 'She had gone to Heaven' they said. I wanted to go too but no-one would tell me the way. I searched, I looked in the places we had hidden when we played Hide-and-Seek. I pretended she was only hiding. One day trying to squeeze behind the wardrobe, I thought I felt her hand. That was frightening, after all she was dead, so I didn't play that game again. I knew I couldn't find her.

We were six years and nine months old. I didn't go to the funeral, I think I was viewed as too young so I didn't ever get to say goodbye.

All our toys, like the 'motor' bikes we had been given for our birthday were the same. The see-saw was no good for one so they all went. The teacher never asked 'How is your twin?' any more. I was given her school books to take home. I wanted to covet those books but they were put away. I didn't have anything left of her.

Life went on. I heard the adults say 'You will lose the other one now'. I was frightened of what that meant as I knew that I was 'the other one', but if it meant being with my twin then good. Some of the children at school hit me and said that if one twin died so should the other so I should be dead. I wanted to be. Some people who still couldn't get the names right called me by my twin's name. I was used to that happening but it seemed wrong when she was not there. Some just called me 'the twin'. Singular. One without the other.

My mum missed my sister terribly. I always knew that and of course I was a constant reminder to her of her loss. When I looked in the mirror I, too, saw the twin that I so missed. I loved my twin and I knew she was my mother's favourite, the smaller of us, the 'baby'. Loveable and loved. My mum told me I had taken all the nourishment in the womb. I had weighed in at 4lbs and my twin at 2lbs. 'Like a bag of sugar', my mum said. I was the 'fat' one. It was my fault.

Years later, having had a baby girl and before my mum died, she gave me a tin. I call it the 'tin of memories' as it contains photographs, letters of bereavement, a dish my sister won at the fair, a small toy (her favourite) and school books, including mine. I realised that my mum also mourned the loss of 'the twins' that had been so special.

The twin relationship is unique and the loss of a twin is unique. No other relationship can compare with it. Marriage, motherhood, friendship, all special but none the same. Only a twin can understand the depth of feeling that exists between a twin pair. We suffer losses, parents, siblings, friends, none the same. Every loss brings back the memory of the loss of a twin.

Communicating with other lone twins has helped as I know that others feel the same intensity of loss. I do not have to try and hide the fact that I was born a twin as I will never be anything else.

I still love and miss my identical twin sister. Forever.

LINDY PIERI

THEME 2
ON REPLAYING THE EXPERIENCE OF LOSS IN LATER LIFE

Many themes tend to overlap, because life-long experiences of grief following severe loss can be expressed in so many different ways. One of these is when loss feelings experienced in early childhood re-emerge when the surviving twin has children of his or her own reaching the same age as the twin who died. Sometimes a twin becomes ill at this time without even being aware of the reason. This theme confirms the belief that the loss of an Attachment figure can be of such utmost significance that even when the original feelings of loss appear to have been overcome, they lie dormant in some people, able to be triggered by events that bring back the memories.

Story 1
A woman in her seventies who lost an identical sister at five years
My identical twin died from diphtheria when we were five years old. I remember her being carried out to the ambulance and how my father took the live coal from the grate in my parents' bedroom to add to the kitchen range downstairs. (The luxury of a fire in a bedroom was diminished somewhat by its being associated with illness.) When the news came through that my sister had died, I was told she had gone to Heaven, and I remember a vivid dream I had not long afterwards, of her coming down a long ladder with a number of other boys and girls to play with me in the street. They were all wearing carpet slippers so they couldn't be heard in Heaven! That is the only time I remember dreaming of her until two or three weeks ago. In this dream, I was waiting alone in a foreign restaurant for my parents. I waited a long time and was about to give up (the disappointment was profound) when my mother came in with my father just behind. I ran to her and hugged her and then realised it was myself I was hugging because she was wearing some of my clothes. When I awoke I thought my dream must have been due to the fact that I realise how much like my mother I have become in my old age. Then I felt in a flash it was my lost twin and she had been brought to mind because that day I had received the LTN Newsletter. The dream left me with a feeling of warmth and comfort. Was this because I know there are all those other lone twins feeling as I do?

I was a very lively child until my twin died. From the age of five until I was about eleven I suffered greatly, physically and emotionally. I had many nightmares of being sucked away in a vortex and can remember, despite my screams, the sound of my father rushing upstairs two at a time to comfort me. I also frequently walked in my sleep. Sometimes I was aware of it, and sometimes I knew it only because I would find myself under the eiderdown instead of between the sheets. Also, which must have been awful for my mother, I would talk to my twin, that is, my reflection in the polished brass doorknobs which were the right height for me at the time. I don't remember doing this, but was told about it many years later. I still 'feel' us playing cab horses on the stairs, our legs covered by a rug, and we played dolls using shoe boxes as cradles. The only other things that are vivid in my mind are the funeral with the little white coffin across the front of the first carriage, and visiting the grave, on my following two or three birthdays. At the head of the grave was a wooden cross inscribed with a name and 'Able bodied Seaman'. I was fascinated by this and imagined Gracie being comforted in his arms.

When I had children of my own, I had 'lost child' dreams and began sleep-walking again. When my daughter was five and my son two, I had two and a half years of group psychotherapy which helped me a lot. Nevertheless, I still get upset whenever the subject of my twin arises, and I have always found parting with loved ones very traumatic, my husband during the Second World War and my sister after her many visits from California where she has lived since 1929. I have now experienced many partings through death and I find that I do not feel grief so much at the time, but eventually when I am alone, I give way to it – even as I write now. To believe in an afterlife must be comforting.

ETHEL MATTISON

THEME 3
ON CONNECTING WITH THE TWIN IN SPIRIT

One of the beliefs held firmly by some twins is that their twin not only survives in spirit, but is in some sense available and guiding them through life. I believe that this is a way for some twins to deal with the intense loneliness so many of them feel, as losing their twin in childhood means that they only have fragments of memory of their being together.

Bowlby would probably explain such beliefs as a totally human way of expressing longings to be Attached and a way of lessening the sense of loss, through the idea that at least in some sense, their twin feels available to them.

One twin describes his endless-seeming experiences of 'coinci-dences' as evidence that his twin is 'with him' and continues to guide him. Other twins can feel quite distant from such beliefs as they struggle to survive on their own.

Story 1
A man in his forties who lost his brother at three years

I lost my brother at the age of three. When I was young, I was always looking back, when I was supposed to be walking forward. When my brother was alive, I had to pull him to keep up with me and it was years before I grew out of this. Michael was the one who started things and I finished them, so when he died I stopped learning for a time. Because of lack of communication, there was a big gap after he died where nobody knew what I was going through. How could I know! When the teacher was telling me something, it just didn't register so they thought that I wasn't paying attention but that wasn't true. The only way I could learn, if it was a woman teacher, was practically if she sat down right next to me and spoke directly to me.

I have experienced so many coincidences in my life, which I believe are brought about, or guided, by my brother Michael. To have dreams come true when I was young seemed to me to be 'just normal'. I was pulled out of the sea and saved from drowning when I was four years old: thirty-seven years later I met my rescuer's son on a football field. When I was twenty-one the van I was driving ran out of diesel: a man stopped and gave me some. The amazing coincidence to me was that five years later and 200 miles away I met him again. Fifteen years later I helped a coach driver change a wheel – then I recognised him as the same man!

Once, in St Albans, when I was having a pint, I asked for a thirty-year-old, obsolete record to be played and discovered I was standing next to the man who'd played the guitar on the original record. He invited me back to his house – which, coincidentally again, was where I'd parked my car!

PAUL HARTLEY

Story 2
A man in his thirties who lost his identical brother at birth

(This is included in this section because it illustrates the theme of connecting with the twin in spirit.)

My twin was, and is, my first relationship – a companion I was born with, and at that time an equal in all respects. Before we were born, our development created a bond, a trust, a responsibility, a sharing nature. Perhaps other characteristics, which some might describe as 'the negative side of things', are also initiated during our time in the womb, such as jealousy, conflict of interests, or peer pressure.

Until recently, the relevance of my special 'relationship' did not keep repeating itself so often – it seems that in times of trouble or stress from other causes its existence gives me strength and encouragement to put things right.

These may seem very adult characteristics, but I believe the model from which we grow, despite later events and circumstances, is made during this time.

I cannot speak of those negative points, because my twin died at birth. That is not to say that these feelings have not or do not continue to appear in me many times – they do.

As a child, friendships with other children were of two sorts: those I knew well and those I did not. The second of these I might meet irregularly and in 'adult' terms the relationships might seem 'thin'. However, members of the first group were closer. Small in numbers, we played together much more, and they necessarily had to have a similar temperament and hobbies to me. It was as though, subconsciously, they had to achieve certain criteria, and keep to them.

Because of the numbers, and the time it took to make friends, it was so much harder when we had our differences and arguments. We made it up the next day, of course – why? I believe that I was trying to achieve something in friendships that I was unable to achieve with my twin. Even at this age, each friendship was important, significant, and was expected to last 'forever'. Yes, that seems an extraordinary word to use, and children do believe in such things – but that was the genuine feeling, they were part of my family, and belonged to me almost. If my friends had friends themselves, likely as not I was a friend of theirs as well. It was a close band (or gang at times) of friendships.

Looking back, at junior school, the 'real' friends I had were few, and always lived close by, and could be called on when needed in some way. It was much easier at this age to be helpful at school, organising clubs and activities, the teachers were keen to enlist my help and I felt that I was giving something to the school, that I made a difference. My twin would be proud of me, as were my parents.

Moving to a larger house in a different area meant that at the age of twelve it was necessary to 'start again'. At the time, the significance of such a move only seemed to relate to starting secondary education and having more room at home. It was exciting having new surroundings, but the school was not in the same area as our home. Consequently, school friends did not live near us and shyness and nerves played their part in making the task of making friends that much more difficult for me.

In addition, many of those at school with me knew each other from junior school or being neighbours; as a consequence, I began making friends from what seemed at the time a disadvantage. I felt that they were somehow looking down on me and might very easily repeat or blab things I might say to the others. Consequently, very often I did not even try. Making or breaking friendships did not seem so earth shattering to them.

Since leaving school, friendships at work were important in that in order to work well and achieve the tasks involved, it was important to be in happy and pleasant surroundings – the purpose of going to work was work – if friendships were found whilst at work, well fair enough, but the number one purpose was to work – I very often work alone, creating my own goals and deadlines – I can and do work with others, but do they achieve the levels of perfection I expect? Do I pass my own criteria for good work? Not often, and the questioning of why and trying to analyse what to do next can sometimes be very frustrating.

Friendships in adult life can be just as difficult – yet when one does come along, which has those qualities you respect and need, that is when you know that 'someone' must be important. Never a replacement – that suggests that somehow you are embarrassed or wish to hide or deny your twin's existence; this suggestion, by many non-twins that we should somehow be getting on with our lives and put the past to bed, is one of those irritating things said to us. We are remembering our relationship with our twin as a past and/or present entity, one we are both proud of, and glad to have happened despite any difficulties it might have had.

MIKE WESTLEY

Story 3
A woman in her forties who lost her identical sister at fifteen years
Philippa and I were identical twins and spent 24 hours a day in each other's company, happily playing our own games together and interacting with the outside world as a pair. We were very alike, neither was dominant, and we very rarely quarrelled, but she was more socially outgoing than me.

Suddenly aged six, she developed a life threatening brain tumour and my world changed forever. I went to stay with a school friend for six weeks and she became my substitute twin. On my return home Philippa had changed. Our experience of our time apart was very different, she was physically fragile but more self confident due to all the attention she received from family and hospital staff. I felt I was the less important twin but did not feel this was her fault. I was physically well and I felt I had to get on with everyday life without making a fuss. Strangely for me for the first time we didn't look alike, she was very thin, we weren't identical any more!

I had to learn to be by myself at school (as my substitute twin moved out of the area shortly afterwards) and be a semi-twin at home. The non-verbal communication was still there but our lives were very different and as the years went by Philippa seemed much younger than me in some ways. Although she had no serious lasting brain damage, she had several further operations due to the tumour growing again which weakened and slowed her such that she rarely returned to school. Sadly she died when we were nearly sixteen. I grieved then for my 'little' sister, not really my twin, who in many ways I had lost when I was six.

After I was six I tended to try to get too close to a particular friend and then eventually got rebuffed and hurt and became very wary. As I grew older I got this balance better but felt there was something wrong with me that the relationship never got close enough in what I later realised was a twin-like way. I hid a part of me, the deep emotional feeling part. I wanted my friends to be very like me and felt rather threatened by our differences. In my early twenties I met my husband, Graham, and although wary at first in case I got hurt, I was able to draw on the trust that I had had with Philippa to gradually build a wonderful deep partnership. Remembering my very positive, close and equal twin relationship, the trust and mutual supportiveness, I was able to have the self-belief that I could achieve this again albeit differently. I respected that he was his own person but still felt insecure about myself.

I really grieved for the loss of my twin in my mid-thirties, which is when in many ways I stopped looking for another twin relationship for me and my children. I tried to build a greater sense of self by writing about my feelings daily, doing yoga, and allowing myself to feel and think while listening to music. I started talking about my twin, learnt to openly value my relationship with her and all I had learnt from it, and move on. As a result of this opening up my friendships became much deeper, which was lovely as I had always feared this would lead to rejection. I learnt to acknowledge and appreciate other people's differences as well as similarities to myself and feel comfortable with these rather than just accepting them as I had before. I had listened to my non-twin friends carefully in order to understand how differently they feel having always been a single individual as opposed to a twin, the inner security they have within themselves. It seems to me that they do not firstly and automatically, think about how the other person feels in any situation. Nor do they project and perhaps empathise as I do, and therefore find it difficult to know how they feel themselves. They seem to have much more inherent sense of self, feel more strongly who they are and what they feel, and need less affirmation from others. They have never known the security of a constant reflection of oneself that twins have and the feeling of not being alone in the world. Gradually discussing and understanding these differences has made them much less threatening, in fact a good thing!

I have now realised I do not have to follow either my twin's individual strengths, for example social confidence, or alternatively that these are unattainable goals for me. I can choose my own path, as can my children.

I have come to realise that I can never replace my twin relationship, indeed I now don't want to, but I can make new and strong friendships based in appreciation of difference as well as sameness. Balance and equality are very important in a relationship to me. Happily I now have much more sense of myself and enjoy my own company but still greatly value that of my husband, family and friends.

BELINDA BRADFORD

THEME 4
ON THE LOSS OF A TWIN AFTER A VERY LENGTHY PERIOD OF ILLNESS

Story 1
A woman in her forties who lost her sister at the age of nine years
Dear Susan,

Tell me what it's like being dead then?

How's Christmas? Do you miss the celebrations? (Not that we had many, did we?)

How did you manage it? You screwed up Christmas and my birthday – oh, sorry, 'our' birthday.

Are you lonely? I can hardly bear to ask; I think of you lying or sitting or watching and waiting under that bush.

It's so cold; is anyone kind to you?

People were kind to you – kinder than they were to me, but I don't think you should have used up a whole lifetime's or deathtime's kindness, just by being conveniently ill – should you?

Do you wait for me? Do you feel abandoned? That image of abandonment is like a clean shining tapered knife (one of Granny's) cutting into my guts, surgically removing my heart and putting it into cold storage – for future use? For research?

Describe Christmas Day to me – alone, cold, crying, abandoned, lonely, in despair? – or hopeful?

Are you an optimist like me?

Will someone come and rescue you, some loving parent to warm you up? Don't be fooled – they have their needs too. No one is going to be totally altruistic about this Susan.

I could have warmed you up; but I'm not the warm bit either. Can two colds make a hot? I left you anyway. I was afraid to come, to unthaw you, in case you reproached me for all those hundreds of years' abandonment. You left me and I got my own back on you kid, but I never wanted us to be lonely.

If we'd died together like the story of the ghosts in The Tower, would we have walked around that bush holding hands? I would always have needed other people, you know YOU WERE NEVER ENOUGH, in life or death. Your image was tarnished after your death by your twinness with me – some of the filth got onto your bit. I never found the other bit I needed. My children are enough, but I can't drain that warmth to thaw me; the buck must stop with this generation sunshine! – you dead cold, me frozen alive.

ANONYMOUS

Story 2
A woman in her sixties whose sister became ill when they were seven

This story comes from *Rosa's Child* (1996) in which Jeremy Josephs writes about the life of Susi Bechhöfer, telling how she (re-named Grace) and her twin sister Eunice were smuggled out of Germany and brought to England to be fostered by an English couple. Eunice became seriously ill and later died. The extract below describes Susi's experience of coping with attention given to her sister.

Mother and daughter, estranged from one another as they were, had one thing in common: neither had anyone at all with whom they could share their sense of isolation – least of all each other.

At the same time, despite Grace's concern for Eunice, all was not sweetness and light between the twins. For many years there had been considerable tension, for although she rarely said as much, Grace resented the fact that her sister had become both disfigured and incapacitated. Previously they had talked, walked and run together, whereas after the tumour was diagnosed these activities had ceased abruptly. As young children they had played happily together, with Eunice invariably the leader of the two, often protecting her more fragile sister in minor skirmishes at school. But those days had long since gone. The sad truth was that from the moment she had set eyes on her sister neatly propped up on pillows in her hospital bed after her first craniotomy, Grace had felt that her twin had already passed from her.

Eunice's illness had prompted Grace to make a painful reappraisal of their relationship. The situation had not been at all easy to accept, and when Grace was back at home from boarding school she would occasionally take out her frustration on her sister. There were frequent arguments, often concerning the family piano, a dark upright model to which she was very attached. Grace loved to play it, but Eunice could not bear what to her ears was a string of ugly, discordant sounds.

With Grace out of the way at school, Eunice naturally came increasingly under the influence of her mother, on whom she had become entirely dependent. As a result, during the school holidays it would not be long before Eunice was herself pointing her finger at her twin sister. 'That's a very unchristian thing to do,' she would often remark. And then, just to remind Grace of the many binding rules of the Mann household, she would warn her twin: 'Mummy and Daddy wouldn't like that.' For Grace, it seemed that her best and oldest friend had ceased to exist. Once again she had been abandoned.

THEME 5
ON BEING OVER-PROTECTED

Very over-anxious parents can set up such fears in the surviving twin that this can lead to them being driven to prove unreal levels of toughness, courting danger in the process. It can also lead to the surviving twin, out of anxiety for the parent, taking on responsibility to make up for the loss and to try and live for two, with intense feelings of failure when this unrealistic goal cannot be met.

Story 1
A woman in her seventies who lost her twin at three years
Looking back to my early life, I can see with hindsight how strongly I buried my feelings about the loss of my identical twin sister who died in our early childhood. There was no family 'taboo' on speaking about her and my mother did sometimes recall the times when my sister was alive. I knew that she kept a little dress and matching knickers that she had made for her wrapped in tissue paper in her chest of drawers. On the rare occasions when I saw them, some strange, uncomfortable feelings surfaced in me. They were always accompanied by simultaneous sensations of huge 'distance' as though I was looking at objects that had nothing whatever to do with me.

Very many years later, I was surprised by the depth of the distress and anger that I felt, on going through my mother's things after her death, that she had got rid of them. Why had she not consulted me? I had nothing of my sister's. I would have liked those. I do not blame her now, for I feel sure that she considered that they represented her connection with my sister and not mine.

My mother was very protective of me in ways that at the time, made me feel terribly 'over-fussed', though I now understand something of what she must have felt. What I now find quite amazing to recall are the lengths that I went to, in an effort to defy the fear hidden in the 'fuss' – both hers and mine.

Because my sister died of meningitis following an ear infection, my mother's attention mostly centred on my ears. I was never to go out in the winter without a beret on. I was a very thin child and 'catching a chill' was to be avoided at all costs. I had to wear a liberty bodice as well as a vest, and the most hated garments of all were gaiters, with what felt to me like hundreds of little buttons that I struggled to do up. Eventually I rebelled so strongly that I was allowed to wear my older brother's cast-off socks-to-the-knee. I always looked different from the other girls at school, who wore very proper-looking lady-like stockings.

I was perceived as a tomboy, between two brothers. I loved tree-climbing, roller-skating and playing a mouth organ. These activities were accepted by my parents but there were some much more dangerous activities that they never knew about, which, had they known, would have been strictly forbidden.

We lived in a flat above a shop and a small balcony which led from the kitchen at the back overhung a tradesmen's alleyway. I used to climb over the balcony railing and drop down onto the coal shed roof of the shop below. From there I could jump down to the alleyway. This had to be done surreptitiously, while the adult who was 'keeping an eye' on us, as our parents were both at work, was engaged elsewhere. Later my younger brother joined me and we made friends with the cooks in the restaurant a few doors along. We used to sit on stools well hidden in the alley, shelling peas or pulling the shells off prawns. I loved every minute of it, peeping into the steamy kitchen, the shouting of the chefs and the clatter of the equipment excited me, especially knowing in some sense that it was a clandestine activity.

From this simple climbing, I admit now with some feelings of shame, that I embarked on much more dangerous climbing. From the same balcony I could climb round the side of the flat, gripping on to down-pipes and re-enter via the kitchen window. I joined an 'adventure club' set up by my closest friend at school. She lived on a scale far beyond that of my family, in a very large house where I was often invited to visit for the day. She was much braver and more daring than I was. She would climb out of her bedroom window and from there could get out to slate roofs slanting in all directions. With plimsolls on we could scale these like monkeys. She had only to 'dare' me, to scorn me as a 'cowardy custard' and I would follow. My most vivid memory of her is with a finger to her lips, she gave me a message not to make a sound. She then pointed down with a grin to where her mother lay gently rocking on a huge garden seat under a canopy. Later such seats came to epitomise for me the 'luxury life', as I compared her mother's afternoons with those of my mother.

I was always very frightened throughout all these adventures and yet it was as if I was compulsively driven to confront the fear. I remember shaking like a leaf on those roof tops, deeply fearing that I would never get safely back into the house again.

There is one phenomenon that used to startle me, which may be more common than I am aware. It seemed to develop out of this urge to climb – to go out, rather dangerously and to experience the fear that I 'could not return', which was what actually happened in reality to my twin. This fear that I would 'not be able to return home' was the essence of the debilitating agoraphobia that I was later to battle with in my early adult life. Now I understand it in Attachment terms, as a form of severe Separation Anxiety.

This fear was expressed by me in the form of a daydream, which occurred repeatedly over very many years. It never differed in content. In the dream I was vividly outside our rooftop garden where we played safely and happily as children. The brick walls that surrounded it were further protected by strong trellis. The roof garden had a large area at the front overlooking a main road, and there was a small area at the back where washing was hung out, which was reached by passing a door that led back down into the flat. From this back area we looked down to a big block of flats and their dismal paved gardens. As the daydream flashed into my mind – often at times that seemed most inappropriate – I was suspended in mid-air, trying desperately to get back into the roof garden. I could neither move up over the top of the trellis, nor sideways onto the roof garden next door, from where I could have easily reached my own. In this daydream I was a child unable to reach a place of safety.

I thought I would have this daydream for life, until some years ago I went to a 'taster' art therapy session and for the first time painted a picture of the child trying to get in and spoke about her. I drew her with wings, for how else could she stay suspended in the air, but I denied emphatically that she was an 'angel', a perception of my dead sister trying to return, as was suggested to me. This was both too simple and too conventional a view. Surprisingly to me at the time, the daydream became more frequent after that, until a year or two later I decided to re-visit my old home. Our family had left the flat rather precipitously in 1939 when my mother's firm was evacuated to Surrey and I had never returned.

When I began to make enquiries, I was astonished to find that the flat was empty and up for sale. I arranged to go and visit it. In spite of great resistance from the man who showed us round, I insisted on going up to the roof garden. It was changed beyond recognition, with a vast air-conditioning system taking up most of it. I moved very shakily into the back part of the roof garden and had a sense of acute vertigo, as, after a gap of more than forty years, I looked down again at the flats and gardens.

For a short while after this visit, I dallied with the idea of trying to buy the flat and move back there in my retirement, but I soon came to my senses. One cannot 'move back', it is an illusion! What I found most interesting was that my daydream had gone. I could not conjure it up even if I tried.

One of the reasons for writing this account is because I think it illustrates how the unconscious part of our mind is often striving to take care of our deepest needs – if only we let it. There is a sense of a process occurring, that may seem strange, even bizarre at times, but which can carry us through to where we need to go, if we can just hold faith in it and try neither to block it, nor hurry it up.

ANONYMOUS

5
TWIN LOSS IN ADULT LIFE

INTRODUCTION

I believe that there is a very important difference in the experience of a loss of a twin in adult life from those losses that occur very early. The adult lone twin has had all the 'ups and downs' of an actual relationship and is facing the end of a long attachment. The process of adjustment to this ending can sometimes be long-lasting and very difficult.

There are twenty-two stories in this chapter. They tell of the enormous depth of sadness and pain in the loss, but they also tell of the huge struggle involved as these twins find their own way to survive well, without their twin. This struggle is particularly acute for those twins who tell the first six stories, as they describe how much their sense of self was largely sustained through the twinship. This is why the loss for these twins is often expressed in terms of feeling 'only a half'. It seems that the loss is felt equally painfully whether it is a sudden one, or slow and expected because of a long drawn-out illness. If the loss for these twins has been in early adulthood they may have difficulties in forming a very close relationship again, as it can feel like a betrayal of the twin who died, or that no one can match the relationship that they had with their twin.

Eight stories follow in the second theme. These are told by twins who, except for one, also felt very close and experienced their losses very deeply, but they have chosen to emphasise the ways they have individually 'moved on'. I believe it is of particular interest to understand from first-hand accounts the process of mourning, and how the stages of both denial of the death and a searching for the lost twin overlap with each other. As the loss is fully faced, the stage of despair is experienced and from this, new ways of living are slowly found. Some of these twins felt able to develop aspects of themselves that they were unable to own before, when their twin was alive, as if these belonged to their twin and were by definition unavailable to them.

The third theme holds three stories that show how these twins found a way of regaining their sense of self through a deep appreciation of having had a twin, even though that stage of their life was over. The fourth theme carries this concept even further, as two twins tell their stories of how their lives have been prolonged through learning about the cause of their twin's death. This has led to medical intervention for themselves and new hope of their own survival, but it inevitably creates quite complicated feelings for them.

The fifth and last theme includes three stories of twins whose twins took their own lives. This seems to result in the most complicated response of all, as it sets up so much conflict for the surviving twin. It shows in an extreme form how strongly some twins are forced into polarised positions, particularly when one twin is emotionally disturbed, as this tends to threaten the other twin who fears being 'dragged down'. It also tends to produce the accumulative effect described in Chapter 2. It shows in a stark way how twinship can sometimes be perceived as being unable to provide sufficient 'space' for two. The stories also sadly tell how little appropriate professional help was given at the time when it was so urgently needed.

THEME 1
WHEN THE TWIN'S SENSE OF SELF HAS LARGELY BEEN HELD WITHIN THE TWINSHIP

Story 1
A woman in her forties who lost an identical sister at forty-two years

MY TRUTH

The scene that possibly describes the best the relationship between me and my sister is: both of us walking to school and from school in parallel lines on opposite sides of the road. When we were ten years old our family lived about a kilometre from school so we walked. The tension was high as each of us knew what the other one wanted but it was unachievable because the desires ('wants') conflicted. I wanted to walk in an orderly way as good girls do but she wanted to have fun on the way – jump, run, play hide-and-seek and jump high enough to pick leaves off trees. I was ashamed and wished I was not associated with her. We were given the nicknames of Tarzan and Jane. In the afternoon she would sometimes manage to get on a horse with a cart and then, having had the approval of the owner, she would call me to join. That was great! I did not, selfishly, make any judgement, because we were tired and it was hot! She was daring, looking after herself and me.

I would like to mention here facts that had an impact on us or me. Our parents were survivors of the Holocaust and had had a daughter five years before we were born, who died of starvation and dysentery. Even though there were two of us I always felt that we could not reach the level of whatever she meant to our mother. Our mother was always ill, so there was a great fear of her dying, a wish to compensate and protect. Up to the age of ten we lived very closely with four other families of survivors sharing all facilities and thus they had a big influence on our lives. My sister had non-identical twins, Shimon and Yair. Yair committed suicide three months after my sister's death and Shimon did the same in exactly the same way as his brother, five months later. I have a niece who is married and has a baby boy, a surviving twin from a twin pregnancy. Since her mother died she has kept our relationship distant. Even though I understand her, it hurts a lot.

In our twinhood we were two halves. Each had characteristics which the other one did not or, even more than that, could not have, and of course it was always the opposite. Each one of us was the scale by which the other one was measured, assessed. The most extreme example for that was the fact that she was very sport-minded and a participant; the only sport she did not do was swimming – that was the only sport I liked and practised. Furthermore, those were divided into good and important, good and not so important, and bad, that needed change. In the overall picture I was the good, lucky one and needed no help. She was the bad and naughty one, who needed looking after. Our parents trusted me and relied on me. They made me feel responsible for her, for her achievements, moods and misbehaviour. The main aim was to keep her happy so she would be better. It was our parents' and our teachers' decision to separate or reunite us three times in our primary school years in order to make her do better at school. Every time the choice was hers as to who goes where. To me all that mattered was that if she is not with me then I will not be responsible for how she does, so I was pleased to be separated. I was given piano lessons while she had ballet; when she was expelled for bad behaviour, my piano lessons were stopped too. When new items of clothing were bought for us, she chose first. The interesting point about it is that I accepted it all. When I was asked if I was not jealous, my answer was no, and I wholeheartedly believe that twins are not jealous because whatever works for one twin works for both twins. It reached a point where I thought I could think for her, that I could feel for her and change her. That feeling went on even after her death. I was always full of guilt feelings for not being able to improve her and her life. She used to cry a lot so I knew she was unhappy. As children do, we fought. She used to punch and hit me black and blue, being the physically stronger and I used verbal abuse. As adults, she used crying and I used criticism. The only area I thought she was really good at was in her instincts as a mother.

At the age of thirty-four my sister sat the equivalent to A levels in Israel and took a teachers' course immediately after. I was very proud. I remember that on her first day of teaching, all I wanted was to stand behind the door of her class and listen, as if that was the proof of her capability and MY success, the step out of the image of unable to learn and so that part of the guilt I was carrying could be put to rest. This to me today is evidence that she made some progress as an independent person.

When Miriam was diagnosed as having malignant cancer and she was told that she had only six months to live, my first thoughts were that it was impossible, that it was not true, it could not be. My second thought was, who am I? Her imminent death was something I could do nothing about and I questioned myself why Miriam and not me, and how come not both? I got frightened. I felt part of me was dying. I felt I wanted to spend as much time together as possible and talk and talk and talk to make up for all the years and to hear from her how she felt and what she thought. I did spend a considerable amount of time with her. Now I wanted to do whatever she wanted me to do. Her demands were very little, the only thing she really wanted and which I could not give her was to live. At every stage of her illness she said, 'Even if I stay alive as I am now, it's OK.' We did talk. I was looking for the alleviation of my guilt feelings, for her forgiveness and found out that she did not think I needed forgiveness. I asked many questions and was surprised to find out that many things I thought I knew, actually I did not. I put the question of how did she imagine our lives would turn out! Her answer was that I would be a doctor and she would be my nurse. To the next question, how she felt about it, she said 'Fantastic'. A few times we discussed our parents and were able for the first time to express anger about them. There was a great deal of anger in me towards my mother in particular, as I have lived with fear of her death for all my life, and here was my sister dying so young. Very curiously she was very worried about her boy twins' futures and not her daughter. She kept asking me what I thought their future would be and if I would participate in major events in their lives. I had plans for a suitable, good future for them and I promised I would always be there. Yes, I was there when they were brought to burial. I know this was not what she meant. I am very angry at them and I miss them.

My sister died on 5 December 1988 at the age of forty-two, and part of me died with her. The part that is still alive, that half-person, has realised that no half can really live life to the full. It feels like being disabled. I have come to admire her and her part to the degree that I want it in myself – the other half, which includes being naughty, having fun, being imperfect and making mistakes, making choices and certainly not thinking or feeling for anyone, not even my twin sister whom I love.

Since Miriam died I have been asked many times if I am now living for both and if I sometimes do things for her. My answer is absolutely NO. I want her image to stay as she was with all her failures and achievements. Just like a photograph captures a certain time and every time you look at it, the picture is the same – you may just see it from a different angle. Because I think I knew her very well I sometimes wonder what would she say, or how would she react. I do miss her very much and use my imagination as to how our lives would have turned out had she been alive: our relationship would have been wonderful, her sons would be alive and I would not feel so lonely. On the other hand, as painful as it is, had she lived, I may have not come to the point of claiming the freedom to be a full person.

When our mother died two years after my sister, I was asked to write the inscription on the tombstone. I was advised that by Jewish law I could not mention dead people, meaning my sister. At the time I felt I had to put my sister in the inscription, and I did. I am not sure if it was my denial of her death, my missing her and feeling so lonely, or the part in me that felt dead and so gave her the right of the living in my mind. A year and a half later our father died. The inscription on his tombstone does not include my sister.

Five and a half years have passed. The pain is still very strong. I still miss her and I am still very lonely.

© HANNA LEVY/WILCZKOWSKI

Story 2
A man in his thirties who lost his identical brother

I used to wonder that other men and women were alive when death had come to my brother, whom I had loved as though he would never die. Even more I wondered that I, who was his other self, was still alive when he was dead.

Someone once spoke of his brother as 'the half of my own soul'. I agree, for I felt that my soul and that of my brother had been one soul in two bodies. So I had a horror of going on living, because I did not wish to live on as a half-person and perhaps, too, that was the reason I was afraid to die – lest he, whom I had loved so much, should die completely.

STEPHEN PIPER

Story 3
A woman in her forties who lost a brother at thirty-eight years

FOREVER TOGETHER

> Two at once on 10th May,
> Side by side they did sleep and play,
> As soon as one walked the other followed,
> If one was hurt, the other sorrowed.
> In the midst of a happy family they grew,
> They travelled and worked and married, time flew.
>
> Nothing prepared her for that terrible night,
> When asked 'Why are you calling, is everything all right?'

TWIN LOSS IN ADULT LIFE 89

His wife was so sorry, he had died around four,
He'd been feeding the cattle, the machine had jammed,
He'd tried to clear it – and that was the end.

The loss was gargantuan, the bereavement enormous,
Her heart had been torn out in a manner so careless,
Her family surrounded her but didn't exist,
She still loved them dearly, but as though through a mist.
Nothing made sense now, why was she here?
She couldn't be living without her twin there.
And now it's been six years without him on earth.
I have come to terms with his terrible death.
I thought he had left me and never again
Would I be loved unconditionally and kept safe till the end.
He has died, and part of me is with him.
He seems to be there whenever I need him ...
Are we together again?

Battered, beaten and bereft
Lost, lonely, half of me left
You've taken my confidence and my support
You've gone on without me
The ball's in my court

I don't want here without you
I wish you'd not gone
But just for you twinny, I'll fight and go on
For me your shadow will never grow less,
Just stronger, and dearer, and always, the best.

LINDA COOKE

Story 4
A woman in her fifties who lost her brother at twenty-four years

We were born prematurely in the early hours of 23 December 1936. My mother
was attended by a midwife – in those days unqualified. My mother had a three-
year-old son and was looking forward to perhaps a daughter, but not until
February! She had a difficult delivery and my twin's arrival was not only a shock
but also a breech birth. My mother haemorrhaged and was very weak, and
when the placenta delivered she heard the midwife exclaim, 'I think there's a
third one!' My father was ill with tonsillitis. It was Christmas and there was this
active, excited three-year-old.

The family rallied round, knitting tiny clothes as we only weighed 4 lb each
and nothing mother had ready fitted and there was not enough for two. The fire

was kept alight in the bedroom and we were laid back-to-back in the crib. I fed all right, but my brother needed a lot of persuading to suck. Today we would have been placed in incubators and tube-fed, but we were surrounded by love and care and we survived. I have heard this story of the night we were born so many times. It was a Christmas not to be forgotten by our family.

My mother says people were sorry for her having twins: the first time my grandfather saw us he said how sorry he was and offered my mother a ten shilling note. She was very angry and said how proud she was of us, and that feeling stays with me today. My older brother would tell everyone which twin was which, to anyone stopping to look in the pram, that was when he wasn't unscrewing the wing nuts that held the two hoods in place. I believe multiple births were less likely then than they are today.

We grew up in difficult times and my parents decided we would be safer out of Dover during the war years, so my mother, grandmother and us three children went to Wales for a year and then to Faversham in Kent where we had relatives, for the remainder of the war. We were very protected and I didn't really know what 'war' meant, except it meant we only saw our father at weekends and sometimes my mother was unhappy. I remember lying quietly in bed on Monday mornings and listening to my father's footsteps getting fainter and fainter as he walked to the station and we were all sad.

I was lucky, I had my twin, I always had someone to play with, to sit next to me in school, to walk with, to share my fears with and to make sense of the grown-up conversations we overheard. We always knew what the other one was feeling and thinking. I always had someone to stick up for me, who was always there. I didn't need anyone else. I loved him. I never felt envious or jealous of him. I know my parents loved us both.

After the war we came home to Dover and slowly we had to start separating. When I was seven my sister was born, so the boys slept in one room and when she was old enough my sister moved in with me. I was glad, she filled the physical gap made by the creation of the boys' room, but our childhood was still the same – we always had each other. We made friends with another set of twins – a boy and a girl and the four of us spent all the school holidays together. They were not as close or content with each other as we were, but it was fun.

At eleven the separation went further, I went to the girls' grammar school and my twin joined my older brother at the boys' grammar school. Then, at seventeen, he went to agricultural college and I left home to start my NNEB training in a residential nursery. The first month I was so homesick I felt 'severed' and I didn't know if I could do it, but of course we did, and how we enjoyed catching up when we got together. When I qualified I came home to live and work at our local maternity hospital and then my twin was doing his National Service. It became a joke between my mother and I during this time because I always knew when he was coming home, even if he had previously said he wouldn't be able to make it – I always knew. The feeling was still the same between us, although naturally more mature. We would consult each other about various friends of the opposite sex, seeking each other's approval.

My mother would never allow Christmas to begin in our house until after our birthday on 23 December. We would have a party and I would invite the girls he wanted and vice versa. He was still my best friend. We became even more separated geographically because of our careers. I married in 1959 and my twin was not happy that day. We did not have telephones, but kept in touch and visited. The closeness was always there.

One Sunday in October, a couple of years later, everything changed. I didn't know what was the matter with me, I felt ill, but I wasn't ill. I went to bed and cried and cried. I felt so wretched, words do not describe how I felt. I was living in Lincoln, a long way from my family, and again, no telephone. On the Tuesday a letter arrived. I didn't recognise the writing or that the letter was addressed to my husband. It was from my father, asking him to tell me that my twin had accidentally been killed in Oxfordshire. Now I knew what that feeling had meant. I recognised what I already knew and had been afraid to admit. The awfulness and the aloneness filled my days. I remember little of the funeral in Oxfordshire. I kept my feelings to myself. My parents were distraught. He was twenty-four years old. We were all living far apart, my brother, my sister with parents, and me. We all grieved separately and we protected our parents. They had lost their child, a son, but I had lost my twin and I felt that no one knew or could understand how I was feeling. I felt half of me was gone. I was alone and there was still so much to say and share together All the traditions we had made together were meaningless and gone. I didn't want any more birthdays without him. I didn't want to do the things we always did together. I didn't want to remember. I hurt so.

The years have slipped by now, there have been many things I wanted and needed to share with him. I tell him many things. There were some unhappy years. I divorced my husband and spent some years alone with my two adopted children. Sometimes I am sad because ten years ago I remarried, and there are many happy things, and I hope he knows I am all right now. My only regret is that my children missed knowing their uncle and they have no physical likeness or mannerisms that perhaps children born to me might have had, that would somehow be a living memory of him. I am sad he doesn't know my husband, they would have been good friends: I always remember him at my first wedding and this time things were so different. Since his death there has been a great void in my life. I have spent years filling it with my work. I know if he had lived my life would have taken a different direction, but I am not unhappy.

Being a lone twin for me is like having a part of me cut out. The wound has healed but if I touch it too hard it will still bleed. It was so special being a twin. He was a lovely person, loved by all who knew him.

DOROTHY REVELL

Story 5
A woman in her fifties who lost her sister at fifty years
I feel like half a person. The emptiness and grief has left a hole in my heart that can never be filled. She is on my mind every hour of every day. And I feel guilty that she was the one to die. You have to be a lone twin to understand, as twins are so much closer than other sisters and brothers, which is why the loss is so hard to bear.

UNA PARKINS

Story 6
A woman in her thirties who lost a brother at eighteen years

HALF A WORLD AWAY

Sitting in the darkened cinema, the two boys were huge in front of me as they played in the boat. I couldn't look away as one boy fell in the lake and struggled for the surface. His watery eyes seemed to bore right into me. The frozen box I'd lived in for the past year melted as I watched the other boy searching desperately for his now dead brother.

I couldn't stop crying the whole way home from Pitt Street to Parramatta in the train. Images of Graeme were flooding me, memories I'd pushed away from the year before came back in wave after wave. My chest was exploding. At one o'clock in the morning I bashed on Sam's front door. Seeing my face he let me in.

'Talk to him,' Sam, a psychiatric nurse, encouraged me, as he told me to imagine Graeme sitting on the chair opposite, 'say all the things you never got to say to Graeme'.

I had never talked to Graeme like this. He was so real in front of me, I longed to reach out and touch his face. As a child, I had not been able to put into words what my father had done when he drove me in his red car to the deserted house. Graeme only knew that something was terribly wrong. We would cuddle together in the dirt between the stilts under the house and cry, our safe place where grown ups couldn't come. But now he was no longer here and I felt as if my whole world was tilting crazily off centre.

Graeme's face had always been fixed firmly in front of mine. It was his image I pictured when the men had finished using my child's body and I crawled along the floorboards to hide in a corner. Squashing myself under the chair, it was Graeme I imagined holding on to, and not my own arm. It had always been like this. It was Graeme I wanted and not my mother. She was a distant shape, that only loomed up in front of me when I had done something wrong, a ferocious scowl on her face.

When Graeme was killed we were eighteen. How could I start to explain to Mum how I felt when I had never been able to talk to her! Mum, desperate in her grief, demanded that I cry, and help console her in the loss of her special son. I was silent, just like I'd been as a child, when Mum wasn't able to notice what Dad was doing to me. I had no words and no tears for crying that week I went home for Graeme's cremation. My one rebellion was buying two carnations, a red and a white. Giving one to my sister, I threw the red carnation on top of the coffin as it disappeared into the hole behind the curtains. In front of the packed room of people who had come to wish Graeme their last respects, it was my silent statement declaring our special relationship.

I wanted to ask for the Hawaiian figure I'd given him, that he wore on a chain round his neck. But Christine, his girlfriend who'd sat trapped beside him as he died in the crumpled car, asked for it. I didn't feel as if I had any rights as a twin. And now that Graeme was dead, I didn't have a place in our family. It was only through him that I felt I belonged.

After the week's leave, I returned to the orthopaedic ward where I was training to be a nurse. I was confronted with young men, limbs smashed from automobile accidents but still alive. A man in his late teens, both legs in plaster, bored and playing practical jokes on any person who came within range of his bed, held a particular fascination for me. If I had any spare minutes, I wandered over to his side to chat. It was the first of many bad ward reports I was to receive, criticising the way I favoured certain patients.

I felt lost, with no direction, becoming more and more outrageous in my behaviour. Sitting on the balcony at the nurses' quarters, I tempted fate as I leaned over the edge. Cycling haphazardly in and out of the lanes of Great Western road, I longed to be hit by a truck. Australia no longer felt like home. I was cut off, disconnected from the land I'd always been able to snuggle into when events in my family home were too crazy to bear. Listening to the waves crash on the sand had soothed me when I was hurting. Now they teased me to come in and melt with their rhythm.

I left Australia with an American juggler, cycling up through Malaysia and Thailand. Riding into new places every day, life became very simple. Where was I going to sleep that night and what would I eat? I was searching, but I didn't know what for. Maybe I would find it in the next country. India freed up my western inhibitions as I played tag with the local rickshaw boys and pushed the boundaries of the relationships with my friends. I was desperate to re-create that special closeness I'd felt with Graeme, but only served in alienating people by my intense need to feel joined to them.

I didn't have a self. I existed only in the eyes of another. Even I knew this wasn't enough. Sitting on a home-made bench, at the fire of Blue Gate at Greenham Common, I realised how hard I had been pushing myself to get out there, to find it. It wasn't working. I hadn't found the answer and I was exhausted. I couldn't die but I wasn't living. I didn't know how to live, only to survive, to keep wandering, getting through each day. I had to do something different.

Moving to Glasgow, staying in one place, and being loved by a woman, started my looking inside of me for the answers to why I felt I was such a mess. Gradually I pieced together the events of my life and began to make sense of them. It was only when a gentle psychotherapist stated how central my relationship with Graeme had always been, and still was, that I realised why I couldn't move on with my life.

No one had ever validated my feelings towards Graeme. I had always been seen as too much, too demanding of his attention, and we had to be separated for our own good. After he was killed, I was told to get on with my life. Misguided therapists said I had to learn how to be a single person, to stand up and say I was glad he had died and I was alive. I couldn't say these words. And I would never be a single person.

It was only by recognising and sharing my need and my longing for Graeme that I began to feel proud of the important bond that we shared. At age thirty-two, fourteen years after Graeme's death, I finally felt special as a twin. I finally felt seen in my grief. I could now get on with my life, being able to enjoy and value my different twin way of looking at the world, knowing that I was OK, and that Graeme would always be a special part of me.

GRAEME

He was cremated
in a 5'5" coffin.
Room enough
for his 6'2" frame.
The many pieces of him
collected by a stranger
and made ready
for burning.
Only his blood had been left,
seeping through
the flattened metal
of the yellow corolla van.
The liquid drank by red ants,
unperturbed by the black crows,
agitated by the smell of death
they couldn't reach.
Graeme, each time I pass
a curve in the road,
lined by bunches of flowers,
wilting and sweating
in their plastic wraps,
I say hello to you.

And remember your long skinny body,
tanned toes pushed out in front,
bandaid ankles and sure hands,
the muscles of your arms bulging
and your grin, red lips, and sweep
of dark hair falling into your eyes.

WENDY GIBSON

THEME 2
'MOVING ON'

Story 1
A woman in her fifties who lost a sister at forty-eight years

What was it like to be a twin! You note I said 'was'. I think quite a few bereaved twins would say they still are a twin, but I definitely feel I am not. For the latter part of my life I am one whole person, not half a one as I felt when my twin died, and I am enjoying it enormously.

I am more self-confident, have new skills and am, I think, a very different person from nearly eight years ago when my twin died. Whilst she was alive I was struggling to be different, but now I'm much more like her – what I feel I would have been if I had not been born a twin. I still miss her very much, but mostly as a very good mate or companion, not an emotional support. As my husband has pointed out, it is a great shame she is not around as we now have so much in common and would enjoy talking about it.

As a child I didn't like being a twin. It was a claustrophobic relationship, with my conscience (my twin) always with me. We were expected to do everything together – in fact we were dissuaded from being apart. This involved being dressed alike, the constant centre of attention, and yet if we got at all uppity, we were sat on very hard. I was always in trouble and being spanked for it – though in fact my sister was often the brains behind the misdeeds, I was the one who actually misbehaved. I was, by the standards of the day, cheeky – that in fact meant questioning! My sister was quiet and by all accounts 'saintly'.

After my twin died I felt resentful that all the maturing processes that are undertaken by singletons are denied twins, such as the first day at school, and that a lot of the maturing had to be done in bereavement. I'm not quite so sure that is true now. Maybe one gets a stability from having a loving person with one at such times. I think I did, but suspect it wasn't the same for my sister. She was the one who looked after me, and I think may have found the responsibility burdensome. I can easily cry, but my twin never could, even in adult life.

I would not have chosen to be a twin, but I am very grateful for the experience of a truly loving and close relationship.

JUDY MOFFITT

Story 2
A woman in her fifties who lost her twin at forty-eight years

LIFE AS A TWIN – AND AFTER

As war broke out in 1939 my parents found themselves with three tiny children, born within sixteen months, a son followed by twin daughters.

I was the first-born twin – always the leader it seems, though I was not conscious of the fact. We were born at home with the help of a midwife cousin of my mother's, who came to stay. We were very small and needed feeding round the clock. Although we always slept in the same cot or pram together our mother took to heart the words of our doctor: 'Remember that although they look so alike they are two different people and you must let them develop their own personalities.' What wise words, for looking back, that is just what our mother did, fortunately. It must have been difficult, for together we made one whole being, it seemed.

As new-borns we sucked one another's fingers and toes as if we did not know where one ended and the other began – oblivious of our separateness. We looked so alike we had to be dressed differently for there to be any hope of distinguishing between us, though I did have the bigger jaw and a determined look, even then. So, despite being identical we were never dressed identically and made to be one item, a pair.

We had a happy childhood together, always together. During the war we spent some time away from our parents, which did not really worry us. We went to stay with grandparents in the west country, and began to live in a world of our own. We both had vivid imaginations and developed games that only we could play, we made them up as we went along without conferring. We had our own language and codes that would have us laughing at our own private jokes, some of which I remember were quite unkind.

Our schooling was delayed until after the end of the war, by which time we were quite an independent little couple and very hard for others to understand. I remember that we found it strange that other people could not communicate in the same way as we did, and I am afraid we did not suffer fools gladly. Fortunately our family at home was growing and we were soon absorbed into the love and rough and tumble that makes life in a large family so healthy and we were able to begin to develop our own relationships within the family.

However, we remained absolutely identical and by the time we attended a school where we had to wear uniform the problems of identity returned. These were really about mistaken identity, and it was suggested that we wear our hair differently, one was to have plaits while the other had bunches. This was fine until we realised the confusion we could cause when we chose to change without telling anyone, though, later, our friends did know how to tell us apart (I'm not sure how).

It is strange, as a growing child, to have someone else who looks like you being there all the time. This became harder as we became teenagers. I did not want to look like Lizzie – I did not want to look like ME either! We were gawky little girls and my nose kept growing and I didn't like it, especially as hers did not seem quite so big! Was she getting prettier than me, I remember wondering? It was a worry, but I do not recollect being jealous of her at any time.

People must have found us very hard to cope with – they just could not understand that we were two normal children growing up together, like all children often mischievous, sometimes sad, and again thoughtful and kind. Why was it so hard to believe that each one of us could be all of these things some of the time. It was decided that one of us must be the 'good' one, kind and thoughtful, whilst the other one must be the 'bad' one who led the other astray. I am afraid that I was cast as the 'baddy' whilst Lizzie took on the mantle of the saint. As we grew up I wonder how much this influenced us.

I do recall being very frustrated by grown ups' pathetic inability to understand that we were two separate children who shared very closely certain characteristics. Our unfortunate headmistress, a well meaning nun, asked me one day where my 'other half' was. I was so angry that she, whom I had respected, should dare to think of me as half a person. 'I am not a half, I am a whole, and so is Elizabeth', I remember shouting at her, poor woman. Little did she know that she had touched on a raw nerve that all other twins must experience at one time or another. WHO AM I, apart from being a twin? It is not so much who we are perceived to be, as who we know ourselves to be; yet, deep down we know there is more.

As Lizzie and I reached our mid-teens, we made an unconscious decision to be different – it followed my encounter with the headmistress. Lizzie became the artistic one, always in the art room at school. I became the scientific one, always in the lab. Fortunately the art teacher would not let me give up art at O level; she was the only person I am aware of who knew what was going on.

Having hoped I had done well enough at O level to be accepted by Guy's Hospital to do physiotherapy I decided I had had enough of the nonsense that school meant to me. I went to our local hospital and got myself a job – 'Could I start on Monday?' So I came to leave school without consulting anyone. It was a wonderful relief to know that I could be independent, not only of my parents, but of Lizzie too. For the first time in my life I was in a situation where I was an individual in my own right – I had broken free. I loved it. It was very hard work. The shifts did not fit into any normal life pattern, which separated me further from Lizzie and the rest of the family. She, meanwhile, stayed on at school and did her A levels and we drifted apart. I was dealing with people who were sick and dying, she was still a schoolgirl. We did not really communicate any more, I felt that I had left her behind. We both started our training in London at the same time, she at the Lycée Français, doing bilingual secretarial studies, while I was at Guy's. She did nice things with the Young Conservatives, while I helped raise money for World Refugee Year by doing less proper things, like busking on London Bridge station.

Our boyfriends were so different – hers were very nice chaps, mine were medical students who played rugby.

At twenty-four I married a dentist and Lizzie went to France. There she continued and developed her relationship with a missionary group and during a training session for African bishops, she was asked to go to Rwanda to help run a group of parishes. None of us had ever heard of Rwanda and I worried for her going into the unknown on her own I had been the adventurous one. Now she was undertaking a far greater venture than anything I had ever contemplated, and I realised almost too late what a fine woman she had become.

During the subsequent twelve years I had seven children and was rather busy. Lizzie used to come home every three years and just fitted into whatever we were doing. Often we were both just too tired to communicate properly. My husband felt uncomfortable in her presence, but the children used to hang on to her legs because they were just like mine and sometimes when she picked up one of the little ones they were not quite sure which was Mummy, just for a moment.

The harshness of Africa began to take its toll on Lizzie. Although I used to send her moisturiser for her skin it was never enough and she often gave her things away or they were stolen. She became thin and very wiry. She had been having malaria attacks and did not tell us. She asked if I was having heart problems: she was; I was just exhausted. The time she communicated most was when she was not able to write. The whole country was in the midst of tribal conflict in the late 1970s. Her community put themselves in jeopardy as they gave shelter to the Tutsis who at that time were under attack from the Hutus. I knew her fear and would often find myself praying for her and I held her in my heart. I am so glad that by the time the Tutsis returned in 1994 to wreak the appalling havoc that we witnessed on our TV screen at the time, that she had died.

It was just before our forty-ninth birthday, in 1988. I had been feeling too ill to go into town to get Lizzie some cotton clothes for her birthday present. I did not know why I felt so rotten, I could hardly drag myself around. I had been like that for several days when I felt compelled to lie by the phone. During the afternoon I received the first call I had ever had from Rwanda. It was from one of Lizzie's friends to say that Lizzie was in hospital – they thought that it was a bad dose of malaria but it seemed more serious. Later that day I got the news that she was jaundiced, in a coma and probably had hepatitis. The decision was made to fly her to Europe.

What was I to do? I was ill – was it because she was ill? – I still don't know. Should I leave the family? A doctor friend said, 'Follow your instincts.'

There is a large Catholic University hospital in Brussels that specialises in liver conditions. This is where 'they' decided to send Lizzie on the only airline that linked Kigali to the high-tech medical care that could save her life. Feeling so helpless, and having already booked my own flight to arrive at the same time, I rang the airline and was connected by some computer whiz-kid to her plane. He told me that she was in the care of a Dr Luke, that she was still alive but unconscious. That was an enormous comfort to me.

Our old mother decided to come with me and the whole family pulled together to make it all possible, and we arrived at the hospital in Brussels within twenty-four hours of the first call. I am glad that we had one another, it was so hard, we do not speak very good French and no Flemish. Eventually we managed to make the receptionists at the hospital aware of who we were to see and were directed to the intensive care unit. There we were, dressed in masks and gowns and ushered into Lizzie's room. She was all wired up to monitors and drips and drains – she was unconscious still. I took her hand and said, 'Lizzie, it's Clare', and for the one and only time she opened her eyes and mouth and looked so pleased, before sinking back into the coma. The readout on the machine attached to her brain went wild at that moment – her brain was working – good news.

But that was to be the only good news we had. That precious moment caught forever in my mind and on some electroencephalograph record somewhere, is the last and most poignant moment of our lives together. Yet there were three long days to endure, all the few times we were allowed to see her. 'They' decided to operate, to do a liver transplant. Then when that failed, to do another one – against my will. She was my twin, I felt that my feelings should have meant something, but no. I wanted 'them' to give her back to me so that I could care for her for the few hours that she had left. I wanted to rub oil on her worn feet – I took some with me to do just that. But no, her feet were wired to machines too. We must go, they had work to do on Madame. 'Her name is Elizabeth', I said, 'please call her by her name' – but no.

Before we left her on the night of her last op. I insisted that the hospital chaplain be called and in a simple, sad little ceremony we gave her back to God, the love of her life.

The next day as I kissed her cold face goodbye I wept years of tears of sorrow for the times I had not been there for her, for the times we meant to have together, for all we did not do or say. Thank God I had that time.

I do believe that being able to let go of Lizzie, to give her back to God, was the beginning of the healing of the loss. However, looking back, I am amazed by the depth and intensity of the grief that overtook me, that would come upon me in different guises – of intense loneliness and isolation (despite a large loving family), of confusion, of anger and of illness and intense weariness. After the months and years this has all changed and peace has come. I had felt I wanted to do the work Lizzie had done, physically rather than spiritually. The opportunity came when the Lone Twin Network needed someone to organise the developing network. I felt it was the sort of thing that she would have taken on and so I did so, rather in her memory and often, I felt, with her help.

I no longer see Lizzie when I look in the mirror, I have grown older, but I do wish she could share the love of the new little ones in the family, that we could chuckle together as they hang on to our legs ... but who knows ...

To coin a phrase, 'It is better to have loved and lost a twin than never to have had one – whatever the loss may cost.'

CLARE FAY

Story 3
A woman in her forties who lost a brother at twenty-two years

I was born unexpectedly, on All Fools' Day, and my twin brother died unexpectedly, twenty-two years later, of an enlarged heart. I was staying with a friend and I had gone to bed, feeling rotten, when the police rang. The family GP gave us a bottle of Valium to share. Just over a year after his death I left England and travelled to Australia and South America. I look back with amazement at my parents' generosity in letting me go like that. I bummed around for two years, hitching lifts, working in a bar in the Outback, typing in Alice, selling magazines in Melbourne, pretending to be tough and hard, thumbing my nose at convention and respectability. I felt daring and Jack-the-Laddish, because, I reasoned, no one else could ever hurt me. I'd had the worst pain possible, nothing else counted.

Since my brother's death I'd felt painful, contorted emotions towards twins: I remember the shock, like a physical blow, of seeing a pair of girl/boy twins, about eighteen months old, at the Riverside, in London. They were sitting on the floor, at right angles to one another, their shoulders and rounded bottoms touching, so they were looking in different directions, but they were behaving as one creature. There was an aura of profound concentration around them – they were creating something with building blocks. Neither of them spoke, but they worked together, very seriously and in perfect unison. There was an air about them of a very old, settled, contented, married couple. They looked as though they'd been together for lifetime after lifetime. I stood and stared at them with such powerful feelings – love, hatred, kinship, envy, fear, yearning – I'm surprised they didn't drop their bricks and run for cover. I felt so drawn to them, but so horribly envious of them. That was ten years after his death.

Fourteen years after his death I read a book by Dorothy Rowe and, as she suggested, I wrote a letter to my brother. It was only then that I recognised, acknowledged and released an enormous black boulder of anger. I'd felt guilty for having survived, but I hadn't realised how furious I'd been – and with him! It was a shocking and cathartic experience. I'd loved him, depended on him, looked up to him, relied on him, checked everything with him. And he'd left me, abandoned me to fend for myself. It was preposterous and I was outraged. The angry words flowed out of my pen and the tears streamed down my face till I could hardly see what I was writing. It was a turning point and I felt 10 lb lighter when I'd finished.

Nineteen years after his death I heard of the Lone Twin Network and was overwhelmed to learn that I wasn't the only one in the world. Even the name was helpful: in my head I'd blundered around with declensions, 'I was a twin/I had a twin/I am twin/I used to be a twin' in a pathetic attempt to define myself. I couldn't, so that part of my life – which was tremendously important to me – I kept quiet about.

It's hard to think back to those first LTN meetings: I longed for the meetings, yet as the date grew closer I thought up a thousand reasons not to go. I came home feeling as though I'd been run over by a bus, but I couldn't wait for the next one. That comfort of being in a room full of people all in the same boat was wondrous. I remember an elegant stranger coming up to me, holding a cup and saucer, like at a tea party, but instead of small talk she said, 'How did yours die?' It was like plunging into an icy pool, but I remembered I could swim, and I told her my story and she listened, and then she told me her story. No one was embarrassed, no one changed the subject. It was so liberating. And so levelling, too. It was only by hearing others' stories, face to face, that I could really relinquish my deadly-secret but long-held belief that I had suffered more than anyone else in the western world. (Well, Sheffield, then.)

About the same time I began going to Buddhist classes. Nuns and monks talk cheerily about death and dying and we are encouraged to meditate on death. As a sweeping generalisation I think the whole of western civilisation is in a state of denial, so any death, no matter how ill or how old the person was, comes as a shock. Death is this century's taboo. But Buddhism helps us to come to terms with death and to face the fact that everybody dies. The death of a twin is a very powerful lesson in mortality. It's a very painful lesson, but a very useful one. Buddhism teaches the transience of all things. We are taught not to take ourselves too seriously, and that there is no nobility in suffering. The real wisdom is joy and happiness.

I still feel slightly odd when I meet twins, but the feelings aren't as powerful as they once were. I'd love to join in and say 'I'm a twin' – by rights I belong to that special club – but I pull back. It's more an embarrassment now – I'm the spectre at the feast – I'm here to tell twins that the unthinkable can happen. We arrive together, and in a vague and unthought-out way we expect to leave together.

I'm sorry I wasn't with him when he died. I wish we could have said goodbye. I wish I could have been there. But I'm so glad to have been a twin. It was a wonderful experience.

JEN COLDWELL

Story 4
A woman in her fifties who lost her brother at forty-eight years

To be born together and then to part leaves a deep sorrow inside my heart. It has been six years since we lost Allan, and the pain is deep inside. My help has been quiet times to myself, writing each day, going for walks, talking to Allan about the birds and the flowers, deep, intense counselling, going to church and the caring and sharing of the Network and a supportive family.

We are always together, Allan and I. We live together in each other's heart.

MARIAN BRAY

Story 5
A woman in her forties who lost an identical sister at thirty-five years

At my sister's funeral I wanted to scream out 'there has never been a Rosalie'. I had never thought much before about us growing in the womb together, in phase at every stage. Neither had I thought much about growing old without her. I was 35 when my twin died, and neither of us had a single grey hair and only the beginnings of aches and sags of encroaching middle age, hers amplified by two pregnancies.

I think I was aware from the age of at least seven that we would be compared by our looks and that photographs would be pored over: 'Rosalie's that one with the freckle on her ear' (from school friends), 'I think Rosalie has a fatter face' (from my mother). Who was taller, broader, had a larger shoe size. My elder sister's boyfriends would pretend to joke about which of us was 'the pretty one' (big sister being 17 and us 7 when this started as a joke about a 'rule' for telling us apart, not about 'falling for us' instead). At our first school photo, just before we were 5, I refused to sit on the bench with my twin, so she had her photograph taken alone. This may have been toddler pique, but as I grew older I certainly began to hate having my photograph taken. From the age of about 10 there are far fewer photos of me than my twin. (It is ironic now that this school photo of my 5-year-old twin is the one that I treasure most.)

We went to different universities at age 18, then at 21 I went as a postgraduate to where my twin had been an undergraduate, and I chanced across a group of her friends, all cavers (potholers). One of these friendly and forthright people told me outright that they initially thought I was Ros, but that she must have been ill over the summer (i.e. lost weight). However, not having known us together, they were prepared to accept me as a separate person, and though I stayed with these friends for years there were never any further comparisons.

I think I am now more relaxed about having my photograph taken. Is this because there is no 'prettier' twin to be compared to? I wonder if my twin would age as I am ageing. What would we have looked like if our photographs were taken at age 40, 60, 80? This is not just vanity (though a small part is) – mainly a morbid curiosity about the difference that would remain, and the loss of a comparison 'yardstick'. I do wonder about when my eyesight will become poor enough to need glasses. Is that twinge in my knee a sign of a genetically determined 'all downhill from here'? Would those lines around my mouth be there on my twin's face? I scrutinise my elder sisters' faces for similar lines and signs of ageing. I'm sure I look more carefully at their faces now than I did before, searching the likeness that is not quite there. Actually, it was only while writing this that I realised my siblings may have painful moments in seeing me age, relating this to the twin who will never age.

The medical comparison aspect plays games in my head: I worry irrationally that the cancer my sister died from could be genetically linked (I think the fear is more about the drama this would entail than anxiety about my own mortality). I became extremely sensitive when my eldest sister (even more of a hypochondriac than I) blithely called me to say she has self-diagnosed a rare skin disorder that may have a genetic element, and she thought I should know. I wonder how she can be so impossibly unaware how this makes me feel, that statistically, I share far fewer genes with her then I did with my twin, that any true genetic yardstick is gone. Oh and by the way, I miss having my twin to laugh with about these moments of paranoia and ire with our legendary insensitive big sister. I'm sure everyone has madcap thoughts that usually get dismissed by recounting them with a girlfriend ('you'll never guess what she said to me...') but I've lost my only outlet for 'having a bit of a moan' and I find such thoughts linger longer.

I keep the school photo of my five-year-old twin on my desk at work, next to one of her with her then 11-month-old son. If people ask about 'my little one', I just tell them it is my sister and her child. I don't think anyone knows the five-year-old is her too. I look at these five to ten times a day in passing, perhaps closely once a day. I'm ashamed to say that I can't imagine I would have kept a photo of her in full view when she was alive – only photographs of her children.

I mentioned that I look over my elder sisters' faces to search for the mirror identity I am used to seeing, and to see how I might age. I also scrutinise the faces of my twin's young sons – to whom my genetic inheritance has passed, since I have no children what will they look like at 5, 10, 30? Will they be a visual reminder of my twin at each life stage?

GILLIAN LINDSEY

Story 6
A man in his sixties who lost his identical brother of fifty-two years in the Paddington Rail crash

My 52-year-old twin brother, Andy, was killed in the Paddington train crash of 5 October 1999. The effect on me was unimaginable. Those close to me witnessed the external effects but the internal ones felt almost unsurvivable. I cried every day for 18 days. I was inconsolable and in a state of complete mental and emotional distress. I couldn't work for almost 12 months.

When making tea at 7.30am on 6 October 1999 I was stopped in my tracks by a bright orange flash and woken at 3.00am on 7 October by dreaming of suddenly hitting a black wall. I woke scared and sweating. With the best of intentions my relatives and friends spent a great deal of time trying to convince me that death would have been instant and that he would have known nothing about it, although I was advised not to see his body. Only at the inquest six months later did surviving passengers reveal that a fireball went through the carriage.

I felt utter stunned disbelief – not denial as such, but complete inability to imagine life without Andy; a numb devastation. I knew the truth but my mind wouldn't accept it. There were no tears at first. I didn't want to sleep. I wanted to be told that it was all a mistake. I could not take it in, but I knew he wasn't coming back.

I felt timid and frightened. I had an external cavern in my stomach which was aching unbearably. I felt cut in half and used the word cataclysmic. I was imploding with an unimaginably deep sense of pain. It seemed to go right through me and have no end – as if I'd been hit by a demolition ball.

I remember feeling like a zombie, with disorientation and continual feelings of being detached from everyday life – almost wanting to be a recluse. My mind was consumed with imaging what had happened to Andy. I felt I needed to find some help from other twins – or at least information about where to turn.

Via the Lone Twin Network I was fortunate to receive very wise advice: Please don't listen to well meaning people who tell you it is time 'to move on', as if you have to somehow leave Andrew behind. I believe you have to find, over time, ways of keeping Andrew with you in the best, richest, warmest sense and that is what makes it possible to feel less pain and regain your sense of self.

The last eight years have proved how valuable such advice was. I managed to execute his estate. We are now grandparents and Andy would have been a grandfather. I spoke at his daughter's wedding and wear his retrieved watch for family occasions. I dream about him only once a week now and tell my wife the silly stories these throw up. But still I can't allow myself to think he suffered any pain.

'The Lone Twin' should be compulsory reading on any psychology/social services course where spouses, relatives and friends need to understand what twin bereavement really means to the one left behind.

GRAHAM THOMPSON

Story 7

A woman in her forties who lost a brother in tragic circumstances four years earlier

17 October 2005 – my brother had been sent home from work ill the night before. He lay dead on the floor. He was supposed to meet me for lunch tomorrow 18th, I waited to hear from him …

He had just returned from a holiday in Spain with his close friend Dawn. He had been complaining of having food poisoning and feeling unwell – I teased him about not wanting to return to work after his break and said to make an appointment with the doctor if he still felt unwell after a few days. I was expecting to hear from him as to where to meet for lunch. But his text and call never came and he didn't return my text. I presumed he'd had a busy night at work and left it until the next day. I texted and called again, then called his friends, they'd not heard from him either – Dawn was away on a course for work so I began to feel uneasy … After driving to Dawn's flat and hearing his mobile upstairs when I rang it, I got his friends and the police to break in – that's where I found him … lying face down … in a warm flat, after two days, not a pleasant sight … my mind swam, I didn't really know if or how I took it in – I went into a trance – I signed all the paperwork for the police – I made several phone calls to my sister Mandy, my mum and my ex-husband, he came to sit with me while the undertaker came.

I sat with David for the longest of time – just talking and stroking his leg, I felt empty and alone as if part of me was draining away. I drove home in the early hours not wanting to leave David's side. I didn't really show any emotion for days. I felt totally lost and empty. I arranged the funeral, my family live in North Wales, my sister Mandy travelled down on Friday to stay with me and arrange the service. The days up to the funeral I was traumatised by seeing horrid faces in the darkness of my windows, I think it was my way of dealing with what I'd seen. I put photographs around in the hope that these would ease my state of mind. The day of the funeral I was still locked away in my mind until I followed the coffin. I placed a single rose on top and I at last felt my barriers break, along with my heart into a million pieces, I do apologise to all at the funeral – they are not the easiest of occasions and the sight of me must have broken everyone, I was in tears the whole way through.

In the days that followed conversations go on in your mind, the 'what ifs' and 'maybes'. We were lucky David was very musical and had recorded many tracks in a music studio; my sister had these professionally made into a CD for friends and family. I can now listen to this and if I close my eyes I can picture him sitting with me, strumming his guitar – he had come to live with me a few years earlier and stayed five years. He was full of life and practical jokes, I now tell my own 7-year-old twins the antics he got up to at my expense. The word 'twin' will always be around me with mine too. They miss him very much.

I can now look back and reflect, it was my place to see him at the end, a private moment between us, I no longer visualise the horror, I just accept it as our moment we came into this world together and I sat with him in his death. I must thank Joan for all her comforting words that really helped me along the road, I would be willing to talk to anyone in similar circumstance, it does help to talk with other lone twins, who understand your loss.

SUSAN GREEN

Story 8
A man of seventy who lost a non-identical brother at thirty-five years

War must have seemed an unlikely prospect when in April 1939 my brother Ian and I were born in the small town of Ilkley, in West Yorkshire. Born at home we were both under 6lbs in weight. I was born first and Ian followed twenty minutes later by breech delivery. My mother never spoke about her pregnancy, but at 34 it was her first and I imagine a far from easy one. Certainly, in an early photograph with a baby in each arm she looks exhausted.

One of the early advantages of being a twin is the instant availability of a playmate and there are photographs of my brother and me playing happily together. We shared a pram and such was the novelty value of twins that neighbours were more than pleased to take us out for display on The Grove, Ilkley's prime shopping street.

A very early memory is of being with my parents at the doctor's surgery. Ian was lying on the examination couch and my anxious parents were told he had asthma. It was something which was increasingly present in his life. In 1945, when our sister Rosamund was born, the focus moved off us.

We were not quite four when we started school. We always sat together but had mixed feelings about being referred to as 'the twins'. Before we were 11 we had attended four different schools and at the last of these we became close friends with twin brothers.

For twins, one of the main tasks is to develop separate identities. It was something we were never told to do, but somehow we knew it was important. Perhaps it was easier for us, because we did not even look like brothers. Until we were about eight we were dressed differently. At school Ian played football; something I never enjoyed. I learned to swim, which Ian never did. Ian was better at maths than I was and I excelled in English. Perhaps we were avoiding competing with each other, although it did not feel like that at the time.

During adolescence we grew further apart, developing different interest and different friends. An even more significant difference was that I became interested in boys, rather than girls.

Not surprisingly we had different careers. Ian became a buyer in an electrical engineering company. After a few months in a publisher's office, I heard I had passed the Manchester City Council entrance examination and started working in the health department.

Falling in love for the first time in my late teens was something else I did not share with Ian. In the 1950s same sex relationships were not usually understood or generally tolerated. Looking back, it seems strange my sexuality was never discussed within the family and boyfriends were accepted, usually without question.

The age of 21 was a good time to leave home and I moved to London to continue my career in local government with three different local authorities. Ian continued with the company in Lancashire he joined on leaving school. I became disenchanted with local government – I was never very enchanted – and left to join a new government organisation where I stayed for the next 14 years.

In 1971 my parents retired to live in a small village outside Preston, so that my brother could live at home full-time. The long-term effects of asthma had taken their toll and the following year Ian retired on grounds of ill health. Rosamund, who is a qualified nurse, got a job in a nearby hospital to help our parents care for him. I did not realise how ill Ian had become, or perhaps I was partially in denial about his illness.

One Saturday morning in October 1972 my mother rang to tell me Ian had died, unexpectedly, shortly before. I was profoundly shocked and felt as I was born at the same time as Ian, I should have been with him when his life came to such a sudden end.

Later that day I was not prepared for the extreme distress of both my parents and Rosamund, who had been away from home when she also heard the news. I found I was more concerned about my father, mother and sister than about the loss of my brother. Somehow, I felt there was an expectation that I would make everything all right. I was painfully aware of being told by my father, more than once, that I was the lucky one who would always 'fall on his feet'. At quite a profound level, I felt I had escaped.

Soon after my return my mother became ill and we thought it was a response to Ian's death. Somehow she managed to attend his funeral on All Saints' Day. She was admitted into hospital shortly afterwards and it was discovered she was riddled with cancer. Ten weeks later she died.

The loss of my mother compounded my grief and perhaps did not allow me to experience fully the death of my brother. I was not at that time aware of what being a survivor means and the feelings of guilt this may give rise to. From time to time I suffered depression, so perhaps there was a price to pay for feeling I had escaped. Or did I ever really escape?

Since the deaths of my brother and mother I have experienced a number of other significant losses. My father, an aunt and an uncle died within weeks of each other during the winter of 1977/78. I felt the 1980s would introduce a period without loss, but in 1981 my long-term partner died from lung cancer. He gave me immense support during the losses of the previous decade and, following his death, I felt at times very alone and depressed.

In 1981, I felt a need to change my life and decided to take advantage of a re-structuring of the increasingly bureaucratic organisation where I worked to apply for voluntary redundancy. Towards the end of the year I left my job and started a full-time course in counselling at the Westminster Pastoral Foundation. Subsequently, I specialised in bereavement counselling.

I do not think I had ever thought of myself as a lone twin until, in 1985, a colleague told me of a research study of lone twins. Joan Woodward came to see me and I attended the first meeting of 25 lone twins and a number of subsequent annual meetings.

A number of times I have been asked if I felt it was an advantage to be a twin. I do not, and I think firstly of Ian as a brother, rather than a twin. I believe twins very often early in life rely on each other, which makes it more difficult in life to think and act independently. Frequently there is no one to ask and no need to consult. Not surprisingly, twins do not usually make effective leaders.

Ultimately, I believe we all have to make sense of our own individual lives and this can be more difficult for lone twins than for 'non twins', or for twins who have not lost their twin. Perhaps for me becoming a bereavement counsellor was a way of making reparation or as John Donne put it in 'The Dissolution' –

> This (which I am amazed that I can speak)
> This death, hath with my store
> My use increased.

GORDON STRANG

THEME 3
ON APPRECIATING HAVING SHARED SOME ADULT LIFE WITH A TWIN, PLAYING A PART IN INCREASING THE SURVIVING TWIN'S SENSE OF SELF

Story 1
A woman in her forties who lost an identical sister at thirty-four years
This is a unique experience that has to be learnt, only the lone twin can do this! My twin Gill was always the stronger willed of the two of us, no one was ever allowed to hurt me physically or mentally, it was something she would always sort out, and when you are left as one a new way of life eventually takes over. Or maybe I was meant to have had all the pain in my life to have become the stronger person – I do not know.

When I think of the thirty-four years that we shared together, this is an experience that not many people are lucky enough to have had – how can you explain being a twin?

Now there is no one to share those special feelings that we shared, those secrets we would never tell anyone else, the personality we shared. No, I cannot share this with anyone else -- this is something I only shared with my twin.

So I have learnt a new way of life – I would not have survived the last nine years if I had not. Maybe in some ways I was very lucky to have had two very small children to bring up when she died – I had to be strong for them – and I also have a wonderful husband who, luckily, knew my sister very well. I feel there have been moments when I did not want to survive without her, but somehow I have and I must, for the people who love me.

I still do not like being on my own for long periods of time and I feel that will never change. The loneliness I feel without her will never go away, so I think I have become a busy person, filling my life as much as possible. Whenever a gap appears, I fill it.

But I still have so much – if only she could have had the same as me, instead of such an unhappy marriage and a terminal illness – life does not seem quite so fair for her. After all these years I still cry for her – I have so much to tell her.

I hope I have survived being one even though I never will be just one – I do not know how! We must be very special people to be this unique.

JAN WATSON

Story 2
A woman in her fifties who lost her brother at fifty-one years

A TWIN RELATIONSHIP

We were born in a small village in the Rhymney Valley in South Wales in January 1938. I was born one hour earlier than my twin brother. My mother was very ill after the birth and it was the doctor who named us Ann and Alun.

Our father died at the age of thirty-four in 1943 when we were five years old and so we went through the trauma together. Alun developed asthma shortly afterwards, and my mother and I experienced great anxiety over his health as he used to have severe asthma attacks. He never complained about his ill health and was very courageous. When we were nearly seven my mother remarried and gradually we adapted together to having a stepfather. We were eight years of age when my mother gave birth to a baby boy, named Anthony. These changes in our lives we shared very closely. We shared the affection of numerous aunts and uncles, cousins and a grandfather living nearby. We were very much aware of each other's feelings, especially as children.

The closeness of twins, especially in childhood, is observed and remembered by friends and relatives. It is very difficult to imagine what it would have been like to have been born a single child. The positive side of being a twin was the close sharing relationship and the negative side was the comparison by some people, especially in later life. I think the personalities of twins are usually different and complement each other.

My twin brother married when he was twenty-one years old. He had two children whose childhood I shared. I remained single. He died at the age of fifty-one having been chronically ill for eight weeks. When he was so ill I experienced feelings of extreme stress and anxiety. I could see him gradually deteriorating, but he was very courageous and always gave visitors to the hospital a great welcome and showed appreciation for their visits and for anything that anyone did for him. It is almost impossible for me to describe my feelings when he was unconscious in intensive care. It was a feeling of utter despair and gradually being torn away from a brother with whom I had shared life, even before birth.

Now five years have passed and I am able to compare two big losses of my life – my father when I was five, and my twin when I was fifty-one. I have always felt the void left by the loss of a parent as a child and am grateful that my brother lived for fifty-one years.

I am grateful for having been able to share times of happiness and sadness with my twin and know that it is one of the closest of all human relationships. The pain of the loss is the price lone twins have to pay for such a close bond, but the memories of a courageous twin give me strength, especially when circumstances in my life are difficult.

ANONYMOUS

Story 3
A woman in her seventies who lost her identical sister in her late forties
In my time I have been asked to speak and write about the medical history of identical twin girls – my sister and I. We were born unexpectedly in 1922 weighing 3 lb 4 oz and 3 lb 2 oz. We were identical twins, born two minutes apart. This was before the invention of incubators of course.

For many years we believed that we were found one morning during a snowstorm nestling among a basket of snowdrops on the front doorstep!

Our mother, who was not prepared for twin babies, was subsequently seriously ill. One baby therefore was put to the breast, and one completely bottle fed. This produced medical statistics in regard to the babies ... and this was monitored throughout our childhood. Interest was also shown in the bonding of the babies to their parents, and it became evident that the breast-fed baby bonded to the mother, and the bottle-fed baby to the father. Indeed, my sister and I did consider that I was 'Mummy's girl', and she was 'Daddy's girl', which incidentally we both accepted, and enjoyed, as we both considered we had the best bargain! Maybe this is the case with all twins.

Other topics I have found myself involved with are whether twins should be dressed identically (we were until we were seventeen years), and educationally should twins be expected to be at the same class standards, although academically not apparently equal? These I know are often considered in regard to all twins – but what I hadn't expected was the query as to whether there is a higher divorce rate amongst twins. I divorced my husband in 1967 after twenty-four years of marriage, and four children. One factor he introduced into the proceedings at the time was he always had felt that there was another human being closer to me than he was – my twin sister! This was despite the fact that my twin and I led our own married lives – miles apart – and rarely intruded on each other. Also, unbelievably, he stated that subconsciously he was also in love with my twin – and couldn't handle the situation!

Thereafter I had to continue the career which I had begun in the Second World War – when I had trained as a nurse. Consequently, as a paediatric nursing officer until my retirement, I had an influence when twins, or lone twins, were admitted to hospital. On occasions parents arrived with both twins – insisting that they couldn't be separated even though it was one that was seriously ill. On occasion parents demanded that twins should be nursed together in the same cot, or bed. It did help them, and the staff, that someone could understand and put the problem into perspective. I was particularly interested in being involved in the cases of anorexic twins, there did seem to be several at the time.

My twin sister, Dorrie, died of cancer of the colon, a week before our fiftieth birthday. We would have been twins for half a century. I was privileged to have nursed her exclusively for a week before her death. Strangely, since her funeral, it was decreed by my mother – at the service – that 7 January would no longer be acknowledged as the twins' birthday, as they were no longer twins! The date therefore was of no consequence and would no longer be recognised as a birthday and it never was!

JOAN HADLEY

THEME 4
ON THE DEATH OF A TWIN LEADING TO THE PROLONGING OF THE SURVIVING TWIN'S LIFE

Story 1
A man of fifty whose identical brother died at forty-three years
Peter, my identical twin, died suddenly, six years ago, aged forty-three.

On that fateful Saturday morning my sister-in-law telephoned, in tears, to tell me that Peter had complained of feeling unwell, and abandoning their shopping trip they returned home, where he died before help arrived. He died of a heart attack.

In the past I had instinctively known when something was wrong, whether it be physical or emotional. How could he be dead? I had felt nothing.

Soon afterwards my wife and I travelled the forty miles to Peter's home, in total silence and disbelief. The journey seemed to take an age. Upon arrival we were met with the sight of Peter's body being removed by the undertakers.

Having experienced my father's death when I was seventeen and my mother's when forty, it would seem fair to presume that my experiences would help me overcome this latest tragedy. How wrong I was.

At the funeral an aunt who was trying to console me said, 'It must feel like losing your right arm.' That would be insignificant compared to the pain I was, and still am, experiencing.

I find it difficult to express my feelings but my immediate family recognise, only too well, my mood swings. I have one older sister, whom I love dearly, but Peter was not only my brother, he was my twin.

An advantage of having an identical twin is that you can pretend to be each other, a ruse we kept up, using a favourite uncle as the target, for nearly forty years. A disadvantage is that I can see the anguish and pain in Peter's family's eyes when we meet. Are they thinking, 'How can Peter be dead when he is standing in front of us?'

In the month immediately after Peter's death, my own family wrapped me in cotton wool. Every ache and pain was treated as a major illness. I do not blame them for this as they had seen the devastation caused by a sudden death.

Some time later I joined the Lone Twin Network and although I'm not a very active member the comfort I receive is immeasurable. Knowing people who have suffered in similar circumstances, even though each is unique, is profoundly reassuring.

I know my life can never be the same again, but with the love of a very supportive wife and family I feel that I am slowly coming to terms with my grief.

If any good has arisen from Peter's death then perhaps it is the fact that I am still alive today. Some time ago I experienced severe pain in the left side of my body. On visiting my GP I was diagnosed as suffering from angina. Subsequent hospital tests recorded blocked arteries. I have since undergone quadruple heart bypass surgery and am now fully recovered. This disease, in my particular case, was found to be hereditary and was the probable cause of my brother's death. Had it not been for Peter's death then I would probably have ignored the pains and would not now be looking forward to a new lease of life, albeit without my twin Peter.

However, tragedy struck again: Peter's widow Gillian died recently of cancer, leaving two grown-up children and two grandchildren. I feel both love and responsibility to them all, almost as if they were my own.

People ask, 'When do you miss your brother?' My answer is, 'Always, but especially when I look in a mirror.'

DAVID JAMES

Story 2
A woman in her late fifties who lost a sister in her forties
Twelve years ago within weeks of the diagnosis of my identical twin's ovarian cancer I was operated on to have my ovaries removed. It was thought that as we had the same genes it was a good idea. This has been proved correct. I have now been found to have the BRCAI gene with a greatly increased risk of ovarian and breast cancer. My twin had breast cancer at a later stage.

I found the news that I had the gene devastating. The risk of breast cancer is so high with this gene that most people go on to have a double mastectomy, which I had two years ago. It has been a difficult two years as it has not gone very smoothly and I have to exercise my right arm a lot to keep it mobile and pain-free, but at least all the badminton and swimming backstroke are making me fit!

When my twin was dying she said she would live on in me. In some ways I think that is true. I realise how lucky I am to have had the knowledge my sister's illness gave me. It has enabled me to make decisions which have let me live long enough to enjoy my three grandchildren. My twin was not so fortunate.

ANNE HARRIS

THEME 5
LOSS IN EXCEPTIONALLY TRAUMATIC CIRCUMSTANCES

Story 1
A woman in her thirties whose sister died at twenty-six years
Talking to other lone twins, it seems common for there to be some sort of imbalance; one twin is considered or considers themselves to be more extrovert or strong or confident or a better 'coper' than the other, for example. Although the truth may be far more complicated than this, they often seem to behave as two halves of one unit, compensating for each other's weaknesses or strengths accordingly. In our case this imbalance was exaggerated by the dramatic events which happened to us as children and which forced us into very strong roles with each other.

Our early life was in London. We were born in 1959, identical twin girls of two young painters. When our parents separated we were two, and we stayed with our mother in her basement flat in Kentish Town. We had cats and other pets and although unconventional, my memories of that time suggest that we felt loved and relatively secure.

According to my father, Soph was already considered rather eccentric. She had a precocious vocabulary and a grasp of ideas way beyond her age, but she was oddly clumsy, her pronunciation was slow and she had strange mannerisms, whereas I was pretty normal. Various theories were put forward as to the cause of this, including slight oxygen starvation at birth, but none was ever confirmed.

She responded to situations more fearfully than me; she was terrified, almost phobic, about gates and having to climb them, whilst I relished that sort of challenge.

Our mother died when we were five on a remote beach in Turkey, where we were on holiday with her and her boyfriend. She had had a dangerous allergy to wasps, and although she had the antidote in England, she had left it behind. She was twenty-four.

Her death was sudden and horrific and apparently we spent days travelling around with her body in an old car, trying to find help.

We were returned to England to live with our father, his new wife and their baby daughter. What had happened to us was a bond that only we shared after our mother's boyfriend disappeared from our lives shortly afterwards. Our memories of it became identical through reliving it together over and over again, but we also 'cut out' at exactly the same moment, moments after we had seen our dead mother being carried into an Istanbul hospital over someone's shoulders.

Back in London, we wrote her letters, addressed to Heaven, which we would throw out of our first-floor bedroom window. We exploited the situation, the compassion and anxiety that it aroused in grown ups, but we were also traumatised by the experience, and the different ways that we expressed this moulded our twinship irrevocably.

Soph became very obviously disturbed. Her first attempt at suicide was at the age of seven, when she swallowed a bottle of cough medicine. She started running away from school and jumping on trains to distant places, paying her fare with money she stole or persuaded kind people to give her. She was devious and desperate, often walking eight miles across London to be with her grandmother; at home behaving like a caged animal who sometimes had to be locked in to prevent her from escaping.

Our father and stepmother, who were caring, intelligent people at their wits' end, tried everything they could think of to remedy a situation which was becoming increasingly nightmarish for the whole family, only baulking at professional help. In retrospect it seems obvious that this was what was needed, but in the late 1960s it might not have seemed as evident as it would do now.

At school, I was instructed to prevent Soph from running away and was told to chaperone her to the outside lavatory. I could not physically restrain her, even if I had wanted to, and was summoned in front of the headmistress when I failed.

This was significant because it underlined the roles we were developing with each other. I was considered in control, normal, assumed to have a degree of power over her and was generally seen as a 'good girl'. Soph was bad, wild, eccentric and gifted.

I buried my feelings about my mother, my resentment over my role with Soph, my need for attention, and was introverted, but inwardly angry and distressed.

There was no room left for any extra demands to be made on a family already at breaking point. Eventually we emigrated to Italy, the main incentive being to try and save the family from a situation which was veering out of control. Soph started compulsively washing her hands, convinced that everything was poisonous. She continued to run away and made another 'suicide attempt' when she was about twelve.

She wrote her first short novel at this age and by now it was clear that she had an extraordinary gift for writing. I soon started seeking respite from the family, turning to boys and drugs. Soph found religion in the Catholic community in which we lived. She felt threatened and shocked by, but also jealous of, my exploits, and I started to deny our similarities while she actively sought them. In spite of being sent to boarding school in England, our lives went off in different directions for a while.

As grown ups, she became a writer, and I a painter; we had been encouraged as children to develop our differences, just as we had been encouraged to dress differently. In fact Soph's drawings, totally opposite to mine, were often brilliant and I had an ability to write school essays in a way that pleased the teachers. Hers were erratic and misspelt, though full of original ideas. She idealised my ability to 'cope', which to her was completely mysterious. As a grown up she wrote one of several short stories based on our relationship, which was called 'Tricks for Survival'.

We loved each other deeply, but her love for me was verging towards incest, and this was in spite of strong mutual irritation and exasperation, largely caused by a kind of jealousy. She wanted my perfectly ordinary attributes, whilst I felt like a cardboard imitation of her, lacking her passion and depth and perception.

She often said she felt suicidal. I couldn't allow myself to properly identify with an idea so threatening to my own life, and yet she longed for me to know, to feel what it was like to be her. She often asked me too if I feared madness. She wanted me to.

My guardedness was frustrating, but she did sense the enormous burden she placed on us, and that gave her an extreme sense of self-hatred and guilt.

We saw each other regularly, even shared a flat for a while. I had married early and divorced shortly afterwards, and some of our lightest moments were spent giggling over indiscretions about the men we knew, usually in restaurants and usually over a bottle of wine. She could be hilarious, she loved people and had a rare gift for friendship, while I couldn't really love, had few friends, and used sex to confirm that I was a valid person, exploiting men in a way that she was incapable of. Nevertheless, sex and love was a rich vein to be tapped for laughs and confessions. She was a marvellous listener too, always relieved not to be focused on herself, which was her natural inclination. Similarly, she once told me that physical pain was a welcome distraction from the mental hell she increasingly lived in.

Even in happier moments, the shadow of the depression which could suddenly grip her threatened us. It felt fragile, you never quite knew what was lurking beneath the surface.

After her death, I read her journals and learnt quite how much more she could have rightly demanded, feeling the way that she did. Her mental pain was beyond my imagination.

A few months before she died, she came to visit me in Norfolk, where I was living at the time, and one evening something snapped. I could no longer cope with the feeling of impotence, mixed up with anxiety and claustrophobia which she gave me. I told her that I couldn't shoulder the burden any longer. Somehow it felt as if my own life depended on it. She went very quiet over the next few months, ringing me less often than usual, and when she did she was uncharacteristically reticent about what she was feeling. This made me relieved and guilty in equal measures.

One night, installed in a strange flat in the suburbs of London, where I was doing some freelance decorating in the flat below, I decided to ring her. I knew that things were getting dangerously bad. I walked about a mile to the nearest phone box, but once inside hesitated. I anticipated Soph's badly disguised anguish with such dread that I simply didn't feel able to deal with it.

I walked back to the flat.

The next morning my half-sister, who was living in the country, suddenly appeared in the shop where I was about to begin work. Tears were streaming down her face. She said 'Soph's dead.' That was in 1985 when we were twenty-six.

The shock induced a breakdown, hospitalisation, then four years of agoraphobia and a gradual and painful rebirth into something approaching a whole person, helped enormously by the birth of my daughter, whose second name is Sophie. I still dream about her, nearly always about trying to save her from some horrible fate.

But just days after her death I dreamt that she was sitting on the edge of my bed, and with extreme tenderness she said, 'I will never leave you.'

My breakdown taught me, ironically, what it had felt like to be her.

I let go of my resistance to being her twin because for once I had no choice, and discovered that under extreme stress we were identical twins. I discovered the reality of having been one egg which had split, because I was no longer reacting in one way or another to her.

Then I had to find another unknown part of me which could survive as an independent identity. It has taken years to even start to tackle the guilt I felt, and still feel, over her death, but in so doing I have had to try and dissociate my life from hers and nurture the new shoot growing from the amputation she caused.

I think some twins hang on to that amputation because it is evidence of their halfness, a halfness they partly desire. Rebirth is no exaggeration; we have to discover who we are as independent human beings for the first time, but in that there is the excitement of discovery mixed up with the disintegration of the selves we knew.

Soph will never leave me; from what has happened, I hope to discover more, and eventually to be able to see her with the clarity of a whole person.

© KATE BEHRENS

Story 2
A man in his forties whose brother died at twenty-four years

I'd always imagined I would automatically know if someone close to me died, and especially my twin brother Julian. There had been so many instances during our childhood when we appeared to be in telepathic communication – unusual, perhaps, since we were non-identical. But when Julian died I was totally unaware, despite the fact that it didn't exactly come out of the blue.

For nearly seven years Julian had been suffering from a mental illness that had never been properly understood. I was very nearly dragged down with him, and it was a long struggle coming to terms with the whole thing. For the sake of my own sanity, I was forced to keep my distance from him, so that on one level we rather drifted apart.

The distressing nature of Julian's illness can best be gauged from the effect it had on the health on my father, who developed a severe anxiety state. At one point my parents were actually forced to go into hiding for a few months to give my father a chance to recover without having to cope with Julian's constant violent outbursts. Had I stayed close to Julian, I would no doubt have become every bit as ill as my father did, and probably more so.

Julian's manner changed markedly during the few months leading up to his suicide. Physical violence gave way to long periods of weeping that sometimes went on for days on end. By this stage he desperately wanted treatment for his illness, but was refused it point blank. The only possible explanation for this is that the hospital psychiatrists decided they couldn't treat him and turned him out on a sink-or-swim basis. (The only time he was actually admitted was after being arrested for causing damage to property.)

People who saw him during the last week of his life said he seemed a lot calmer, and police enquiries afterwards revealed that he had embarked on specific suicide plans at lease a week before his death. A series of copy-cat suicides by burning had been reported in the press, and this had presumably given him much the same idea.

In the meantime, I had moved to Tyneside to do postgraduate studies.

After three weeks I was just beginning to feel OK about things there. So on Saturday 28 October 1978, while Julian's death hit the news in the south, I was blissfully unaware, walking along South Shields beach and enjoying the balmy warmth of an Indian summer. That afternoon is still etched on my mind because of what followed. I remember getting a free ride on the journey back because the ticket staff were on a work-to-rule.

As I was out for the day, my parents couldn't get hold of me when it happened. Fortunately they got through as soon as I got back. Otherwise I might have found out from the radio news. It was probably best that I wasn't around at the time. It was bad enough seeing a detailed account on the back of someone's newspaper in the train only two days later.

The trauma was indeed made worse by the insensitive press coverage of an event that the journalists themselves had encouraged. The national press soon found other fish to fry, but the local papers kept on about it for what seemed like ages. I suppose we should have been grateful that they didn't print any actual lies!

It wasn't until the Monday that I travelled south. People thought it strange that I didn't drop everything and run, but that has never been in my nature. My parents were getting plenty of support, so there was nothing to be gained by rushing. Besides, I needed to sort out a number of practical matters such as laundry, college and other commitments. Routine often helps when you can't get your mind around something.

Perhaps the most difficult part was the funeral. So many people had been involved in helping the family through all the traumas that a small private ceremony was out. The result was a packed church with many friends, but also with some who had clearly come to gawp. At the crematorium committal I suddenly found myself looking for Julian, and it finally hit me that he had gone for good – up until then his death hadn't been real.

The Aftermath

My memory of the year or two that followed is understandably hazy.

Julian died only three weeks after my arrival on Tyneside, and my father died of cancer in the summer, only three weeks before I moved to a job in Northampton. My main impressions are of long weekend journeys, frequent blizzards and several bouts of flu.

A month of so after my move to Northampton, life reached its lowest ebb. No one seemed to understand, and people seemed to think I should be 'getting over things' when if anything I felt much worse. It was during this period that the news broke that Lord Mountbatten and several of his family had been killed, and I soon heard that two of the victims were his twin grandsons, one of whom was killed.

In my muddled state most of the details passed me by. What interested me was that here was someone who had lost a twin too, and in a manner that was perhaps even more traumatic, and even more public, than Julian's death. When I met Tim Knatchbull, the man himself, at the Lone Twin meeting in March 1993, this all came back to mind.

I remember seeing a picture in the press of Lord Mountbatten's grandson, and assuming this was Tim. It must actually have been his elder brother because he was of a similar age to mine. But such a mistake would have been natural given my state of mind at that time. It was vitally important to know that there was someone else out there who had lost a twin and would therefore understand.

This is why the Lone Twin Network is so important – knowing there are other people who understand. Every relationship is unique and nobody completely understands, but there is an important element to the twin relationship that can't be taken away.

I remember how annoyed I used to be when people asked, 'What's it like to be a twin?' I usually replied with, 'What's it like not to be?' I can even remember once standing next to Julian while somebody walked all round us as if we were prize exhibits! Being a twin was no big deal until Julian died, and only then did I realise what I'd lost.

I remember a recent heart-to-heart with a friend, who couldn't understand why it was so important that I was a twin when to the outside world I wasn't any longer. Well, perhaps that's what it is. I'm no less a twin than a widow or widower is someone who was married.

A Flashback

How much Julian meant to me is probably indicated by the fact that my very earliest memories are of him and not of my parents. I remember us both chasing round the greenhouses in a park when we were only two. What I don't remember is my poor mother trying to catch us before we did any damage. She tells me we had deliberately chosen two different greenhouses in order to foil her attempts at capture.

As a baby I had been rushed into hospital with a strangulated appendix, and nurses there accused my mother of spoiling me. My behaviour, they said, was that of a baby who was never left alone. My mother of course knew the answer to that: Julian and I gave each other constant attention, sometimes to the extent of her feeling excluded.

As children we quarrelled a lot. Like many twins, we were in strong competition. But underneath all that we were inseparable for most of our childhood. This was partly because we didn't have much in common with our contemporaries. While other children deafened their parents with the latest Beatles number, we deafened ours with piano, oboe and flute practice, and raucous renderings of songs from Gilbert and Sullivan operettas!

I used to think I was no good at music because Julian was so good at it.

But looking back on it I suspect he was somewhat of a musical prodigy. I remember seeing people staring open-mouthed when he played the piano in a concert at the age of seven, and wondering what all the fuss was about. Later on

I benefited from his talent because he was such a good accompanist. We made a good musical team with me on the oboe.

We were inseparable but individual and very different – we knew that, but other people often didn't at the time. I began to develop a strong aptitude for languages, especially German, which I taught myself with the aid of television programmes. Julian was good at languages too, but he found it an effort to keep up, just as I found it an effort to keep up with his musical abilities.

As I entered a rather stormy adolescence, I began to resent Julian's increasing dependency at times. His lack of assertiveness meant I was always being left to fight his corner for him. When we left school I went to Germany for a year, where I enjoyed myself tremendously despite missing Julian. After six months he followed me there, and I noticed how his mental state was deteriorating in various ways although at the time I put it down to delayed adolescent rebellion.

The truth was much worse. The sky fell one Christmas Eve, when he had the first of countless violent outbursts. That was the point when the 'siege' began. My conviction that it was an illness of some sort stems from the fact that right up to the end there were short periods when he was the old Julian again – almost as though a dark veil was being removed briefly, showing the real Julian underneath all that agony.

The last time I witnessed this was during a game of Scrabble only a month or so before Julian died, when he told me I was stupid for some reason or other. My father commented afterwards that he would never have expected to see me pleased at being insulted by Julian, but he too had noticed the same thing: it was a relaxed, teasing kind of insult such as Julian hadn't indulged in for years. Such brief moments gave us hope even at the most desperate moments.

Why?

Why did Julian end his life? He probably simply wanted to end all the agony. The change from violence to weeping also had something to do with it. He was acutely aware of how many people he had hurt, and how badly he had hurt them – which made it even worse. The final blow was the refusal of psychiatrists to treat him in any way at all.

Looking back on it, I suspect that for him it was the only way out. Had he lived longer, he might possibly have recovered, but he might equally have prolonged the agony for all concerned.

Life Since Then

In the meantime life has moved on. About a year after my father's death I met Phil, and we have lived together in Leeds for twelve years now. Those years have been mainly happy despite all the problems that life inevitably tends to bring – some of them directly associated with the loss of Julian.

One problem has been agoraphobia, which, though comparatively mild, was difficult to deal with because I didn't realise what it was until many years later. It's much easier to manage when you know what the problem situations are going to be. As a freelance translator and book editor I've been lucky in having plenty of work to do from home. At the same time, I have far too many friends and various commitments to allow me to stay at home all the time.

Perhaps the most difficult thing of all was the bereavement process itself. It was at least five years before I began to function normally again, partly because my own personality seemed to change in some ways. From being a fairly gregarious person, I have become a bit of a loner – more so than can merely be explained by the process of getting older.

And all the while there was that feeling that the length and intensity of the bereavement was abnormal: I should have got over the loss. Just when I thought I had indeed got over it, my grandmother's death brought everything rushing back again for a while. And I gather that it's only in the last year that I've stopped talking to Julian (or about him) in my sleep.

Is this because we were twins, or because of the way he died? Probably a bit of both. There is one particular way in which my mother and I feel much the same about the loss. Both of us feel strongly at times that my father isn't very far away from us, and that he's probably happy that we've managed to rebuild our lives since he and Julian left us. But there has never been that feeling about Julian. Maybe it will happen eventually. I hope so.

I sometimes get annoyed with people who try to pin these things down and say you ought to be doing this or that to work through things. Everyone has to find their own path. However, we probably need the odd nudge at times. Maybe when some well-meaning person has annoyed me by saying what I should be doing, it has nudged me into doing something positive, even if it was definitely not what they suggested!

One thing I've discovered is that I am in many ways stronger as a result of what has happened. I always feared becoming embittered, and there is, I suppose, an underlying resentment still there. But too many good things have happened since to allow that mood to take over. In so many other ways I've been fortunate in life.

ANDREW SHACKLETON

Story 3
A woman in her forties whose identical sister at thirty-six was murdered by her husband leaving four children
When we were growing up people always used to ask us 'what's it like being a twin?' I remember Maddy and I just looking at each other, grinning and replying 'what's it like not being one?' Having your best friend there all the time was brilliant and I felt a bit sorry for the other boys and girls who didn't have a

best friend like Maddy. Little did I know that I would find out the answer to our question much sooner than I or Maddy would have ever envisaged.

On 30 December 2001 my identical twin sister was murdered by her husband in her home in Rotherham, South Yorkshire. She was just 36 years old. Her husband stabbed her to death in front of her four children. I remember my brother telling me the awful news – I was sitting in bed panicking a bit because I had tried to phone Maddy and couldn't get her on the landline, or her mobile – I instinctively knew something terrible had happened. Paul, my brother, rang and said, 'Are you sitting down? Maddy's dead'. I screamed and screamed and screamed 'no, no, no' but no matter how loud I cried it was still true. I remember it to this day as if it happened yesterday.

My husband and I travelled to my parents' house where the family gathered and Maddy's children were – it was a completely unreal scenario. I felt like it wasn't true and I would wake up at any minute from my worst nightmare. Of course as the days went on I didn't wake up and I had to start dealing with the awful truth, I was now alone for the first time in my life, and I hated it.

At the funeral I was strong for my parents and Maddy's children – I don't really remember a lot about it. I do remember one of the ladies from church gave me a hug and said 'it must be worse for you'. I remember not allowing myself to think like that – how could it be worse for me? What about my brothers and sisters, my parents and Maddy's children? I felt guilty for even thinking like that. With hindsight the lady was completely right of course – Maddy was my identical twin, 3 minutes older than me. I had been with her since before we were born and had a unique relationship with her – a relationship I would not share with any other human being on the planet because I had only one twin, and now she was gone.

For some time I was on autopilot – I lost over a stone in three weeks and struggled from day to day. My over-riding emotion once I had recovered from the immediate shock of the situation was anger. How could someone I loved and called a brother have done this to my lovely Maddy? How could he then set everything in motion to protect himself and get the lightest sentence possible? How could he use my mother and father in their grief to strengthen his own case (he did this by writing to them just one week after he killed Maddy saying he couldn't explain his 'madness' that had happened and would they go and visit him in prison)? His actions worked wonders though and he was sentenced to 7 years in prison – eventually serving just three and a half years before being released.

My husband struggled to cope with my levels of anger – he said that the angry person I was at times wasn't me. I knew what he meant but needed to be allowed to be angry and express myself – it was then I decided to see a counsellor. It was one of the best decisions I made – it allowed me to rant and rave if I needed to, let my feelings out instead of bottling them up. I also experienced immense guilt that I had not been there to save Maddy – ridiculous as it sounds, I lived over

400 miles away. I felt guilty that I was still alive and had a chance to fulfil my dreams. My husband Kevin was a rock but even he needed a break sometimes. I think if I hadn't had Frances my counsellor our relationship would have definitely suffered – there is only so much one person can take on board but he did what he could without question and I owe him my life and my sanity. Words cannot explain how much he means to me and how much I love him.

In July 2002 I discovered that I was expecting our first child. We were overjoyed and it brought some positive aspect to that year when all we seemed to have was negative issues surrounding the court case and our battles with the legal system. Of course I was overjoyed at the news but it was tinged with sadness knowing that Maddy would never see my baby and we would never be able to swap stories of our experiences. I was upset that I would never have a card or present from her after my baby (a son called Sebastian) was born so I decided that I would buy a present myself and say it was from Maddy. I would know when I found the right gift – and that it is exactly what happened. The gift became my son's coming home outfit on a very special day.

I also decided that I needed to channel the negative feelings of anger and frustration into something that would eventually become positive. I decided to campaign for a change in the law and for better treatment for families of murder/ manslaughter victims. Once again Kevin was a great support and encouraged me in my efforts – none of the changes that are ongoing in law will affect our case but they will hopefully mean that another family will not have to endure the added trauma of a legal system that represents the criminal rather than the victim. I think that is what Maddy would have strived for – to help others in the future, and it is something that is positive rather than negative. I am very proud of what we have achieved – if it helps just one person in the future then it will have been worth all the effort, and I know that Maddy's name will be associated with the changes and that makes me immensely proud.

Over the last five years I have lost my beloved Maddy, two brothers, my closest Aunty (all within ten months), my sister-in-law (in traumatic circumstances) and my father (as well as having to deal with the court case and my brother-in-law's release from prison). I wonder just how I have survived and often people ask me how I've managed it. When I think about it I had two choices – go to pieces and become engulfed with anger and grief or try to make the most of life and live it to the full. I chose the second option – and it was the hardest option, believe me, but I had to do it. I had to do it for Maddy, she would have done the same for Kevin and my lovely Sebastian, for my family, friends and work colleagues. But most of all I had to do it for myself. Imagine letting myself become so down that life wasn't worth living – I have been there and it's not a nice place. A psychiatrist helped me get through the darker times. It hasn't been easy taking the second path – there have been plenty of times when I just want to stay in bed and cry all day, my work colleagues became quite used to me crying at my desk! But the only option is to carry on, no matter how hard it is. I try to focus on positive things – my beloved Kevin and Sebastian, the progress we're making in getting the law changed, family and friends. I have so much support from everyone that I know it has enabled me to pull through so far. The worst thing I could have done was to bottle up my feelings and deny them – the best advice I would give to others is don't be afraid to ask for help, I needed plenty and it helped me cope at times when I thought I was genuinely going mad. I don't think I'll ever get over what has happened to Maddy but I'm hoping that it has made me a better person. I know that she is with me still in spirit and I have happy times thinking about when we were together – every now and then I get 'a sign' from her that she approves of me carrying on and being happy. You probably think I'm mad but it's the little things that keep you going (normally a piece of music at a particularly appropriate time – like when I was buying the present from her for my baby).

I'm still adjusting to being me and not us – that has been the hardest thing. Things like saying my birthday instead of our birthday. Seeing twins in the street and not being upset by it or wanting to run over and tell them that they should hug each other every day and tell each other how much they love each other because you never know what's around the corner. It's still hard, and I still don't really know who I am as a single person. I can't describe how much I miss her or how lonely I am sometimes, despite the fact I have my family and friends around me. Even to this day I still sometimes forget that she's dead – when I see something nice in town when I'm out shopping I think 'I'll get one of those for Maddy' and then it feels like a slap in the face again as I remember she's dead.

I think I'm going to be adjusting to my new life for the rest of it – but I feel like I am doing OK. What keeps me going is the thought that I know it is what Maddy would have wanted me to do – be strong (easier said than done), live life to the full and try to be a good person who values others and treats others as she would have treated them. I'm lucky to have had my precious Maddy with me for 36 years physically, I know she is still with me spiritually and one day we will be together again, the old team reunited. Till then I'm trying to concentrate on positives – a hard thing to do but I know that's what she would have wanted. I just wish that a lot more people could have known Maddy and seen her outer and inner beauty. I tell my son Sebastian all about Aunty Maddy and I know he'll love her as much as I do when he grows up, even though he never got the chance to meet her. She is watching over us, I'm convinced of it, and I feel privileged to have called her my sister, but more importantly my best friend. Maddy I love you.

PAULA WATT

6
THE LONE TWIN NETWORK

THE BEGINNING

Throughout the Bereaved Twin Study a register was kept of those lone twins who participated in it. Every six months the twins received an update of names and addresses which built up gradually to a final list of 217 lone twins, with only two out of those interviewed asking not to be included.

Those twins on the final register were invited to meet with each other in 1989. Dr Elizabeth Bryan, Director of the Multiple Births Foundation, offered the Unit at Queen Charlotte's Hospital as the first meeting place. Twenty-five twins came who were all known to me, but none of them had knowingly met another lone twin before. I organised this first meeting so that twins were grouped according to the stage in their lives when their twin had died, with an additional group of those who lost their twin in a particularly traumatic way. I stayed outside the groups, making myself available, in case anyone felt too distressed to stay in a group and needed individual time.

The two-year gap between the publication of the Study and this first meeting of lone twins was an indication of my anxiety about whether bringing lone twins together, possibly in large numbers, was intrinsically a 'good thing' to do! I felt quite nervous at that first meeting. I knew that I had found some of the interviews for the study extremely emotional, as some twins spoke for the first time in depth about the loss of their twin and the effects it had on them. I knew that the accumulative effect on me of hearing 219 stories of twin loss over a period of two years had brought about a complete writer's block, at the point when I was due to write up the data for presentation. This was because I did not know how to reduce all the anguish I had heard into a very short paper to be presented in ten minutes at the International Congress of Twin Studies. I had never previously experienced such a block but was finally able to break it by writing a poem. I needed to face the core of the sense of loss for me, which is that one's twin is irreplaceable. This sounds absurdly obvious, but it left me uncertain of the outcome for other lone twins, not meeting each other one at a time, as I had done, but facing a number of other lone twins all at once in a group.

As it turned out, my fears were groundless and at the end of that meeting no one was eager to leave. We were offered a future under the umbrella of the Multiple Births Foundation, which we accepted gratefully.

THE CURRENT SITUATION

Since that first meeting the name of the Register has changed to the Network, numbers have grown from 25 to nearly 500 and a further six Annual Meetings have been held, either in London or Birmingham, with some smaller regional meetings in between. In 1996 the Network was taking up too many resources of the Multiple Births Foundation and we were requested to become independent, in view of our size. We remain at present an informal network, dependent on the readiness of the lone twin members to contribute as they do with great generosity, their time, energy and donations, so that the Network List is maintained, proper accounts are kept, Annual and Regional Meetings are organised and recently a Newsletter has been started. Members have joined us from Canada, the US and other European countries.

I believe that the Network fulfils an important function for many lone twins. The membership will inevitably change as some twins want to move on and yet others choose to stay, to build up friendships and retain the Network for newcomers. The different role that the Network has played for some of the twins coming to the meetings is described in this chapter, beginning with a shortened account of the first meeting, originally published by the *Independent* newspaper (26/7/89), written by the lone twin journalist Rosemary Stark.

The everlasting sadness of the lone twin

To lose a spouse is a tragedy, to lose a child perhaps the greatest tragedy most of us could imagine; but everyone had some identity before becoming a spouse or a parent. A twin is never anything but a twin until separation by death, and there is no way of untwinning except by death.

In that most intimate of bereavements, the surviving twin finds the foundations of his or her own identity undermined, because twinhood bestows the singular oddity of a plural identity. Even before birth, doctor, nurses, family friends of the parents and the mother herself come to think of and refer to the contents of her swelling uterus not as he, she or even it, but as they and them.

The first name of all twins is The Twins, and the only answer twins can offer to the question, 'What's it like being a twin?', is another question: 'I don't know – what's it like not being one?'

In childhood years, when this metaphysical conundrum is first confronted, it probably never occurs to either twin that one day one of them will find out the answer to that question, and when this does happen the sense of isolation of the newly untwinned is absolute.

Two years after my identical twin sister, Sheila, died in 1983, I learnt through a letter in the press of a study of twin bereavement being undertaken by Joan Woodward of the West Midlands Institute of Psychotherapy and made contact with her. I asked how many lone twins she had seen. 'You are the hundred-and-nineteenth', was her astonishing answer.

Being the only bereaved twin in my own world, I suppose I tended to see myself as the only one in the world itself. If I ever did address the fact that of course there must be others, I certainly had not the slightest idea of how to set about contacting them, had it even occurred to me that there might be a point in doing so.

Earlier this year, twenty-five of Joan Woodward's interviewees met, first with the intention of sharing our own experiences of life untwinned, and then perhaps to see how we could best offer our shared awareness to support other lone twins.

My first shock at that extraordinary gathering was to find that the tall and elegant young woman to whom I had found myself talking over coffee lost her twin brother at birth. What, I thought, was she doing here? How could she know what it felt like for me to lose in early middle age an identical sister with whom I had shared every growing-up experience until I was well into my twenties? How could she sympathise with the shock encounter, peculiar to identical twins and still poignantly painful nearly six years into lone twinhood, with the unexpected mirror? What did she know of the joylessness of birthdays now unshared? The fact that she had travelled from the West Midlands to this event some thirty years on from her own bereavement indicated a continuing sense of significant loss, but how could it compare to my own, and how now were we to help each other? Embarrassment, mutually felt, dominated this first encounter.

The next and greater shock was when we were assigned to groups, varying in size from just two to about half a dozen: those who had lost brothers and sisters at birth; those whose bereavement had been in childhood or in adult life; and five of us, whose uniting factor was that our bereavements had been traumatic.

Finding myself grouped with three bereaved by their twins' suicides and one whose identical twin was murdered, I tried to run away, convinced I was in the wrong group.

Sheila was alcoholic. Her death followed the slow and painful estrangement through lies and deceit that all alcoholics inflict on those who love them most and who must, if they are to keep them, keep them away from the thing they most crave. Only after the death of an alcoholic do those who are closest to them discover, in clearing the detritus of a life, the extent of a dependant's furtive skill to deceive. For twins, who grow up sharing everything, often even (as in Sheila's and my case) a secret language, the discovery of the deviously hidden bottles, and the treachery they speak of, is particularly painful. I was persuaded to stay with the group in which perhaps I did belong after all.

First – and quite spontaneously – we all identified whether we had been the stronger or the weaker twin, dependent or depended on. None of us was in the least doubt about this: two of the suicide victims had been the weaker twins, their survivors the stronger, as indeed I was also. Half a pound heavier at birth and always physically healthier, I was put in charge in childhood, given the bus money and minded my own sister from our first menstruation not quite simultaneous, but certainly within the same monthly cycle. Sheila was given to fainting, and I would be let out of school to look after her on the way home. I was always the responsible one.

On the night before our finals Sheila, who brought the gaiety into my life, threw all care to the winds and went to stand on her head at the end of the pier of our Scottish seaside university town, bringing me back a bag of chips to sustain my swotting. She did not graduate with me, and that separated us for the first time since she had gone into hospital aged seven to have her tonsils out. Family lore has it that then, taken to visit her, I tried to swap places, accepting that it was my turn now to do the nasty thing.

In our group, a young man whose stronger non-identical twin shot himself at the end of their teens had recently begun therapy. None of the rest of us had had any counselling or therapy at the time of our bereavements or since, and he alone among us felt no guilt over his twin's death, though at the time, having found him dying and picked up the gun, he came briefly under police suspicion of having occasioned it. In fact his brother had become engrossed in eastern mystic religiosity and had convinced himself it was time for him to move on to another life; he had left a letter to this effect.

For the rest of us there was a lingering, possibly permanent, sense that there was something we could have done, and not necessarily just in the latter stages. For a bereaved twin, particularly one who was the stronger of the partnership, there can be a sense that we somehow all along drank more deeply from some common pool of strength and well-being. Often the stronger twin is, like me, the first-born and the heavier at birth, so the guilt goes back to the womb, where we must imagine that we grabbed more of the goodies, giving us the superior strength.

At lunch we found ourselves spontaneously huddling back into our assigned groups – even I, who had tried to run away from mine. It was inevitable that when we reconvened to report back our group findings, those bereaved at birth were at one end, with more recent bereavements graduating up the room.

Then came, for me, the real revelation of the day. As each group reported back, the profoundest emotion, the unstoppable tear-shedding, was from those whose loss was at birth. As we, the later bereaved, reported back, there was the dawning shock of realisation that what was coming from their end was a shuddering sense of deprivation expressing itself in open envy: at least we had had our twins for a while, some of us well into adult life. We all spoke of how we had loved being twins, had cherished the sharing, the intimacy that knows exactly which dress a sister will choose in a shop, had enjoyed the exclusivity of twinhood as well as the mischief, never in the least minding being mistaken for each other and called by each other's names. They who had never known twinhood had been searching all their lives for that.

Memory, it seems, begins in the foetus at the age of six months; for the last three months in the womb a twin has knowledge of another presence. If that womb-mate is lost at birth, the surviving twin may grow up with an inexplicable sense of the most profound loss. Many birth-bereft twins were not told about their brother or sister till later in life, one of our number by her mother who, in an outburst of anger blamed her for her twin's non-survival. It is experiences such as these which may need to be shared by lone twins as a matter of sometimes desperate urgency.

ROSEMARY STARK

THEME 1
ON SHARING AND GAINING A SENSE OF 'BELONGING'

This sense of belonging to a group of people who have a very important shared experience, is the theme most frequently mentioned. It is of great significance to many lone twins to discover that they are not the 'only ones', but that there are many others facing similar feelings.

Story 1
A woman in her thirties who lost her sister at birth
This was a really amazing day for me. My first Lone Twin meeting. A bright and sunny day, and the venue comfortable, safe, easy to find. Being greeted by friendly faces. The room full of people, can all these people be lone twins? How great!

We started after coffee, by dividing into small groups. There was a written agenda, and an information sheet about grief and its stages. There was also other very useful and interesting information on various printed sheets. This is one of the things I feel I have lacked – simple, basic information. The accounts and quotes by other lone twins really summed up some of my own feelings and experiences. My twin sister, Elizabeth, died shortly after she was born, and

I was not told about this until I was eighteen. Of course I 'knew'. Searching, one of the stages of the grief process, is something I have been subconsciously and consistently doing for ages. It felt so good just to sit and talk and listen to other lone twins, have a chance to express some of my own deep feelings, feelings that I find so powerful and so familiar that they have, in the past, overwhelmed me. It was wonderful to hear the strength, the grief, loss, thoughts and ideas of others and to identify these feelings within myself. For me the therapeutic value of expressing these feelings is without parallel, for these feelings seem so special, as if they belong not only to me, but to my dead baby sister too.

We all came together again for lunch; by this time I had spoken to quite a few people and felt more at ease. I spoke to a man who had had an identical twin brother who died in a fall: he showed me photos of his brother – there was something so great about seeing someone's photos – so precious. I also learned that people had travelled from all over the UK. One woman had even come from Canada.

In the afternoon we again split into smaller groups. We had five 'headings' to choose from, and I wanted to be in two or three groups at once. Our small group was very valuable – further listening, discussion, just sitting with some of my painful feelings and hearing the stories of others.

Afterwards suggestions were made about a support group for mothers of lone twins. I really hope this group gains strength and support, and that sometime in the future I may be able to help with this. Because (I cannot help feeling) if my own mother had been able to talk to someone, had something of this nature been offered to her, and had she taken the opportunity to have some sympathetic counselling, she would have been more able to deal with telling me about my sister, Elizabeth. I would then have been able to grow up with and deal with these feelings before now. I know many other lone twins feel the same way. I hope this mothers' group grows in strength.

As the day came to an end I was reluctant to leave. There was a Quiet Room too; I did not use this myself, but found it very comforting to know it was there.

I feel a great sense of relief that there are other lone twins out there, hundreds of them who have travelled the same road as I. These words seem inadequate to express my true feelings. I hope other people new to the Network, other lone twins, will know something of how I feel.

RUTH HEALEY

Story 2
A woman in her seventies who lost a sister at sixty-six years
Kay, my identical twin sister, and I were very fortunate, we shared many wonderful years and somehow we imagined we would reach the stage when we would be together sitting in our rocking chairs!

Alas, that was not to be. Suddenly in November 1988 I was a lone twin. A telephone call from England told me the devastating news that my sister had collapsed in the street and was dying. No warning, my twin was dying and I was thousands of miles away. The next few hours were ones of extreme sorrow, thinking it was a bad dream from which I would awake. Suddenly I was with her in spirit and was with her when she walked through a tunnel and waved goodbye. It was seven o'clock in the evening in Toronto and midnight in England when she passed away.

Fortunately I had the support of a very understanding husband, a daughter (living in Toronto), a son (living in London) and friends to help me through those days of shock and sorrow.

Weeks went by, I walked around in a daze at times, wondering why I felt more than a little strange, then I realised why: I was a lone twin. Part of my life was missing, but part of Kay's life was now mine. Not easy to understand, not easy to explain to anyone who is not a twin. How I wished I could talk to another lone twin who perhaps could understand just how much I was missing Kay. Our lives had been spent as one person, in that we could share so much – and never be lonely. That very special relationship we had shared would always be with us even now we were not able to communicate as in the past.

How I longed to speak to another lone twin. One day I happened to see *The Times* and I could not resist browsing through an English paper. The first page I turned to was an article about a lone twin who was trying to cope with being on his own after the tragic death of his identical twin about ten years previously. I immediately phoned my son in London and he made enquiries about a very special organisation relating to lone twins.

Within a short while I was able to make contact with the group and arranged to go to a meeting in March 1990 which was being held in Birmingham. With trepidation I ventured forth, not being quite sure of what the outcome would be. That meeting proved to be a turning point in my life, and each year I return to England to meet many lone twins as friends, and make new friends.

Call it Fate, or what you will, reading that article in *The Times* in Toronto in May 1989, was the first step for me in sharing with others.

NORAH BARRABLE

Story 3
A woman in her forties who lost a brother at thirty-seven years
I returned home emotionally drained, yet elated and so glad that I had gone.

The morning of the Lone Twin Network meeting dawned a bright and sunny one, which was just as well as I had 'cold feet' at the last minute before going. However, I pushed this aside telling myself the benefits would be many, as they had been when I attended my first meeting the previous November in Surrey.

I arrived at the Quaker Meeting House in Byng Place, London, to find it already bustling with people. We were greeted warmly with tea or coffee and handed a name badge and information pack. I immediately got chatting with the lady behind me and found we had a lot in common, despite the different circumstances of the loss of our twins. This was very encouraging, as was the whole atmosphere of the place which was one of sympathetic friendliness.

Once everybody had arrived, we split into groups depending on what time in life we had lost our twin, i.e. at birth, in childhood or in adulthood. I lost my twin four years ago, at thirty-seven years, and therefore joined the third group. It was very helpful to hear what others felt about their loss. As Philip and I were not identical twins it was very interesting to talk to those who had identical twins to discuss any differences in the level of bonding, etc.

After lunch I felt the need to be alone and headed for the Quiet Room – as had a few others. It was a lovely, peaceful room with the warm sun shining in and some beautiful spring flowers on the table, along with the Book of Remembrance and various other books, poems and articles on twins. I must say that having chatted away all the morning about my loss and the loss of others this finally took its toll, much to my surprise, and in the peaceful atmosphere of the Quiet Room I couldn't hold back the tears as, once again, I missed my brother so much, wishing he was still here to share the sunshine and the flowers with me.

I dashed to the loo and on the way was hugged and comforted by the other kind, caring lone twins. I emerged red-eyed but ready for the afternoon session, when we split into the various groups we had chosen at lunchtime. Fifteen groups in all, covering many aspects of being a lone twin and how it affected us. There were only two of us in our group, but this didn't matter as we found we had so much in common and were able to relate to our feelings of guilt, anger, loss and sorrow over the way our twins had died and how we were coping now.

After we had broken for tea, the meeting turned to the business side of the Network. Ideas for a logo were discussed and we were updated on future articles about lone twins appearing in the press and asked to put our names on a list if we felt we were up to press interviews.

Having met so many kind and friendly people, the overall feeling that I took away with me was that we may be lone twins, but we are not totally alone, there are those who understand.

ALISON HOW

THEME 2
ON BEING 'PROPERLY HEARD'

For some twins the Network meetings have offered then the first opportunity to tell their version of their loss and to have the existence of their twin validated.

Story 1
A woman in her forties who lost a brother at birth

Finding out about the Lone Twin Network was a big plus for me. For two or three years I received notification of the annual meeting and somehow forgot about it. Then two years ago I told myself I couldn't put it off any longer and said I would go. On the day as I was driving up I kept on thinking of excuses to turn back, finally saying to myself, 'Well, if it's causing this much upset, then it shows how much you need to be there.' When I got there the first thing that struck me was that here was a room full of people with half the people missing, as though everyone was there with an invisible twin. The small groups were a revelation. It was so nice to be with people who could relate to my feelings after all these years, almost a sense of coming home. Even the people who had lost their twins in later life seemed to have a bond with those of us whose twins had never lived. I went back the next year. It was a whole lot easier to get myself there this time, and I certainly intend to get to the meeting as often as I can in years to come.

LIZ DAWSON

Story 2
A woman in her thirties who lost her brother in childhood

In 1994, something (someone) made me walk into the paper shop I normally pass, buy a newspaper I no longer bought, and go home and open that paper at a page that was to change my life. As I read about the Lone Twin Network, I hardly dared to believe that here, at last, was something I had searched so frantically in the dark for – understanding.

On 26 March 1994, on a beautiful sunny day, I made my way to London to my first ever annual meeting of the Lone Twin Network. As I walked through the door and received smiles and hugs from lone twins, just like me, I finally realised that I was not alone. I was able to tell my story for the first time. They recognised and accepted the intensity of my grief and loss. My twin felt near again. A candle had been lit and I could begin to see again ...

During the afternoon of that day I joined a group 'For Twins Who would Like To Explore if There Are Any Gains in Being a Lone Twin'. About half of our group consisted of twins who had lost their twin in adult life, myself who had lost my twin in early childhood, and the others who had lost their twin at or around birth. Numerically, at least, we were a fair representation of the Network.

We began by introducing ourselves and giving a brief resume of how and when we had become lone twins. As we talked more, an interesting ambiguity emerged as to how we had interpreted the group titles. For some, particularly those who had lost their twin in adult life, the search was for gains in being a lone twin, as opposed to how life would have been if their twin was still alive. For twins who had enjoyed a wonderful relationship with their twin, this was particularly difficult. On the other hand, twins who had felt constricted, pressured or oppressed by their twin and/or by society's expectations of them as a twin, felt a sense of release at becoming a lone twin – if only the inherent feeling of guilt at feeling this way, along with their natural grief, hadn't been so constricting itself.

For the rest of us, we had looked at the title as meaning the gains we might get from being a lone twin as opposed to never having been a twin at all. This was particularly the view of those of us who had little or no experience of living with a twin and so had been left to wonder 'what if?' To counter this our search for gains led us to talk about the guidance and strength and comfort we received from our twin (and here many of us unconsciously gesticulated to an area just beside our shoulder).

We were surprised to learn how many of us, and those we had been talking to throughout the day, were in the 'caring' professions and it might have been interesting to explore whether this was related more to us being twins or because we were lone twins.

I hope that other members of this group obtained some comfort and understanding, as I did, in this intimate sharing of experiences and feelings. The gains we were searching for predictably weren't as tangible nor as accessible as I, at least, had hoped. But at least for me, through all the pain and trauma of my own circumstances, I can honestly say that being a twin (or 'lone twin') is a very special experience – obviously I wish things could have been different but I NEVER wish that I wasn't a twin. And that must be a gain in itself.

Update

I think it was only when I joined the Lone Twin Network that I fully realised the catastrophic impact of losing my twin in childhood. The wonderful people that I met through the LTN gave me the opportunity to really consider what had happened to me and make me realise that, through all of these years, I had struggled along as only half a person. Then, remarkably, through the support of all these friends, I began to change from half a person, to a whole half. I am now a whole half a person! And the difference between a half and a whole half is that I can now be a rounded individual. I can stand up without the crutch that my twin had become and I have been able to give him the freedom that he needed to find his own peace. No, I will never be a whole person again, but being a whole half is more than enough for me. I cannot thank my fellow lone twins enough for this.

NICKII ROBERTSON

Story 3
A man in his forties who lost a sister at birth

46 YEARS, 157 DAYS, TWO AND A HALF HOURS

For the first two of those years I cried. So I was told, keeping all around me awake. I pined.

Forty-six years, 157 days, two and a half hours later I still pine the loss of my twin. Legend has it that we were both a mistake. My twin never survived the error. My mother almost didn't. There was much of me and little of my twin. I had what was rightfully mine, together with what was rightfully hers.

I made my debut into this world a murderer. So legend has it. That I know not to be true. The physical body of my twin died at birth, but she has always been part of me. We have played together as children, we talk and share many things. We live as one.

For forty-six years, 157 days, two and a half hours, these feelings dared not be shared. Who could possibly understand? Who could believe the way that I feel deep, deep inside, deeper than any other person could ever reach?

A good friend told me of the Lone Twin Network. I wrote. I waited, not knowing what to expect. I opened the mail. The Lone Twin Network and Newsletter. I read, glued. There were others who felt as I did. I cried. I cried for my twin, for myself and for those who have lost twins. Some at birth, others as children, many as adults. Twins all. Taken peacefully, suddenly, restfully, or violently – all taken from us painfully. I tried to write: too many tears. I could not see. I telephoned: conversation was impossible through the sobbing. Forty-six years, 157 days, four hours later I was for the first time speaking of the way I felt about my twin. Somebody was there to help, to understand, to reassure. I felt helpless, but gained strength from their strength and understanding.

I cannot explain how I would have coped with that day without the Network, or even if that day would have ever come. Neither can I write how glad I am that it did come, for now my twin has recognition from people other than me. It is as if a sun has burst into her identity, giving it light and warmth in her own right.

Forty-six years, 157 days, two and a half hours later, both my twin and I have friends who know and understand.

Dawn, I miss you dearly and always will, even though you are, and always will be, such an essential and integral part of me.

DAVID ELVY

THEME 3
ON THE NETWORK MEETINGS REPRESENTING A 'MILESTONE'

Some twins experienced a Network meeting as a turning point, as if it provided a new start, an opportunity for change, in the way that they felt about the loss of their twin, based on the experience that their highly individual feelings about being a lone twin had no longer to be hidden.

Story 1
A woman in her fifties who lost a sister at a day old

I was very nervous on my first visit to a Network meeting, but what an almost indescribable experience that was. I was really worried that there would not be anyone who felt as I did. I could understand how a twin would feel if they lost their twin in childhood or adulthood, but would people understand me, who had lost my twin at only one day old? I soon felt very much at home and was discussing my feelings with other lone twins. I realised that it is understood that the time in the womb makes that special bond and a sharing that you never lose. Listening to others was certainly overwhelming and put a lot of my feelings into perspective. Everyone at the meeting was so kind and special.

When I left that meeting my mind was buzzing. I couldn't wait to tell my family all about it. It was an amazing experience for me.

MARY HEIGHWAY

Story 2
A woman in her fifties who lost a brother around the time of birth
The first Lone Twin Annual Meeting in London was certainly a milestone for me and one I still talk about. Coming together and sharing with other lone twins was very affirming. To realise I was not the only lone twin out there in the world, that there were others similar to me with like experiences who could understand me, was very satisfying. To be able to talk about this huge gap in my life, this void that sometimes seems too big to comprehend and for me to deal with. My attempts at filling this void with possessions, acquaintances, friends, food, and yet it is still there, this emptiness. I can be paralysed by it, leaving me isolated. It seems like a hunger I am unable to satisfy, a searching I am unable to stop, like tramping the earth, walking and walking yet never getting to or finding the final destination. Always something missing.

I have only been to two of the annual meetings for Lone Twins. I have not attended the others, almost too frightened to face that vulnerability in me again. Yet I am there in spirit always, I have been moved to tears by the courage and openness of other lone twins who have written about themselves in the Lone Twin List.

CYNTHIA WHELAN

Story 3
A woman in her forties who lost her identical sister at birth
This, I am pleased to say, is a Progress Report. The whole story started nearly fifty years ago. I had a normal upbringing, but my sense of self at many times in my life was a complete mystery – those small pockets of time left me so unsure of myself; lacking in self-worth and self-esteem.

At the age of ten or eleven I was told I had been one of twins but that my identical sister was stillborn at our birth – no other facts. Even that small amount of knowledge made sense to me – it gave me the missing part of the jigsaw of my sense of self. But as I got older I still could not make sense of all my innermost feelings.

I have no doubt that had I not joined the Lone Twin Network, I would still be where I was prior to February 1989 (our first meeting) just about coping or struggling with my identity at the best of times, but really floundering during times of trouble. At that meeting, for the first time in my life I heard others expressing their personal inner feelings with which I could identify! That meant that I was not odd or peculiar – just that I had involuntarily been following the line of responses to my situation. We all shared in the first good step of self-help group therapy made that day!

This has continued over the years. Not just at the meetings, but also through some individuals writing to each other. This offers an escape route for otherwise bottled-up emotions and feelings.

I never have tried or ever will try through all this, to forget my sister; but only ever to try to effect a stable frame of mind and a feelgood factor about myself. I said this was a Progress Report, and as I think back over the time since the Network began I can identify three significant turning points and milestones for me. The first was, of course, the first meeting, as I have already explained. The second, a couple of years later, came from a resource paper available at the meeting, regarding the relationship between twins. This revealed that the first-born, generally, would be the leader to do things and the second-born would be the follower. My sister was the first-born and apparently as a baby I would sit up but would never crawl, until one day a clockwork doll was put into action and I simply followed without hesitation! Not having my sister around over the years would account for my lack of self-confidence. So having recognised this factor I would in the future have to allow for this. The third milestone came about through a Network member explaining the procedure on how to find the grave. So after a year's delay I plucked up enough courage to do this and after a few weeks I was standing at her graveside. That was two years ago. I didn't feel peace of mind wash through me, unfortunately – more a relief of mind that I had found her grave. What followed for some considerable time, when I faced up to it in my mind, was a mixture of deep emotions.

Now, fortunately, I have peace of mind, knowing she is with God. As for me, now I feel I have come as far as it is possible to do to get my sense of self clear in my mind – after all, the one person who could make me complete is not here. Sometimes I am very conscious of this and that is something that will gradually be sorted out as the years go by – with the help of God and, needless to say, the Lone Twin Network meetings!

LINDA HARVEY

Story 4
A woman in her seventies who lost a sister at a few days old

On my way to my first LTN meeting I felt apprehensive and more than one butterfly floated around in my stomach. My son escorted me to the venue and I felt like turning round at the door, but I took a gulp of air and crossed the threshold. The atmosphere was so warm and friendly and everyone was so helpful. I could hardly believe it – here were other people talking the same language and telling of experiences so like my own, it almost seemed too good to be true.

How sad it was to hear of the opposition some had had from their own families; some had never been told they were a twin until their late teens; for some an elderly aunt or grandparent had let it slip; some parents still refused to discuss the matter: if only those parents could realise that they are depriving their lone twin of their twinship. There were tears and smiles and a huge feeling of relief to find others who were feeling the same profound sense of loss. I was overjoyed to know that those heartaches I'd felt through the years were not just a figment of my imagination, it was all to do with being a lone twin. After the meeting I felt so uplifted – the knowledge that others shared the same feelings was wonderful.

RUTH WEAVER

Story 5
A woman in her fifties who lost a brother at birth

I attended my first regional Lone Twin meeting in Purley in November 1990. I was very apprehensive about going since I assumed it was really meant for recently bereaved twins. But the welcome was so warm and with my 'Twin Lost at Birth' badge I somehow felt that I had found a new family.

Gradually stories of loss began to unfold. It was so strange to look around the room and sense amidst the men and women there twenty-six amputated existences, twenty-six people sharing the hidden pain of losing the closest relationship which can exist, that of being a twin. Very slowly, my own 'twin identity', which had always felt rather like a childhood fairytale, seemed to be creeping out of the shadows into the real world.

PENNY LUMLEY

Story 6
A man in his forties who lost a brother at birth

I want to tell of my first impression on going to my first Lone Twin Network meeting. I sat outside for half an hour and smoked 5 or 6 cigarettes I think, feeling like I was going in for a job interview. I wasn't sure whether I wanted to go in or not!

Many thoughts went through my mind, why am I here, what is going to happen in there, what are the people going to be like? Finally I went in on my own. I didn't want anyone to go in with me, after all, it was me and my lost twin. That was why I was there, I wanted to know if I could find out if some of my life habits and thoughts, the way I react to people and my outlook on life were similar to those of other lone twins. It was really helpful to me that I wore a badge to show that it was my first meeting. This made me feel like I was looked after, after all I did walk in, go straight to the tea and biscuits and totally ignore most people out of total fright! I managed not to burst into tears as I realised when I looked around the room, all the people there had, at whatever point in their lives lost a twin, too! The emotion was overwhelming.

After a brief welcome we had a choice to go into our different groups. For me this was 'loss at birth'. Here I met Joan Woodward, author of *The Lone Twin* book that opened my mind to coming, although from reading the book to turning up has taken 10 years!

Overall I wish that I'd gone years ago, but I believe things happen for a reason and at 39 the time is right for me to bury my twin by finding the grave of my brother and to say 'thanks for making me who I am'.

Since going to that meeting I belong to a very special group of people, some have become friends, one identical lone twin, same as me with loss at birth, has become a friend who understands because like everyone else in the Lone Twin Network, they know what the empty feeling is like. Except now that empty feeling has been filled with the understanding that I'm not on my own, or weird, or a freak anymore due to *The Lone Twin* book and the Lone Twin Network.

GARY ORANGE

JOINT MEETINGS WITH RECENTLY BEREAVED PARENTS

One of the outcomes of the Lone Twin Network being initially under the umbrella of the Multiple Births Foundation was the development of some joint meetings. These brought together recently bereaved parents who had lost a twin baby, either at birth, or in very early childhood, with adult lone twins from the Network, whose twins had died during these stages. The adult twins were able to offer suggestions very sensitively to the parents, telling them the kind of help their surviving twin might need. The parents in turn responded appreciatively to these ideas, especially to the optimistic view that if they could be open and talk with their bereaved twin about the twin who had died, answering questions appropriately and making space for each member of the family to grieve in his or her own way, there was a good chance the surviving twin would lead a full and interesting life, with a proper sense of self.

These meetings were instigated by the Multiple Births Foundation and came directly out of their Bereavement Clinics, set up by Dr Bryan and run in London and Birmingham for parents who lose twins or multiples at birth. Only two such meetings were held and they seemed to arouse even more emotions than the Lone Twin

Network meetings. I believe that they need very careful organising with an experienced facilitator in each group of mixed parents and twins, but they hold enormous potential for helping both parents and lone twins to heal some of the pain of loss. The third story under Theme 1 in Chapter 4 is told by a twin who went to one of these meetings and she elaborates on the effect it had on her. The first story told in this section also emphasises how the twin concerned wished that her mother could have had such help when she lost a twin at birth.

As the Network has developed and more and more twins have shared their experiences, it has become clear how important it is to understand at a deep level the dynamics of twin loss and the factors that lead to some lone twins seeking therapy.

7
ATTACHMENT THEORY AND THERAPEUTIC INTERVENTIONS

INTRODUCTION

In Chapter 1, the 'bare bones' of Attachment Theory were described in an attempt to understand in Attachment terms both the themes that came out of the Bereaved Twin Study and the many lone twins' stories of their experiences that followed.

Unfortunately, so-called 'anecdotal evidence' is often dismissed by theorists as unreliable or insignificant, yet there are only two sources for our understandings of the 'human lot'. The first comes from individuals both willing and able to speak out about their 'truths', as they have experienced them. The second comes from wise observers capable of seeing wider truths which can be tested, and the results are seen to be replicated. From the discovery of these observable truths come workable theories, *open to change,* as more knowledge becomes available. Such observers not only need to be skilled in the hearing of individual truths, but above all they need to have the courage to speak out about them. The purpose of this book is to offer some truths experienced by lone twins, whose stories I believe have not to date been sufficiently validated or understood. Because of this, it is important to look briefly at why and how other groups of people's experiences have also been denied, in order to appreciate the effect this has on our society and the courage it takes to challenge them.

Freud was originally able to believe the truth of his patients' experiences of incest and formulated his Seduction Theory as a way of understanding their symptoms of hysteria. In the face of formidable opposition to this belief from his contemporaries, Freud came to reject the theory and turned to create alternative explanations. He proposed instead that the sexual abuse had not happened in reality, but existed as a fantasy in the child's mind. It was a sexual desire on the *child's part* for the parent of the opposite sex.

I believe that this very serious error of judgement has been the major cause in generations of people having their stories of incest and sexual abuse being disbelieved, with some disastrous results in many cases. Masson (1985) and Webster (1995) both express strong views on this change in Freud's views and elaborate at length on how it led to his creating many more spurious theories. I believe it has also helped to give some level of greater credibility to the current movement which supports 'False Memory Syndrome'. This is particularly strong in the US. This is a complex and controversial field which needs organisations like Accuracy About Abuse to help us all take a responsible position. It does this largely by making case material and court judgments more widely known, but a great deal more work needs to be done.

Bowlby had both the courage and the wisdom to challenge very profoundly some of these later theories of Freud's and those of other psychoanalysts, as he listened to and observed mothers and babies as well as children and adolescents.

THE MAIN WAYS THAT BOWLBY DIFFERED IN HIS VIEWS FROM FREUD

In order to appreciate the role of Attachment Theory in helping to unravel the complexities of twin loss, it is important first to understand the main ways in which Bowlby's views differed from those of Freud and other classical psychoanalysts. Bowlby states throughout his work that he gained his knowledge from direct observations and, as a result, he extrapolated *forward*. For example, he observed a baby crying. The child's mother comes in and comforts the baby and the crying stops. She goes out and the baby starts to cry again. This is a very different way of working from Freud, who worked *backwards*, interpreting information provided by his adult patients during their analytical sessions.

Bowlby evolved his theories slowly and patiently. He took many years to complete his major work in three volumes, *Attachment* (1971), *Separation* (1973), and *Loss* (1980). He was helped in this task by many other workers and was always ready to give them credit. The Second World War provided opportunities for children separated from their parents due to evacuation, to be observed by Dorothy Burlingham and Anna Freud (1942, 1944) in residential nurseries. Their work was followed by observations of children in hospital, also separated from their parents. Two social workers, who later became psychoanalysts, wrote about the effects of hospitalisation on children and played a large part in bringing about changes in hospitals that are now taken for granted. James Robertson, who was one of them, made the now famous film *A Two Year Old Goes to Hospital* (1953). Mary Ainsworth (1962, 1977), who researched, studied and wrote at great length in Attachment terms about the way babies and children related to their mothers, was also one of the first people to write about the importance of the role of the father. Children who have had good Attachment experiences with both parents do best; those who fail to make Attachment to their mothers, but do so with their fathers, do better than those who fail with both parents.

As Bowlby observed, humans express strong loss feelings when separated from their Attachment figures because the characteristic of Attachment behaviour is the *intensity* of the emotion that accompanies it, irrespective of the age of the person concerned. He observed that the type of Attachment that occurred *before* the loss and those available *afterwards,* as well as the quality of other Attachments in the life of the bereaved person, was enormously important in affecting the outcome for better or worse.

This view was confirmed by the data in the Bereaved Twin Study, which showed that lone twins who had a strong and important other Attachment in their lives (for example, a marriage partner) generally felt their twin loss less severely than those twins who had not made another close Attachment. It was also strongly confirmed in the situations described earlier, with those parents who were genuinely relieved that there was only one baby to care for and were able to make strong, loving connections with their surviving twin.

One of the most important ways in which Attachment theory differs from classical psychoanalytical thinking, is that it *replaces the concept of 'Dependency Needs'*. This concept is most clearly set out in Bowlby's last book (*A Secure Base*, 1988). He considered that the way many psychoanalysts refer to 'Dependency Needs' is highly pejorative and as he put it 'baleful' in its influence. He believed that Attachment behaviour is not 'babyish', something to 'grow out of', but necessary for proper human development throughout life. The Attachment that twins can have with each other needs to be understood in these terms.

Bowlby also considered that Attachment Theory replaced another psychoanalytic concept held by such analysts as Klein and Winnicott, known as 'Object Relations'. This, in brief, is the concept that supposes we all have a strong libidinal drive that makes us relate to others (the objects) solely in order to satisfy our two primary needs for food and sex. Bowlby's observations led him to believe that there are different *instinctive behaviours,* rather than one overriding libidinal drive, and that these are biologically determined to meet different needs. The work of other biological scientists such as Lorenz, who studied the bonding patterns in geese, confirmed the role of Attachment in the protection of their young. Lorenz's studies that are most widely known concern the way a newly hatched gosling followed a shoe box pulled along on a string, to imitate a moving figure. The gosling's *instinctive behaviour* made it follow the box as if it was its mother, as being closely attached to its mother is the overriding need of the baby gosling to secure its survival (Lorenz 1935).

Similarly, Harlow's work with baby monkeys showed their need for Attachment to their mothers giving them a sense of security, which took priority over their need for food. He set up two model 'mother' monkeys. One was made of a wire frame with a bottle of milk at nipple level. The other one was made of soft fur without any milk being available. The baby monkeys showed preference for the fur 'mother', attaching themselves to her as if she was real (Harlow and Zimmerman 1959).

Bowlby never dismissed the importance of food or sex, but pointed out that the instinctive behaviour patterns governing these were different, as they determined different survival needs including those of procreation.

Humans take so long to develop, in contrast to so many other animals, and the more 'civilised' and complicated the lives of humans become, so the period of time that they need protection through good Attachment tends to lengthen.

Bowlby stressed, again differently from other psychoanalysts, the importance of adolescence, both in terms of being a time when good Attachments are still needed to provide security and also for being understood as a time when losses of Attachment figures can have very severe and long-lasting effects. This certainly applies to some twins who lost their twin during their adolescence, particularly when the significance of the loss to the bereaved twin was not fully recognised. In describing how different Attachments are from Dependency Needs, Bowlby states that Attachments are always specific, they endure and are not easily abandoned. The pursuit of them continues, though it may change and become supplemented as people grow older and lose earlier Attachment figures. He also made clear that some people's major Attachment behaviour may be directed towards the groups or institutions that they belong to, but he suggested that in these instances there is generally a specific person who acts as the 'head', carrying the role of the Attachment figure.

In summary, Bowlby believed that our Attachments engage us in the most intense emotions during their formation (falling in love) and in their steady maintenance (loving), and that their disruption, or threat of disruption, causes our deepest fears, anxiety and anger. When Attachments are renewed, they bring us joy and their unchallenged maintenance make us feel secure.

This leads on to Bowlby's main thesis, that whether a child or adult is in a state of security or anxiety and distress is *in large part* due to the accessibility and responsiveness of their principal Attachment figures. Bowlby ultimately came to describe four stages of mourning that the person goes through following the loss of an Attachment figure. These are not distinctly separate, but rather overlap and at times may recur, but can be distinguished from each other. The first is numbness, which is relatively short-lived. This may be interrupted by bursts of intense distress and/or anger. The second is one of yearning and searching for the lost figure which can last from some months to many years. The third stage is one of disorganisation and despair as the person realises the lost figure is not returning. Finally, the fourth stage brings some measure of reorganisation. From this stage may come an ability to relate again and to find ways of coming to terms with the loss. Bowlby believed that this comes about only through 'healthy mourning' which occurs when individuals can express their grief over a period of time and have it fully heard and recognised. If this process is blocked and the urge to recover the lost Attachment figure and feelings of reproach remain uppermost, then the person is caught in 'pathological mourning', unable to move on. Sometimes a person becomes completely 'detached' through too many losses, or by experiencing a loss so deeply, with no ameliorating factors, that he or she may develop severe emotional problems and become incapable of making Attachments of any kind later in life. Detachment does not occur in those who have never been Attached in the first place. Both responses of 'moving on' and becoming more seriously detached have occurred in some lone twins.

One other area of difference between Bowlby and Freud that is important to recognise is that Freud perceived 'spoilt children', that is children who were experienced by adults as very demanding, as being made so due to their having had too much libidinal satisfaction. Bowlby's observations led him to come to the opposite conclusion, that demanding children are those who feel insecure because of failures in Attachment. They have felt unsure about being loved and valued, or had inconsistent parenting, which has left them with their security needs insufficiently met.

Many years ago when small children were not allowed to be visited by their parents while in hospital, their mothers sometimes described them on returning home, as having been 'spoilt' by the nurses. These children often were very demanding of their mother's attention. I spent many hours with such mothers helping them to appreciate that their children were in fact suffering from separation anxiety and that far from being 'spoilt' by too much attention, they were deeply in need of reassurance that they would not be separated again (Woodward 1978).

Throughout his life Bowlby faced opposition from psychoanalytical colleagues. Unfortunately, he also faced a lot of opposition from women, as his theories gradually became more widely available in a more popular form (Bowlby 1965). In the 1960s and 1970s, as women were struggling through the growth of the Women's Movement to bring about change in their lives and to find ways of working outside the home, some of them misread Bowlby's message about the importance of the early mother-child relationship, as meaning that he proposed all mothers should stay with their children all the time. This led to the spread of a distorted message in a way that did a lot of damage, though their fears were very understandable at the time. Bowlby actually made it clear that he believed the way Attachment behaviour is reinforced is through the child's carer (mother, father or other adult) responding to the child's *social advances*. It is *not routine care* that is important. I believe that insufficient emphasis has been placed on this. There is no doubt that he was a man of his time and he did find it difficult to believe that men were as fully capable as women of responding emotionally to the needs of young children. Attitudes have changed since then and the idea of men playing a far greater role in the lives of their young children is slowly gaining ground. Some valuable thinking on this subject has been set out by two psychotherapists who describe themselves as feminists and acknowledge the valuable contribution that Attachment Theory has made to their practice (Brave and Ferid 1990).

ATTACHMENT THERAPY

Throughout his writings, Bowlby showed consistently how Attachment Theory could be applied in therapy. He started with his basic belief that therapists need to recognise that the symptoms of Separation Anxiety, which include depression, all kinds of fears and feelings of inadequacy, as well as those of extreme anger and violence, are due to *real experiences of loss* arising from insufficient Attachment in infancy, childhood or adolescence. When clients come to recognise this, it helps them gradually to stop blaming themselves for their symptoms and, in turn, it makes them less likely to engage in further self-harming or more general self-defeating behaviours.

Bowlby also believed that therapists need to be aware that an individual's susceptibility to respond to anxiety whenever he or she meets a potentially alarming situation, is based on the person's forecast or expectation of the probable availability of their Attachment figures. He emphasised that this 'working model' that we all hold is based on our actual experiences over many years and that without therapeutic intervention they tend to remain relatively unchanged. Because feelings of insufficient security in early life are so common, the therapist's priority must be to offer a 'Secure Base' to their clients. How this is done and whether it is purely the therapist's concept, rather than that of the client, is absolutely crucial. There is no doubt that many people who have suffered Attachment failures in their early lives will test out again and again the Secure Base offered by their therapist, to see just how secure or valid it really is.

The purpose of offering a Secure Base is to give the clients the opportunity of a unique Attachment experience, so that they may discover within themselves a sense of their own worth and feel sufficiently valued and respected so that they can develop a feeling of being a worthwhile person in their own right, in spite of earlier Attachment failures. This new sense of their own true identity and the recognition of their own strengths and acceptable weaknesses leads to their feeling able slowly to make other Attachments, which in turn confirm a more real sense of self, in place of the bad or helpless person they perceived themselves to be before.

How all these changes occur in therapy is a complex matter and different therapists hold different views on this. Bowlby stresses that three elements in particular are needed. The first he describes as 'joining the client'. This means making the client feel that the therapist is really with him or her in sympathy, in understanding and in a real sense on their side. In the language of classical analysis it would be described as forming a 'therapeutic alliance'.

I believe that what lies at the heart of Attachment Therapy, is the wish on the part of the therapist to diminish, without denying the existence of, the power differential between the therapist and client. This means doing everything possible never to take advantage of the client or belittle the client's feelings by lack of respect. This is achieved by the second element of forming a genuine relationship with the client. Bowlby goes to the length of stating that unless a therapist is prepared to enter into this, no progress can be expected. This he considers is especially so for people whose parents have persistently simulated affection, to cover actual deep-seated rejection. A genuine relationship does not mean that the therapist unburdens his or her concerns on to the client, but that he or she is honest and open in attitude and does not apply different rules to the client from those applied to him- or herself. The third element is that all decisions as regards how best to construe a situation and what action is best taken, *have to be the client's,* but given help and support the therapist needs to show that he or she believes the client capable of making them. This is particularly true when clients risk taking new steps, or manage to behave more positively than they have felt able to previously.

Bowlby also believed that therapeutic change can only be expected after individuals have become emotionally aware of how and what they are *feeling*. Therapy cannot be a purely intellectual or cognitive experience. He thinks that there is a danger of some therapists thinking that *their* recognition of their client's feelings is enough. Therapist and client need to see together, in a supportive way, what the client's feelings *are* and, above all, what they lead the client to *do*. If, for example, they feel afraid, does this tend to make them withdraw, or to 'attack', and so on.

Bowlby, like other psychoanalysts and many dynamic psychotherapists, believed it was important to help the client to see that the responses and situations that they typically get into *include what is happening between themselves and the therapist*. This can lead to an understanding of these in terms of their experiences with their earliest Attachment figures. For some, these experiences may still be continuing. If they experienced their parents as abandoning them, or never really being there for them emotionally, the person is likely to experience breaks in therapy as very threatening and will constantly be expecting the therapist to let them down. These supersensitive reactions will be acted out in the therapy sessions, but provided the therapist does not take it personally, or retaliate in any way and enables such reactions to be openly discussed, profound changes can occur. This is due to the original feelings being relived, as the person experiences the pain of the early Attachment failures and slowly lets go of the blame for them. All babies and children, unless they are seriously brain damaged, are capable of Attachment behaviour. If Attachments have failed, it is due to the inability on the part of their carers to engage in Attachment behaviour with the child. This may in turn be due to their own histories of Attachment failures.

Unlike some other psychoanalysts, Bowlby thought therapy should begin with the present, so that individuals can see how they tend to respond to particular types of interpersonal situations in a self-defeating way. Expressing their feelings and their expectations leads them to memories of experiences from the past and they see for themselves the persuasive influence these exert in the present. Bowlby is one of the few therapists who not only emphasised the importance of getting into touch with actual experiences, but stressed how much people need help and support in *recovering these memories*. He thought it was very understandable that people do not want to uncover very frightening events; they want to forget them. All the feelings of despair and anger connected with loss are often so strong that huge defensive processes have been at work to stop the person recognising, or even recalling such painful events. I believe that most people can only do this in small amounts and only if they feel sufficiently supported by their therapist to embark on it.

Bowlby considered the yearning for love and to be cared for, experienced by so many people, particularly those seeking therapy, need to be seen by both them and their therapists as a yearning that is not 'babyish', but due to a failure in their early life of the Attachments that they *should have had,* but were not made available to them. In the next chapter I want to describe the work of two other courageous therapists whose understanding of human development adds further dimensions to Attachment Theory, and also some valuable ways of conducting therapy, that are relevant to the experience of loss occurring at any stage of life.

8
THE CONTRIBUTIONS OF
ALICE MILLER AND JEAN BAKER MILLER

INTRODUCTION

Although my original background has been that of classical Freudian psychoanalysis and some formal training in conventional psychiatry, as mentioned in Chapter I, I have come to the conclusion that, overall, neither of these theoretical frameworks has much to offer ordinary people who are suffering from a deep sense of loss. No doubt there are some exceptional individual practioners with training and backgrounds in both fields who, due to their own experiences, have the capacity to work well with some clients. More important is the fact that a few such individuals have formulated profoundly different ways of working therapeutically to help people overcome severe loss experiences. Along with John Bowlby, Alice Miller and Jean Baker Miller are two outstanding examples of such individuals. I believe that their theoretical frameworks contribute a great deal to furthering our understanding of the ways our early upbringing and our life experiences affect how we feel about ourselves. This in turn largely determines how we operate in the world. I have found that their views, added to those of Bowlby, form a very convincing theoretical base for me to work with as a psychotherapist.

ALICE MILLER

Alice Miller was born in Poland, but has spent most of her life in Switzerland. She gained a doctorate in philosophy, but moved on to engage in a lengthy classical psychoanalysis which led her both to practise and to teach it. Like Bowlby, she took a long time to formulate her theories about human development, which led her to very specific conclusions about the causes of violence and mental illness and to her eventual rejection of psychoanalysis altogether, as a valid method of therapy. This resulted in her being personally ostracised and her views being inevitably strongly rejected by the Psychoanalytical Establishment. Unfortunately, her rejection of psychoanalysis has been so extreme that it has been perceived by many practitioners as going 'too far' in the opposite direction. I find it hard to believe that she did not help many of her patients while working as a psychoanalyst and perhaps she gained more than she has been prepared to admit from her own psychoanalytic training. There is also a good deal of evidence that some psychoanalysis has been of tremendous help to some people. Two well-known autobiographies (Green 1964; Cardinal 1993) have provided vivid accounts of the authors' beneficial experiences of analysis and both books became best-sellers. Apart from Alice Miller's criticism, which holds some validity for me, psychoanalysis demands enormous commitment, is very expensive and takes too long, for it ever to be a valid method of therapy, except for a very small number of people. Because of her extreme views the rejection she experienced was far more severe than anything experienced by Bowlby, but it led her to withdraw from the scene of therapy, to become largely reclusive and to devote her time to writing.

In order to appreciate Alice Miller's work, it needs to be viewed historically. She has written seven quite remarkable books. In her first two, *The Drama of Being a Child* (1983a) and *For Your Own Good: The Roots of Violence in Child Rearing* (1983b), she is still influenced by psychoanalysis. In her following books, *Thou Shalt Not Be Aware: Society's Betrayal of the Child* (1984), *Pictures of a Childhood* (1986), and *The Untouched Key: Tracing Childhood Trauma in Creativity and Destructiveness* (1990a) and her last two books, *Banished Knowledge: Facing Childhood Injuries* (1990b) and *Breaking Down the Wall of Silence: To Join the Waiting Child* (1991), she writes with ever increasing emphasis about the destructive outcome of the mistreatment of children and very strongly against psychoanalysis, turning instead towards the teaching of Stettbacher (1990).

Just as Bowlby came to his conclusions by observing the interaction between mothers and babies, so Alice Miller turned first to observe herself in 1973 through free painting, in a way that she had never been able to do through her many years of analysis. She believed that it was through these paintings that she gained access to the 'undisturbed reality of her childhood'. In her later books, she examines in great detail the early lives of many famous people, including dictators: Hitler and Ceausescu, artists including Picasso and Buster Keaton and the philosopher Nietzsche.

From her own paintings she realised not only that her very cold mother had been cruel to her, but that as a little child Alice had been terrified of her and totally unable to express any form of anger or protest, because that only led to more punishment. She realised that all these feelings of hers had been repressed, that is to say, pushed out of her awareness, and the actual process of idealising her mother and taking the blame for being a bad child, was part of the way she had kept her 'truth' at bay. She felt that this very process was endorsed during her analysis, which led her to be 'locked in' to a denial of her experiences.

Her father witnessed much of what went on, but never intervened. This led her to see that rejection, emotional abuse and failure by parents to make children feel loved and wanted, creates an *untenable* situation for children. Knowledge of this has to be repressed for the survival of the child's psyche. I believe this fact, described in virtually all Alice Miller's later books, makes absolute sense, *when it is understood in terms of Attachment Theory*. Children will go to almost any length to try and maintain Attachment, because this is a need that is *biologically* determined to secure their survival. This, for me, is the only satisfactory explanation for the *tenacity* with which adults continue to hold on to what are often very distressing patterns of behaviour, set up in childhood both to achieve and to maintain Attachment in the most adverse circumstances. It also explains why these behaviour patterns are so hard to 'let go' and why so much courage is needed to work at finding ways to do so.

From her own experience Alice Miller came to believe that children only need what she describes as 'one enlightened witness' to believe in them and stand up for them, for children to be able to hold on to the truth of their feelings. She believes that when this does occur, it frees children from the dire outcome of having to repress the knowledge of their mistreatment. Alice Miller never had a single enlightened witness during her childhood to hear her truths.

This concept of an enlightened witness has something in common with Bowlby's idea of a Secure Base, as he believed this must be offered to the adult in therapy, who still has the 'emotionally deprived child within'. Put differently, it means that for adults who have experienced a very low level of Attachment, leaving them with a poor sense of their own worth, the Secure Base can enable their truth to be heard, just as the enlightened witness can do for the child.

Alice Miller moved from observing herself, and how her parents' treatment had affected her, to observing the way many other parents treated their children. In *Banished Knowledge* and *For Your Own Good*, she describes very movingly some examples of children seeking what Bowlby would describe as Attachment, and failing to find it. She describes some apparently caring parents responding in a very teasing way to their small boy, who wants a share of their ice cream and is presented with the empty stick. She also describes very fully a severe example of parental cruelty that a girl endured, which led to very serious self-destructive behaviour.

The more Alice Miller observed parents with their children, the more convinced she became that violent and cruel behaviours were commonplace. She believed that this was so, because they were disguised within parental rights and seen as acceptable. Widespread physical abuse was perceived as good for the child. This perception is both exposed and challenged even by the title of her book, *For Your Own Good: The Roots of Violence in Child Rearing.*

Another concept that Alice Miller writes about is that of 'poisonous pedagogue', which simply means, deadly or dangerous teaching. She considers this to be used authoritatively by many adults in response to children, as though the adult always knows best. This keeps children helpless and unable to acknowledge the truth of their own feelings.

As Alice Miller developed her theories more clearly, she met the problem of moving so far away from the thinking in her early books, that when they came to be reprinted she contemplated trying to change the text. She realised this was impossible and instead wrote a new preface for *For Your Own Good,* which enabled her readers to understand the very different position she had reached. In *Banished Knowledge* she devotes a whole chapter to explaining why she rejects psychoanalysis as a method of therapy. She perceives that the patient lying on the couch, with the analyst sitting unseen on the chair, as the expert holding all the knowledge about the patient, is too like a repetition of the child's experience of the poisonous pedagogue of the all-knowing parent. She also believes that the method of 'free association' used in psychoanalysis exposes the patient's unconscious thoughts to the analyst, which in her view simply exacerbates the power differential between them and leaves the patient talking *about* feelings, but not free actually to *express* them.

In *The Drama of Being a Child,* Alice Miller suggests that there is only one enduring weapon in our struggle against mental illness and that is the emotional discovery and acceptance of the truth within the individual and unique history of our childhood. She uses the word 'truth' in opposition to a concept of pretence, denial or illusion and, like Bowlby, she too acknowledges the pain and struggle involved in therapy, when recalling some of the actual experiences of childhood. She believes that seeing this truth always produces more pain, but it eventually leads to a new sphere of freedom. She sees this as freedom from the false idealising of the experience of mother love. She goes on to emphasise the deep extent of loneliness, and feelings of desertion that occur for many children; not just those brought up in very traumatic or necessarily uncaring families, but rather in ordinary ones.

She has experienced such families producing adults who are at times quite severely depressed. They may be people who are high achievers, admired and envied and yet they suffer feelings of emptiness, sometimes self-alienation and feel at times that life holds no meaning for them. They often suffer from anxiety, guilt and shame. She goes on to describe how, when individuals who are feeling depressed come to therapy and are able to express anger, they may leave with their depression lifted, having been able to express real, deep feelings not previously allowed to be shown. Often she says such people will tend to re-create a situation that plunges them back into depression again, as they feel compelled to re-create their old pattern, whatever it may be, of having to meet their parents' demands. They must be 'sensible' or 'work hard' or feel driven to 'take care' of somebody and, in doing so, deny their own needs. If these needs do arise consciously, they are perceived as wrong or bad, in some way. This understanding is of great importance for those twins who strive to respond to parental messages that require them to 'live for two' or to live as if they were of little consequence in comparison to the twin that has died.

This description is similar to Bowlby's of children who have failed to get good Attachment, seeking it through 'parenting the parent'. Such children strive to meet the parent's needs rather than their own and fear rejection or some punishment if they protest. Because they have experienced so many times *not having their emotional needs met*, rather than face the unbearable agony of this, even the desire for it tends to be pushed out of awareness.

Alice Miller and Bowlby share the same view that children who have been wanted, loved and fully respected, will grow up mentally healthy. As she writes in *Banished Knowledge,* a child who is not injured or abused can tell or show his or her mother when she enrages or hurts him or her. If children have been loved and respected they will never need to abuse themselves or anyone else. She makes it clear that she believes abused people do not necessarily abuse others, but that those who do will always have suffered some abuse that they have had to push out of their awareness as too intolerable to remember.

Over the years that Alice Miller has been writing, she has received very many letters from readers, thanking her for understanding their situation and deeply appreciating her work. Nowadays, she sends out a summary of her views in twelve points. These coincide very closely with many of Bowlby's. The most fundamental view that she holds, is that children need the respect and protection of adults who take them seriously, love them and honestly try to help them become oriented in the world. This is a good description of what Bowlby would define as good Attachment, provided it is offered in ways that are appropriate to meet the baby's, child's and adolescent's needs. When these vital needs are frustrated and children are abused for the sake of adults' needs, by being exploited, or beaten, punished, taken advantage of, neglected or deceived, without the *intervention* of any witness, Alice Miller believes that the child's integrity will be lastingly impaired. I believe that she means by this, that their sense of self is damaged. She goes on to state that if someone is dissociated from the original cause of their anger, helplessness, despair, longing and pain, they will ultimately find expression in destructive acts against others, or towards themselves, in drug addiction, alcoholism, prostitution, psychic disorder or suicide.

When such people become adults, they sometimes direct acts of revenge for the mistreatments in their childhood against their own children, whom they use as scapegoats. This perpetuates the child abuse which she insists is still in many cases sanctioned as child rearing. She believes that if mistreated children are not to become mentally ill or delinquent in behaviour, they must come into contact with at least one person who knows without any doubt, that the *environment* and not the helpless battered child is at fault. She says that here lies the great opportunity for relatives and professionals alike, to support the child and believe in him or her. To some extent Bowlby endorses this view in stressing the need to listen to and believe in the child's experiences.

Alice Miller emphasises that though this knowledge of painful experiences may remain unconscious (that is, out of the person's awareness), it still exerts its influence in adult life and that such experiences are stored up in the body. She states that there is plenty of research evidence to support the fact that 'responses to both tenderness and cruelty start at the foetal stage of existence'. I believe this is of particular significance for twins, as it could possibly determine how they respond to each other before they are born, as well as afterwards.

She believes that even the most bizarre kinds of behaviours in adults can make sense once the traumatic experiences of childhood are revealed. I have certainly found this to be true for many clients with whom I have worked. In the last of her summarised points, she expresses her most controversial view that if society could become sensitised to the cruel ways in which children are treated, instead of denying it, as happens so frequently, there would be an end to violence from generation to generation. From this belief she moves to a macro scale of envisaging people whose integrity has not been damaged and states that they would be intelligent, responsive, empathic and highly sensitive, taking pleasure in life, using their power only to protect themselves and those weaker than them, including their children, because they will not be able to do otherwise, as this is what they will have learned from their own experience. Such people in generations to come, will be incapable of understanding why earlier generations had to build up gigantic war industries in order to feel safe.

Alice Miller has met such criticism of her theories that it seems important to make clear that when she writes about the vital need of children to have their emotional needs met, she does not mean that children should be raised without restraint. She lists what she thinks is needed:

1. Respect for the child
2. Respect for his or her rights
3. Tolerance for his or her feelings
4. Willingness by the parent to learn about the nature of the individual child
5. To learn about the 'child' in the parents themselves
6. To learn about the nature of emotional life

She admits that centuries of constraints of children can scarcely be expected to change in a single generation.

Therapy

Like Bowlby, Alice Miller uses the understanding she gained from observations of herself, as well as many others, to formulate her views on the kind of therapy that she considers helpful for people who have had traumatic experiences in life, leaving them with feelings of loss, despair and self-destructive patterns of behaviour.

She lays out clearly in *Banished Knowledge,* (1990b: 179) the four steps she believes that need to occur in therapy, based on the teachings of Stettbacher (1990). This may seem somewhat simplistic but all therapists and those who have undergone long-term therapy know just how complicated it can be to enable people to change to more constructive ways of viewing themselves when they have a long history of emotional neglect, rejection or abuse.

The first stage she says is 'describing the situation and one's sensations'. This again may sound simple and obvious, but it can take a long time to do and be very painful. The second stage is 'expressing and experiencing emotions'. This essential need to relive one's feelings has already been described by Bowlby as essential for any change to occur, and Alice Miller agrees with this. The third stage is described as 'querying the situation'. This is the only description of Alice Miller's that I have found unclear. Using the word 'querying' sounds superficial, but she leaves us in no doubt about how important she considers this stage to be. It actually entails *challenging* what has happened during childhood and the person concerned being able to let go the concept of being to blame.

At this stage, the client is facing the fact that the emotional deprivation, the demands and possibly the cruelty that they have experienced *should not have happened.* This removes the need to forgive the parent that Alice Miller sees as a concept beloved by psychoanalysts. She thinks, as Bowlby did, that understanding the parents' behaviour in terms of their inability to provide the emotional caring that was needed, being due in turn to *their* emotional deprivation as children, is enormously important. This is because they too can be seen as victims and the mourning can be done for both.

The fourth and final stage is described as 'articulating needs'. This too may sound simple and obvious, but many people have never been allowed to express any such thoughts, so they do not even know what their needs are. I believe articulating needs is just the start and people need a great deal of encouragement and support to discover how to put them into practice. This may mean that individuals who have been driven to be 'ill' or 'inadequate' in an attempt to be cared for, can move on to discover their real capacities and find pleasure in achievement. For someone else, they may have had to be 'invincible' to show that whatever was done to them, had to be perceived as 'not hurting'. When they begin to express their needs, it becomes possible to discover that denying their real feelings is no longer necessary. For others who have felt compulsively driven to care for someone, they too may discover they are lovable, even if they cease always to put the needs of others first. Alice Miller stresses again and again that therapy offers the opportunity for these patterns to change slowly, step by step, and that changes can never be forced or rushed.

Perhaps one of the most important issues to address is why so many thousands of ordinary people have read Alice Miller's books and found them describing a very accurate account of their experiences, yet they have had so little impact on the Establishment – the people who have the powers to legislate and direct policies. I believe this is because in general terms people in this country do not like children. If any readers disagree with this, I would ask them to travel in any bus or train, or go into any supermarket and listen to the way many parents address their children. They are frequently slapped, threatened or shouted at. In the Court Report (1976), set up to recommend ways of improving children's health, it states that 'children have special needs which they cannot articulate for themselves and that society therefore has a duty to ensure that these are identified and cogently represented'. Sadly, like so many reports, very few of its recommendations were accepted.

Professor Court spoke despairingly of giving up on a campaign he strongly championed, of trying to get some carriages on long-distance trains to offer facilities for mothers to breast-feed and change their babies. This is only one small example, but it shows how, in our society, commercial interests tend to take priority over the needs of children. Juan Calvo-Sotelo (1996) goes even further in suggesting that hidden within some forms of psychotherapy, there is evidence of the 'hatred of children'. All this does not mean that there are not many loving and deeply caring parents about as well, who take their role of parenting very seriously, who bring up well-balanced and mentally healthy children.

When Alice Miller addressed the idea of whether there could be 'harmless pedagogue', she came to the conclusion that so much 'training' of children is harmful, because it tends to hide the fact that so much of it *meets the needs of adults*. She thinks this not only discourages the child's development, but actually prevents it. When children are 'trained', she says that they learn how to 'train' others in their turn. Children who are 'lectured' learn how to lecture; if admonished, scolded, ridiculed or humiliated – how to do these things to others. She writes at the end of her twelve points, that if worst of all children's psyches are 'killed' they will learn how to 'kill'. The only question is *who* will be killed – themselves, others or both. This very chilling message could not be spelled out more clearly and seems today to have a deeper significance than ever. Stories of adults, described as 'loners' and 'misfits', killing children and even children killing other children younger than themselves in appalling circumstances, are no longer rarities. These tragic events, when made public, lead to people crying out for vengeance instead of looking seriously for causes and addressing the very complex issues of how to bring about change.

I believe that Alice Miller would acknowledge that the dislike of children that is so often reflected in the way they are treated publicly, as troublesome and a nuisance, is the strongest evidence of the repressed pain from our own childhoods projected on to children in general, who act as unconscious reminders of childhood suffering.

Although some experienced professionals have been working for years to put Alice Miller's theories into practice, her basic message is still largely ignored. I believe this is because it is seen fundamentally as subversive but it at least offers a way to begin working on breaking the vicious circle of violence and abuse which is currently so disturbingly on the increase. This seems to me the most important issue that, as human beings, we need to address with urgency.

JEAN BAKER MILLER

Introduction

I first knew of Jean Baker Miller's work in the mid-1970s, when the first book that she edited was published, *Psychoanalysis and Women* (1973). This was a collection of papers by well-known contributors such as Alfred Adler, Karen Horney and Clara Thompson. They deeply challenged some of the concepts about women's development that were widely held by many classical psychoanalysts at the time.

This was the first book that enabled me seriously to question the 'brainwashing' that I had experienced during my training, concerning women's development and sexuality. When I read her second book, *Toward a New Psychology of Women* (1976), I experienced a strong sense of excitement. Even though in some sense I already 'knew' what she was writing about, I had never before met it expressed so accurately and clearly. I felt here at last was a real understanding of human development that explained so many of my feelings and those of my clients.

Since the 1970s Jean Baker Miller has played a leading role in the Stone Center at Wellesley College in Boston, Massachusetts, formulating 'The Relational Theory', and has now set up a training centre. In her striking paper 'The Development of Women's Sense of Self' (1984) she describes her early formulations of 'Relational Theory'. This has been enormously extended since, both by her and by her many colleagues. Seventeen of the early papers have been collected into a book entitled *Women's Growth in Connection* (Jordan et al. 1991).

In some respects this theory has similarities with Attachment Theory, as it too proclaims that humans have a fundamental need for what Baker Miller calls 'Connection'. Unlike Bowlby and Alice Miller, who ignore the issue of gender, Baker Miller shows that in patriarchal societies it is *societal* forces that play a large part in determining the very different ways that men and women develop psychologically. These differences tend to shape a great deal of how we all feel about ourselves and they affect us throughout our lives. Some of the twins' stories illustrate this clearly.

Baker Miller's work shows how, in western society, very strong forces are at work that distort not only the way people relate, or as she puts it 'Connect' with each other, but the vital need for 'Connections' is generally devalued. She has coined some useful words to recognise the different ways that people relate. She uses the word 'Connect' when referring to ways of relating that are *mutually enhancing*. When this does not occur and the relationship is mainly for the benefit of one person, she describes it as a 'Disconnection'. When there is an imbalance of power with a serious negative outcome, she describes it as a 'Violation'. She describes these in detail in her paper entitled 'Connections, Disconnections and Violations' (1988).

Although all three of the theorists whose work I have attempted to summarise in this book have met some form of rejection by their psychoanalytical and psychiatric colleagues, Baker Miller responded to it very differently from Alice Miller. She and her colleagues have focused on certain aspects of psychoanalytical theory, created in the main by male theorists, which they consider falsify women's own experiences. Far from withdrawing, Baker Miller has attracted around her a group of women of very high calibre, who both practise and teach in the fields of mental health. In the process of developing Relational/Cultural Theory, they have studied and written on many aspects of women's and men's roles in society and have shown how deeply sexism and racism affect our 'sense of self' and so our mental health, which makes their papers extremely relevant to therapists.

Baker Miller and her colleagues have proposed new ways of working on resolving conflict. They show how this can be done with individuals, as well as in groups and very importantly within the therapeutic relationship. Baker Miller has never produced any bland ideas, or suggested that conflict should be avoided; on the contrary, she sees it as holding the genesis of change. She believes that if it is faced with courage and with the purpose of understanding the elements within it, these can be worked on and the conflict resolved.

Baker Miller describes how the way many men have been brought up to reject and deny the importance of feelings, especially those to do with emotional connections and vulnerabilities, has led to women being the carriers of these aspects of human experiences. Eichenbaum and Orbach elaborate on this too, in *What Do Women Want?* (1983). Feelings of vulnerability tend to become areas seen by men as those they must have mastery over and they fear that they will be reduced to some undifferentiated state of weakness, emotional attachment and lose the long sought-after and fought-for status of manhood. She believes that this threat is the deepest one that the notion of equality poses for men, because they erroneously perceive it not as equality for them, but rather as a total stripping of the person.

Baker Miller emphasises how we all experience vulnerability, weakness and feelings of neediness, partly due to our long maturation process and the lack of support that most of us suffer, both in childhood and adult life. She considers that as men are encouraged to deny such feelings, women are pressed to cultivate them. This results in the psychological strength that women gain through acknowledging, expressing and carrying these feelings, in spite of this not being recognised. Women are driven to be the givers of most of this caring and of meeting the emotional needs of others, but they can often feel resentful at having to carry this burden so they tend to fear not giving enough and feeling a failure in this respect. Men have quite a different self-image based on *doing*. The problematic aspect of this for women, Baker Miller believes, is due to the fact that women's activity is seen as passive, because it is rarely in pursuit of meeting their own goals.

Baker Miller does not decry serving others, she sees it as an essential human task, but she stresses that when women are brought up to believe that they can use all their attributes only if they use them for others, but not themselves, it can lead to the martyr syndrome or the smothering mother. On the positive side, women have an ability to recognise and respond to others' needs well. It only goes wrong if doing so detracts from women's sense of identity and they feel forced in some way into serving others and having no way of getting their own needs met.

The concept of *simultaneous* 'self-development' and 'service to others' she believes is a relatively new one. It produces such a sharp conflict for men that they rarely attempt it. Women have been trying to do so but without men doing so too, which is what in Baker Miller's view has led many women today to carry intolerable burdens. She describes how some women come to believe that others will love them and become permanently devoted to them, because they serve them so well. The tragedy of this is that men and children can become so dependent on services that they feel trapped by their dependency. This can become a reason for men sometimes neglecting or even walking out on 'super wives' or 'super mothers'.

What Baker Miller shows is a very complex notion, that in our patriarchal society the very structuring of the relationship to other people is basically different for men and for women. She asks who has declared what is 'masculine' and 'feminine', for it is these formulations that reflect the whole dichotomy of the essentials of human existence. The book ends with a plea similar in some ways to that of Bowlby, which is the urgent need for humans to move towards valuing affiliation, that is, making 'Connections', because she believes, as Bowlby does too, that men and women's individual development only proceeds by means of 'Connection'. She acknowledges that at present, men are not prepared to give this proper recognition. The ability to 'Connect' needs to be more highly valued than a way of life based on self-enhancement, gained at the expense of others. Unfortunately, the characteristics of women do not help them to 'make it' in the world as it is constructed at present. In fact, as she states, the very characteristics like 'participating in the development of others' are specifically dysfunctional for success but it is these characteristics that are really important ones for making the world a different and better place. Women now need to seek power to make changes and to do this they will have to face conflict to get these characteristics valued and seen as leading to a way of engaging with each other, which in turn could lead to the development of us all to our full potential as human beings.

Relational/Cultural Therapy

Baker Miller and her colleagues at the Stone Center have built up a comprehensive understanding of how, differently, both men and women suffer psychologically from the inequalities imposed by a patriarchal society. From the time when her first paper, 'Women and Power' (1982), was presented, she and her colleagues have continued to develop and write about ways that Relational/Cultural Theory can be applied in therapy. She states in 'Connections, Disconnections and Violations' (1988) that 'historically our central formative relationships have not been founded on the basis of mutuality nor have we had a societal situation based on a search for full mutuality'. As major theories inevitably reflect the societal situation, so she points out that psychological theories have inevitably focused on a line of human development which is cast in terms of a series of psychological separations from others.

At the heart of Relational Therapy lies the way in which the therapist and client are able to have a high degree of mutual engagement. This is only possible when the therapist is experienced by the client as giving close attention. Such attention can then enable mutual empathy to develop. J.L. Surrey, in her section of the paper 'Some Misconceptions and Reconceptions of a Relational Approach' (1991), writes clearly that 'mutuality' in therapy does not mean equality, sameness or a simplistic notion of mutual personal disclosure. She explains with great care that any disclosure by the therapist must be based on her decision about whether this will help to move the relationship toward expanded connection.

As Baker Miller and J.P. Stiver state in their joint paper 'A Relational Reframing of Therapy' (1991), they believe that people can only begin to risk moving out of what she describes as disconnection if the therapist creates an empathic and responsive relational context, not if the therapist is distant and affectively neutral. The aim of 'mutual empowerment' is where Baker Miller and her colleagues differ most profoundly from the psychoanalytical concept of Object Relations described earlier, as this carries the notion of seeking gratification only through the 'Object' or other person. In contrast to this, Relational/Cultural Therapy emphasises the need for people to participate in 'Connections' which mutually empower each other. In brief, the better the connection a therapist and client can make together, the greater the sense of development and achievement that occurs for both. In the same paper, they say, 'what we are always seeking in therapy is change, *movement*, out of isolation and/or suffering, to empowerment and fulfilment'.

Relational Therapy as developed by Baker Miller and her colleagues is not limited to individual therapy with women. It can also be applied to groups. Fedele and Harrington (1990), in their paper, show how validating painful experiences can heal the distress suffered through 'Disconnections' and 'Violations'. One of the most challenging Work in Progress Papers (Fedele and Baker Miller 1988) shows how Relational Therapy can be put into practice in the most formally run mental health institutions. This is done by introducing the idea of women completing assessments that list their own perceptions of their 'strengths' and 'needs'. This is very different from defining women in terms of their pathology. Such radical thinking was found to bring about change in staff attitudes too, which in turn leads on to their planning relational structures for their patients at the time of discharge. This makes it less likely for them to return to the very situation in which the mental health problem existed before.

It is rare to find the issue of gender given proper recognition within the 'Attachment Model', though Bea Campbell does so in her chapter in *The Politics of Attachment* (Campbell 1996). What perhaps is most important of all, is to appreciate that research studies referred to by Kaplan (1982) all conclude that the relational qualities between client and therapist are more closely related to outcome than are any particular clinical skills and specific techniques. (See Gurman 1977, Bergin and Lambert 1978, Dent 1978 and Orlinsky and Howard 1980.)

9
WHEN DOES MEMORY BEGIN

This is a question that lies at the heart of opposing viewpoints. It is one of particular interest to the Lone Twin Network as it needs to define 'A Lone Twin' for its membership. So far this has been defined as 'someone who has lost their twin through death at any stage in life'. The application form requests some reasonably objective proof that another twin, apart from the survivor once existed. Problems arise for a few people who perceive themselves as 'lone twins' but who have no objective proof. The Network has tried to remain open minded on the subject and a few 'lone twins' completely convinced that they have lost their twin very early in conception have been allowed to join. The crux of the issue is what 'evidence' is acceptable to the Network. At present the criteria for membership remain unresolved because those members dealing with it have felt reluctant to take a 'hard line' over such a sensitive matter.

Althea Hayton, who perceives herself as a 'Womb Twin Survivor', (the very definition implying there is no objective evidence) has her own web site and has edited an anthology (Hayton 2007). She has subtitled it, 'Perspectives on the death of a twin before birth'. One of the contributors (Nick Owen p. 152) also describes himself as a 'Womb Twin Survivor'. He writes about the role of twins and twin loss in many myths and classical fairy stories and the significance of the idea of 'changelings'. Many writers including Otto Rank (Rank 1994) have written about the trauma that a birth experience can have on a person's later life. There have been many examples of this among lone twins in the Network, as it is a traumatic experience for both the mother and her live twin to have the simultaneous birth of a live and a dead baby. In these cases the existence of the lost twin is not in doubt. As I have already written in the Introduction to this Revised Edition the whole issue of membership of the Network remains unresolved. I would hope that in the future, those people who believe themselves to be 'lone twins' but with no objective evidence of loss, could feel well supported by linking up with like-minded others by contacting Althea Hayton or Nick Owen, as their web sites can easily be found.

I agree with Nick Owen, that 'birth is not the start of consciousness', but I remain unconvinced at this point, that 'personal trauma can begin at conception'. I believe that we need to look at the scientific studies that have been made into memory. These examine when 'memory' begins and what kinds of memory can be shown to exist. Daniel Siegal has a clear and carefully reasoned account of memory (Siegal 1999). He describes 'implicit' forms of memory, being those formed very early in life, based largely on touch, sound, movement and smell, experienced before a verbal account of them could be made. This form of memory he sees as vital to early learning. Their importance may well be linked with the ability to make Attachments. For example, a baby is attuned before birth to its mother's diet. This is known to the foetus in the womb and will continue to be experienced by the baby if there is breast feeding. The rhythm of her heart beat and the sound of her voice will also be familiar when the baby is born. Siegal points out that this form of memory is different from 'explicit' memory, requiring, as he puts it, 'a conscious awareness for encoding',(that means having a neural input in the brain) which produces 'a subjective sense of recollection'.

As we all know, memory is often experienced subjectively as a very strange phenomenon. We can all be surprised at times why we retain some memories so strongly and lose others. As we grow older, our current memories fade and early memories can become much more vivid, enabling us to recall memories of events we have 'forgotten' for many years. In a special edition of Developmental Review 2004 in a particular paper, (Howe and Courage 2003) write about 'Demystifying the Beginnings of Memory'. They examine at depth the question of when they consider our memory for personal experiences begins. They note different beliefs, for example that of Janov (Janov 2000) who considers like Rank, that very early experiences including pre-birth ones can 'shape a child's future mental health'. They also note that there are people who claim that they have 'memories' of a 'previous life'. These ideas raise the question about remembering our birth. Chamberlain (Chamberlain 1990 & 1998) believes that we do all have birth memories deeply embedded in our unconscious minds.

To return to the work of Howe and Courage, they state that for early memories to be encoded, stored and later retrieved, *the brain has to be sufficiently developed for these events to occur.* There is a slight difference of opinion about the timing of this ability, some thinking it only occurs in the last few weeks of foetal life and others that it is a bit earlier, for the event of some memories for example such as auditory ones. P.G. Hepper (1996) writing on foetal memory also notes many different studies. He suggests that as the foetus develops it clearly shows an ability to respond to a variety of different stimuli showing *emotional* responses to temperature, sound and touch, with later evidence of these being 'remembered' after birth. Hepper comes firmly to the conclusion that the foetus does have 'memory' but he considers it of a very rudimentary kind which develops as the individual matures. He states there are research findings that show auditory abilities occurring between 27 and 28 weeks in the pregnancy, with other more complex responses occurring by the 29th or 30th week.

This confirms for me how amazingly forward thinking Thomas Verney was (Verney 1982) whose work I referred to in the first edition of this book. He states that physiological, neurological, biochemical and psychological studies confirm that around six months of age the foetus is 'sensitive to remarkably subtle emotional nuances'. He believes that the hormone known as ACTH affects the oxytocin levels in the blood and that large quantities of it have been shown to produce loss of memory in animals. He concludes that as during labour oxytocin from the mother 'floods her child's system' it is reasonable to deduce that this may be the reason why we have no conscious memory of our birth. Even the doctors disagree, as I have already mentioned, Chamberlain disagrees with this view.

I would like to end this section with notes from a personal e-mail to me from Louis Cozolino, as he is one of the current leading writers on the subject of brain development and its connection with the mind. (Cozolino 2002) He says, that if he were to write about foetal memory, he would focus on sensory and thalamic circuits in the brain, as they have been suggested to contain genetically transmitted images of stimuli that are important to our species. He mentions for example predators. He thinks the 'presence of another' (in other words the existence of a twin) could be of importance in a social species like our own, that some sort of primitive sub-cortical representation would be stored in these systems and later developing right hemisphere circuitry. He thinks these 'memories' could direct awareness or break through into consciousness during moments of stress, intimacy, or loss in day-to-day life, or emerge during brainwave states between waking and sleeping.

This could well explain the fairly common remark made by some lone twins on being informed in a precipitous way that they 'were born a twin', who said, 'it immediately made sense to them'. This implies an awareness at a deeper level of consciousness, leaving them not altogether surprised by the information. On the other hand, some of them may well have overheard conversation that confused them at the time, as perhaps they picked up what they were 'not expected to hear'. On being *told it as a fact*, that they had a twin, they were 'allowed' to know it, could digest it and respond to it as a piece of knowledge that in some sense they already knew.

10
LONE TWINS' EXPERIENCES
OF THERAPY

INTRODUCTION

This section begins with five accounts by lone twins who have courageously described their personal experiences of therapy. They provide evidence of how many of them failed to obtain the kind of help they needed. It is a very unrepresentative group, in that they are all women and four out of the five lost their twin at birth. The fact that no male lone twin has wanted his experience of therapy to be singled out in this way may be due to the fact that men find it much harder to seek therapy in the first place, having been brought up in general to deny their feelings of vulnerability which are associated for them with being 'weak'. Women who are perceived as 'emotional' can express these feelings more readily. I am certain that men do have very similar feelings, but on the whole are more fearful of their exposure.

Story 1
A woman of fifty who lost a brother at birth
It was fifteen years ago that I went to see my GP with yet another ailment when he suggested me seeing a counsellor. I was apprehensive, yet I went, and this opened up a new world for me to experience my emotions in a safe place, to begin trusting people, learning to love myself and giving myself permission to grieve. This has been important expressing the grief for my twin brother. Not easy, as I spend a lot of time avoiding it if I can, as it is so painful. By being able to say how much I miss him, to express my anger at being left alone here in this world to fend for myself is very liberating.

I have found the therapeutic process invaluable in exploring issues concerning all of this. Taking part in a psychodrama I have been able to experience what it was like for the family as a whole to deal with the death of my twin; the unexpressed grief of my father and mother, yet still having to cope with the surviving twin – me – and to take care of me. The impact of such a birth is immense on a family. It is carried by all family members, young and old, at a deep level, yet not openly shared and grieved over in my case.

Through guided visualisation I have gone back to my conception, being in the womb with my twin, and being born together. When I entered the world in the visualisation I knew I was alone and that my twin had left me. I felt I didn't want to be here and there was an instant recognition for me in my present life with that feeling. That I struggle and feel guilty for not wanting to be here and then deny how I feel. Instead of gritting my teeth and getting on with my life saying to myself, 'Yes, I do want to be here', and yet knowing deep down I don't. It has been a releasing experience to own up to this and make the connection with my birth.

I find it difficult to write about the final piece I want to share because it may sound too maudlin, but for me it felt a joyous thing to do. I acted out the burial of my twin brother in a psychodrama session. I had been working on this heavy load I was carrying which turned out to be my twin brother. What was I going to do with him metaphorically, still carry him around with me or not – I decided to give him a loving burial and we were fortunate enough to have a hospital chaplain with us in the group. She led the prayers as we, the group, put my brother to rest. I felt many emotions doing this, fear, sadness, grief, and yet a sense of completion, of a coming together for me which felt very profound. He will always be a part of me and my existence which I will cherish always, for he has enabled me to understand myself more in a loving and accepting way.

CYNTHIA WHELAN

Story 2
A woman in her thirties who lost an identical sister at birth

THE LONE TWIN ISSUE

I have had a variety of responses to the issue of how being a lone twin has affected me. Until I started seeing my current therapist, I had hardly ever explored the impact of losing my twin sister with any of the psychiatric doctors, nurses and counsellors that I had met. In a lot of cases, the subject was not discussed at all or, when I did mention it, it was dismissed.

In the early stages of my treatment, I was not aware that losing my identical twin sister at birth had affected me. When taking my personal history, it was noted that I had had a stillborn twin sister, but after that it was not mentioned.

The first discussion of the subject occurred with the psychiatrist at the Day Unit. She asked me to draw a life line, on which I had to put key events that had happened to me. The circumstances of losing my twin at birth were raised. The psychiatrist discussed this event with me in one session and was interested in how I thought it had affected me. Ironically, I didn't think at the time that it was very important and so the subject was dropped. It still amazes me that I was drawing pictures while I was attending the Day Unit which clearly showed my pain at losing my sister, but neither I nor the psychiatric doctors and nurses noticed the connection.

Both voluntary counsellors dismissed the issue of my twin. Brenda asked me to draw pictures of my family during one session and I automatically included my twin, but she did not comment on it and was more interested in the picture of my mother. By the time I saw the Christian counsellor, I was much more in touch with my feelings about my twin, but she believed that I should forget her and concentrate on getting on with my own life and she would not discuss the matter any further.

My psychologist was sadly ignorant of lone twin issues. In every other way, I found him very helpful and supportive, but he was dismissive about my bereavement. I was even more curious at that time about whether an event at my birth could still be affecting me. Jack said that it may have done in the sense that it could have affected my mother's relationship with me, but that we would 'never really know'. We did not discuss my twin again. It is a shame that he didn't know anything about the issue of lone twins, but he had obviously not come across it before. I'm sure he would be quite amazed to hear how deeply lone twins can feel about their lost sibling. Had either of us known about the Lone Twin Network at the time, I have no doubt that he would have accepted my feelings and supported me through them.

The first private counsellor that I saw was interested in the issue of lone twins and I'm sure she would have discussed it with me further had I stayed with her. My second private counsellor had some very strange ideas about my twin. She fully accepted the significance of her loss and believed that it had affected me. But then she seemed to get caught up in her own feelings about it and pressurised me to find the cemetery where she was buried and to have a memorial service for her. At the time, I couldn't cope with doing either of these things and she became frustrated and impatient that I was not taking any of her advice. Later on, she said that she believed my sister was still around me and that she was sapping my strength and harming me. She continued to urge me to have a memorial service in order to put her spirit to rest and leave me free to get on with my own life. I was horrified that she believed my twin was hurting me and disturbed by her suggestion that she needed 'exorcising' like an evil spirit. I do not feel that my sister would ever wish to hurt me, nor I her, were it in my power to do so. It led to Rebecca telling me her doubts and fears about death in general. I felt that she was putting me last in our sessions, something that happened on more than one occasion.

As for my current therapist, she has supported me through all my feelings for my lost twin. The first thing she did was to believe that my feelings are genuine, which was a huge relief in itself. When I later felt that I did want to find the cemetery and plant a tree there, she encouraged me to follow my instincts, but she has never tried to make me do anything that I didn't feel comfortable with. She has encouraged me to express all my emotions about her death and supported me when those feelings have been intense. I do not often talk about my sister now as I feel I have made my connection with her and I am much more at peace about it all. When I do need to talk about my twin, I know that Erica will not laugh at me or tell me my feelings are imaginary or that thinking about her is bad for me. I am sure that it is through feeling safe to talk about her that I have been able to come to terms with losing my little sister.

Even when I have not talked directly about my sister with my counsellors, I am sure that being a lone twin has drastically influenced my attitude to therapy. I believe that my need for communication at a deep level is to do with me missing the opportunity that I would have had for that type of relationship with my twin. When I am unable to find good communication with a counsellor, I feel frustrated and at a loss. I try not to be unrealistic in my expectations, but I think that it is part of the reason my relationship with my first two private therapists failed. They were happy to talk about things that seemed superficial to me. They could not understand that I wanted to work at a much deeper level, even though I tried to explain that to them on several occasions, and they were shocked when I told them that I felt the therapy was getting nowhere. Neither of them ever understood the gulf that I felt existed between us. Had I not been a lone twin, I don't think I would have been quite so needy of the deep levels of communication that I want in therapy and may have felt more tolerant when understanding my feelings was not forthcoming. Having said that, I think that some of the lack of sympathy and understanding that I have experienced in therapy would have been upsetting and damaging for anyone.

I do feel that I have had the type of communication I seek with both Jack and Erica. What made the sessions with Jack so helpful was that he seemed to be able to tell what I was feeling without me having to spell it out. It was almost like telepathy at times and it made me feel safe and understood. It helped, too, when I was finding it difficult to explain how I felt.

Erica also knows instinctively what I need sometimes and I feel glad when she does. I do find, though, that she doesn't completely understand why I want that intense form of communication. She wants me to ask for what I need rather than expecting her to just 'know'. I am sure that she is right when she suggests that I have never learnt to recognise my needs or consider them important. However, I don't agree with her that this is why I don't want to have to tell people what I need. It may be part of the reason, but I think that much more important is my need for the type of empathy that I would have shared with my twin.

Occasionally, during a session with Erica, our feelings seem to merge. She feels moved to tears, I feel moved by her tears and it seems difficult to separate out whose feelings are whose. There is no need for words and we just end up hugging each other. I love those moments. They feel so safe and natural to me, as if that is how communication with other people 'should be' and I am sure that I feel that way because I am a lone twin. I would have shared moments of intermingled feelings with my sister in the womb and throughout my life, had she lived. Erica doesn't seem to feel quite as comfortable as I do with that intensity of non-verbal, empathic communication. She doesn't withdraw from me as such, but she likes to remind me empathically that it is also nice to be an individual! I just don't feel that way about it.

I find myself asking, 'What have I learnt from all this?', and 'In what way can I help others going through the same struggles?'

I suppose the most important lesson I have learnt is to recognise the power issues between the client/patient and the 'expert'. When someone seeks help, it is usually because they are feeling in need of help and support. No matter how careful the counsellor or therapist is, it is impossible to avoid the fact that they are in a stronger position than their client. A large number of the professionals I have met seem to enjoy wielding their power for their own ends. They seem to enjoy the feeling that they have all the answers and that they can reduce you to a pulp whenever they feel like it. It is all too easy, when you are feeling vulnerable and desperate, to start believing your counsellor when they tell you that you are in no position to judge what is good for you. I have a tendency to blame myself for problems in a relationship, and early on in therapy, I easily found myself thinking that the difficulties I was experiencing in the treatment were entirely my fault. It did not help that several counsellors and doctors readily confirmed my fears. When I lost the confidence to trust my own perception of reality, I lost everything and I am having to work hard at regaining that confidence. I still find it impossible to come to terms with the way that the Day Unit and four other counsellors succeeded in taking away my power and squashing any last remnants of self-respect that I had left.

At the time I had no way of knowing that therapy doesn't have to be like that. At least I am now able to fight back against people who want me to think that they know me and my needs better than I do. My current counsellor never negates my feelings. Erica accepts responsibility for herself and does not put everything down to my psychological illness. She also WANTS to discuss the relationship between us and I am sure that it is by working through our feelings about each other honestly and openly that I have made a lot of progress. It horrifies me to think that so many doctors, psychiatrists, psychologists and counsellors I have met seem to have been intent on systematically taking away from their clients all their power and feelings of self-worth. It is now my opinion that if a client is continually blamed for any difficulties they are having with the relationship, then they don't have to put up with that and they should think about getting another therapist!

ANONYMOUS

Story 3
A woman in her forties who lost a brother at birth

My first patch of clinical depression occurred in my early twenties when my parents went to Canada without me for two weeks. I also become frightened if I am with someone who loses consciousness, e.g., fainting. This to me has a lot to do with 'subconscious memories' of being in the womb with my twin after he had died and before we were born. I am left with a permanent tendency to experience almost paralysing fear and panic if anyone close to me goes away even for a week's holiday.

At thirteen I had an attack of 'school phobia'. This coincided with puberty for me and I now see what happened as a reaction to being forced to accept that in reality I was not him and me, my body was really all female. It was a crisis of identity.

After returning to school, and being labelled a nervous type, I went on to take exams like anyone else and I opted for physics and maths, which led to laboratory work. A few years later on I had my first bad patch of clinical depression and anxiety. Whilst in hospital I remember asking my psychiatrist if what I was going through could have anything to do with having a stillborn twin – he dismissed it out of hand. On returning to work I saw the company psychiatrist and asked him the same question. He described it as a 'red herring'. Because they were the 'experts', I believed them.

I then embarked on several years of Freudian psychotherapy, again because the experts recommended this, and we touched on everything except my twin, probably because it doesn't fall into the classic Freudian frame of reference, life events being related back to interactions between father and, in particular, mother, in the first few years of life, not to the circumstances around birth and before it.

Whilst I was in therapy, I had another bad patch of depression and anxiety. This coincided with my realisation that I was, and am, a gay woman. I was actually very pleased to come out to myself as it explained why I could never get emotionally close to boyfriends, and I was delighted to fall in love for the first time. But it was another shock to my identity. It could be theorised that it was the result of me still wanting to be my brother, to take on a male role – all I can say is that it doesn't feel that way to me. I feel that my sexuality belongs to me, that it is the way I have always been.

In my mid-thirties I hit another bad patch, and, having finished therapy with Freudian therapists several years before, started again with someone who was a lot more human, person-centred, who listened to me and tried to understand what I thought it was all about. I implored him to search out any papers written on the survivors of stillborn and neonatal twins. A week or two later he came back amazed, it was all there, depression, anxiety, survivor's guilt. Eureka, I was a normal surviving twin.

From then on I had the space to explore what it all meant for me – I found that at the age of thirty-five I could not bear to say that my twin was dead. I still clung to the desire to believe that he was somehow alive somewhere. It was a very painful time, but gradually I came to let go – helped a lot by my therapist finding out where Richard was buried, in a cemetery not far from where I live. It felt very odd going into an undertaker's on my own and expressing a wish to put a marble vase on a thirty-six-year-old communal grave, but I did it. The vase says 'FOR MY TWIN 4.2.52'. I still visit it seven years later and talk to Richard there sometimes, I go there when I really need to sort things out.

I have looked back and wondered if my parents could have done anything to make it easier for me, but I don't think so. Their attitude at the time was 'thank goodness one baby lived'. They both wanted a girl rather than a boy, so there was no feeling of me being second best. They had also both come through the Second World War, not many years before, and I would guess that one way of coping with the horrors of war (my mother lived in London for the duration, with all the bombing that went on, and my father was in the army), was to carry on with what was left and make the best of it. In any case, at that time there wasn't the psychological/psychotherapeutic research to alert anyone that surviving twins may be suffering trauma.

My sister is left with a strong feeling that if my brother had lived she would not have been born. This is probably about right as my parents only wanted two children. I am able to talk about my feelings to her, and she is the only member of the family who knows about the grave, but she is understandably ambivalent about Richard. I do not press her to listen, there is no need any more.

I hope this doesn't sound too much like a tale of trauma, more like a quest which eventually helped things to fall into place for me. If I get a bit down or anxious now I look upon it as an inevitable consequence of a difficult start to life and take myself off to have acupuncture, which quickly gets me going again. I have had various interesting technical jobs, then six years ago, because of what I had learnt about myself through experience, decided to become a counsellor myself. I trained in the evenings, after work, and have now changed career completely and am a full-time counsellor in a day centre. One thing I do have to be careful of, though, is to be very sure to separate out my feelings if a client has a twin. There are always pangs of envy, longing and a momentary picture of the perfect fairytale image I have of life with a twin, which I know probably wouldn't have been the case anyway.

LIZ DAWSON

Story 4
A woman in her thirties who lost a brother in childhood
At the time of my divorce I did attend some Marriage Guidance sessions (now called Relate) and the lady did encourage me to speak to her about my twin.

It was all too much for me at the time and I left after only a few sessions. For twenty-four years I had never spoken of my twin and I felt that she was taking him away from me. Throughout the second part of my life he had been at my side (you see Mum, we shared him all the time) guiding and watching over me. My Guardian Angel. Now she had pushed him into the corner of the room, peeping through the door. Not so close at all.

ANONYMOUS

Story 5
A woman in her thirties who lost a brother at birth
I am receiving counselling for my loss. My grief has been great, and the problem has never before been addressed. I feel as though I am only just beginning to understand the effect that my loss has had on my life; I feel that after thirty-one years I am only just starting to learn how to let go of Mark. I do not ever want to forget him, but I do want to come to terms with the fact that we may be separated for many more years before we see each other. I need to talk; I need people to listen. Sometimes it helps to talk to other lone twins, as well as to professionals. One day I may be able to whisper softly to him at his grave, 'I am living my life to the full, Mark; I am doing it for you and for me.'

ELIZABETH DALLAWAY

11
CREATING A DIRECTORY
OF THERAPISTS

After attending LTN meetings for several years I realised there was a need to find counsellors and psychotherapists for grieving twins, particularly after they had attended our meetings and their feelings surfaced.

I discussed this with Joan Woodward and Diana Crook, who was a counsellor and a member of the Network, and devised ways to develop a list of therapists who would be sympathetic and understanding of the uniqueness of losing a twin. We already had reports from some members that they had visited counsellors who were very dismissive of their loss, or who in other ways showed lack of understanding. So I sent out forms to prospective therapists asking about their interest and understanding of our losses and requested references from their counselling supervisors

Some of the therapists were recommended by twins who had good experiences with them, some were lone twins themselves (as I am) and some heard via a 'grapevine'. I then kept their details for use when lone twins asked for referral to a sympathetic therapist. Unfortunately there has not always been someone in the specific area where the twin lives, so in those cases I have sometimes gone to colleagues I know in those areas, or failing that have looked up therapists in the area for the person and suggested that they try two or three for assessment sessions, to find out for themselves if they seem to have an understanding of our issues.

I probably get requests about 5–10 times a year for help and I then send information to the lone twin so that they can make arrangements to see the therapist. I have been asked by other lone twins if we could expand the Directory to include alternative practitioners, this maybe something for such a practitioner to take up in the future, but I personally didn't feel I had enough expertise to take this on myself.

Owing to increasing workload as a counsellor tutor and psycho-therapist, I am about to pass the Directory over to another Lone Twin Network volunteer who I am sure will bring fresh energy to the project and will ensure a future for the Directory.

LIZ DAWSON

12
CONCLUSIONS

There is no doubt that twins hold some fascination, not only for other twins, but also for singletons. Just how widespread this is became apparent when recently a case of 'selective foeticide' led to the creation of a lone twin in the womb. This became headline news at the time and caused intense interest and highly charged emotional reactions in the public, in spite of the fact that such procedures are no longer a rarity in centres where there are *in vitro* fertilisation (IVF) programmes. Unlike abortion, when a single foetus is removed from the womb, selective foeticide is the process when there is a multiple pregnancy and one or more of the foetuses are selected to be killed by injection, in order to enhance the chance of survival of the others.

In writing about this particular case I am not wanting to revive the press sensationalism that surrounded the case at the time, but to bring serious attention to the significance of twin loss and its effect on the surviving twin. There is a great need to increase the understanding of this unique loss, both among the families and friends of lone twins, as well as among professional carers. The latter seem in general to have shown little awareness of the significance to the survivor of twin loss, which I believe is largely due to ignorance.

At the centre of twins' and lone twins' existence lies a quest for identity, or, as I prefer to call it, a sense of self. This sought-after sense of self is not found through 'neurotic solutions', which demand the giving away of self to fit in with other people's needs (Woodward 1988), nor through an attempt to achieve total self-sufficiency. I believe it is found through making mutually empowering relationships, which in turn provide the sense of security and, as Baker Miller describes it, a 'zest for life', which leads to an increasing ability to make more relationships. This concept of being able to give and to receive in a mutually empowering way is, I believe, central to us all for living a fulfilling life.

Attachment Theory provides the biological evidence of our need as humans to form Attachments – as Bowlby puts it, 'from the cradle to the grave'. He shows how both Attachments and the loss of them, or threat of loss, at any time of life, affect our state of mental health. The work of Alice Miller is included in this book, because she brings our attention very forcibly to the damaging effects that parents can have on their children, through the way that they bring them up. This is well illustrated in many of the twins' stories. If we constantly deprive children emotionally, neglect or abuse them, in other words fail to provide them with good enough Attachment, we risk creating many of society's worst problems – violent behaviour and psychic disorders. I believe that the very fabric of society is put in peril when children's truths go unheard, or are denied.

Baker Miller's creation of Relational Theory has been included, not only because it has many similarities with Attachment Theory, but because it adds a vital ingredient that should not be ignored. We need to look with honesty at the ways that *unequal* relationships affect us at the deepest levels of our being. Patriarchal societies insidiously sustain these and over the years this has led to women's truths also being largely ignored or denied, as well as those of children.

Lone twins have their truths to tell too, which are not just about loss, but about the ability to survive and discovering how to survive well. This is why I have attempted to show how the theories concerning therapy, held in common by Bowlby, Alice Miller and Baker Miller, include a basic principle, that effective therapeutic interventions must validate the person's own experiences. This seems of particular importance to lone twins who so often have had the significance of their loss denied.

It has felt to me quite a fearful responsibility to present in summary form the work of theorists whose therapeutic work I respect and from which I have learned a great deal. This is because any such presentation can only be partial and therefore must carry some distortion and risk the criticism that the accounts are superficial or simplistic. Whatever may be missing in the accounts, it is clear that they share Baker Miller's expressed view, that we are now needing very urgently to examine the care and growth of human development. To begin on this task we surely need first to listen to the voices of people whose truths have been extinguished for so long. This book has given some lone twins, men and women, the opportunity to have their voices heard. I believe it demonstrates that we *all* need to have our pain, sadness and vulnerabilities properly recognised. Above all, we need to acknowledge that each lone twin has a unique story to tell.

LIST OF CONTRIBUTORS

BARRABLE Norah
BAYLEY Barbara
BECHOFER Suzie
BEHRENS Kate
BRADFORD Belinda
BRAY Marian
BRINE Joan
COLDWELL Jen
COOKE Linda
COPPOCK Irene
CURTIS Patricia
DALLAWAY Elizabeth
DAWSON Liz
DEELEY Jill
ELVY David
FAY Clare
GABRIEL Ann
GIBSON Wendy
GOODE Bryony
GREEN Susan
HADLEY Joan
HARTLEY Paul
HARRIS Anne
HARVEY Linda
HEELEY Ruth
HEIGHWAY Mary
HOW Alison
HEYWOOD Sheila
KNATCHBULL Timothy
LEVY Hannah

LINDSEY Gillian
LOCKE Judith
LLOYD Liz
JACOBS Cate
LUMLEY Penny
MARCH Sue
MATTISON Ethel
MOFFITT Judy
ORANGE Gary
PARKINS Una
PIERI Lindi
PIPER Stephen
REES Mark
REVELL Dorothy
ROBERTSON Nickii
SHACKLETON Andrew
STARK Rosemary
STRANG Gordon
THOMPSON Graham
TURNER Jo
WATERSTON Sally
WATSON Jan
WATT Paula
WEAVER Ruth
WESTLEY Mike
WHELAN Cynthia
WILLIAMS Simon
WOODWARD Joan
WRIGHT Aileen

REFERENCES

Adams, D.L. and Fettlerhof, C.K. (1971) 'Locked Twins: A Case Report'. *Obstet. and Gynecol.* 38: (383–5).

Ainsworth, M. (1962) 'The Effects of Maternal Deprivation: a Review of Findings and Controversy in the Context of Research Strategy'. *WHO Public Health Papers No. 14.* Geneva: World Health Organisation.

—— (1977) 'Social Development in the First Year of Life: Maternal Influences on Infant-Mother Attachment' in J.M. Tanner (ed.) *Developments in Psychiatric Research.* London: Tavistock.

Baker Miller, J. (1973) *Psychoanalysis and Women.* London: Penguin.

—— (1976) *Toward a New Psychology of Women.* London: Penguin.

—— (1982) 'Women and Power'. Work in Progress Paper No. 1. Boston, MA: Stone Center, Wellesley College.

—— (1984) 'The Development of Women's Sense of Self'. Work in Progress Paper No. 12. Boston, MA: Stone Center, Wellesley College.

—— (1988) 'Connections, Disconnections and Violations'. Work in Progress Paper No. 33. Boston, MA: Stone Center, Wellesley College.

—— and Stiver, J.P. (1991) 'A Relational Re-framing of therapy'. Work in Progress Paper No. 52. Boston, MA: Stone Center, Wellesley College.

—— and Surrey, J.L. (1991) 'Some Misconceptions and Reconceptions of a Relational Approach'. Work in Progress Paper No. 49. Boston, MA: Stone Center, Wellesley College.

Bechhöfer, S. with Josephs, J. (1996) *Rosa's Child.* London: I.B. Tauris.

Bergin, A.E. and Lambert, H.J. (1978) 'The Evaluation of Therapeutic Outcome', in S.L. Garfield and A.E. Bergin (eds) *Handbook of Psychotherapy and Behaviour Change. An Empirical Analysis.* 2nd edn. New York: Wiley.

Bowlby, J. (1965) *Child Care and the Growth of Love.* London: Penguin.

—— (1971) *Attachment.* London: Penguin.

—— (1973) *Separation.* London: Penguin.

—— (1979) *The Making and Breaking of Affectional Bonds.* London: Tavistock.

—— (1980) *Loss.* London: Penguin.

—— (1988) *A Secure Base.* London: Routledge.

Brave, A. and Ferid, H. (1990) 'John Bowlby and Feminism'. *J. of the Inst. for Self Analysis* 4 (1): 30–5.

Burlingham, D. and Freud, A. (1942) *Young Children in Wartime.* London: Allen & Unwin.

—— (1944) *Infants Without Families.* London: Allen & Unwin.

Burton-Phillips, E. (2007) *Mum Can You Lend Me Twenty Quid?* London: Piatkus Books.

Calvo-Sotelo, J. (1996) 'The Hatred of Children in Psychotherapy'. *The Psychotherapist. J. of UKCP* 7 (Autumn 1996).

Campbell, B. (1996) 'Gender Crisis and Community' in S. Kraemer and J. Roberts (eds) *The Politics of Attachment.* London: Free Association Books.

Cardinal, M. (1993) *The Words to Say It.* London: The Women's Press.

Chamberlain, D.B. (1990) *Babies Remember Birth*. New York: Ballantine Books.

—— (1998) *The Mind of Your New Born*. New York: North Atlanta Baby Books.

Court Report (1976) *Fit For The Future*. Committee on Child Health Services. Vols 1 & 2. London: HMSO.

Cozolino, L. (2002) *The Neuroscience of Psychotherapy*. New York: W.W. Norton & Co. Inc.

Dent, J.K. (1978) *Exploring the Psycho-Social Therapies Through the Personalities of Effective Therapists*. DHEW Publication No. (ADM)77–527. Rockville, MD: Nat. Inst. of Mental Health.

Eichenbaum, L. and Orbach, S. (1983) *What Do Women Want?* London: Michael Joseph.

Eliot, T.S. (1982) *The Cocktail Party*. London: Faber & Faber.

Farmer, P. (1996) *Two, or the Book of Twins and Doubles*. London: Virago Press.

Fedele, N. and Baker Miller, J. (1988) *Putting Theory into Practice: Creating Mental Health Programmes*. Boston, MA: Stone Center, Wellesley College.

—— and Harrington, E.A. (1990) 'Women's Groups: How Connections Heal'. Work in Progress Paper No. 47. Boston, MA: Stone Center, Wellesley College.

Green, H. (1964) *I Never Promised You a Rose Garden*. New York: Signet. The New American Library.

Gurman, A.S. (1977) 'The Patient's Perception of The Therapeutic Relationship' in A.S. Gurman and A.M. Razin (eds) *Effective Psychotherapy: A Handbook of Research*. New York: Pergamon Press.

Harlow, H.F. and Zimmerman, R. (1959) 'Affectionate Responses in the Infant Monkey'. *Science* 130:421.

Hayton, A. (2007) *Untwinned*. Herts. UK: Wren Publications.

Hepper, P. G. (1996) 'Fetal Memory Does it Exist?' *Acta Paediatrica Supplement* Vol. 416 pp16–20. Belfast: Foetal Behaviour Research Centre, Queens University of Belfast.

Howe, M.L. and Courage, M.L. (2004) 'Demystifying the Beginnings of Memory'. *Development Review* 24:1–5. Ontario Canada: Dept. of Psychology, Lakehead University.

Itzin, C. (1989) 'My Place' in *Hidden Loss, Miscarriage and Ectopic Pregnancy*. London: Routledge.

Janov, A. (2000) *The Biology of Love*. London: Prometheus Books.

Jerusalem Bible (1974) 1. Thess. 4: 13. London: Darton, Longman & Todd.

Jones, E.M. (1987) *My Twin and I*. New York: Carlton Press.

Jorden, J. et al. (1991) *Women's Growth in Connection*. New York: Guilford Press.

Kaplan, A. (1982) 'Women and Empathy'. Work in Progress Paper No. 2. Boston, MA: Stone Center, Wellesley College.

Lorenz, K.Z. (1935) 'Der Kumpan in der Unmelt des Vogels' *J. Ornith.Berl.* 83. Eng. Trans. (1957) C.H. Schille (ed.) *Instinctive Behaviour*. New York: International University Press.

Lummaa, V. (2007) 'Male Twins Reduce Fitness of Female CO-Twins in Humans' *PNAS* June 26, 104:26 pp10915–10920.

Masson, J.M. (1985) *The Assault on Truth*. London: Penguin.

Miller, A. (1983a) *The Drama of Being a Child*. London: Virago.

—— (1983b) *For Your Own Good: The Roots of Violence in Child Rearing*. London: Virago.

—— (1984) *Thou Shalt Not Be Aware: Society's Betrayal of the Child*. London: Pluto Press.

—— (1986) *Pictures of a Childhood*. London: Virago.

—— (1990a) *The Untouched Key: Tracing Childhood Trauma in Creativity and Destructiveness*. London: Virago.

—— (1990b) *Banished Knowledge: Facing Childhood Injuries*. London: Virago.

—— (1991) *Breaking Down The Wall of Silence: To Join the Waiting Child*. London: Virago.

Nissen, E. (1958) 'Twins: Collision, Impaction, Compaction and Interlocking'. *Obstet. and Gynecol.* 11: 514–25.

Orlinsky, D.E. and Howard, K.I. (1980) 'Gender and Psychotherapeutic Outcome' in A. Brodsky and R. Haremustin (eds) *Women and Psychotherapy*. New York: Guilford Press.

Pionelli, A. (1992) *From Foetus to Child*. London: Routledge.

Raine, K. (1988) *Monessie Gorge: Selected Poems of Kathleen Raine*. Ipswich: Golgonooza Press.

Rank, O. (1994) *The Trauma of Birth*. New York: Dover Publications.

Robertson, J. (1953) Film: *A Two Year Old Goes to Hospital*. London: Tavistock Child Development Research Unit.

Segal, N. (2000) *Entwined Lives*. New York: Penguin.

Siegal, D. (1999) *The Developing Mind*. New York: Guilford Press.

Stark, R. (1989) 'The Everlasting Sadness of a Lone Twin'. *Independent* 26 July.

Stettbacher, J.K. (1990) *Wenn Leiden Einen Sinn Haben Soll (Making Sense of Suffering)*. Hamburg: Hoffmann and Campe.

Verney, T. (1982) *The Secret Life of the Unborn Child*. London: Sphere Books Ltd.

Webster, R. (1995) *Why Freud Was Wrong*. London: HarperCollins.

Woodward, J. (1978) *Has Your Child Been to Hospital?* London: National Association for the Welfare of Children in Hospital (now known as Action for Sick Children).

—— (1987) 'The Bereaved Twin' *Proceedings of the International Congress of Twin Studies 1986*. Rome: AGMG/Twin Research.

—— (1988) *Understanding Ourselves*. London: Macmillan.

INDEX

Compiled by Sue Carlton

Page numbers in **bold** refer to the personal stories